Sarah Stone

Natural Curiosities from the New Worlds

ART *of*
NATURE

Sarah Stone

Natural Curiosities from the New Worlds

CHRISTINE E. JACKSON

MERRELL HOLBERTON
PUBLISHERS LONDON
and
THE NATURAL HISTORY MUSEUM, LONDON

Unless otherwise stated, all photographs are taken from the books
and portrait collections of The Natural History Museum, London.

The Natural History Museum would like to thank the Hayward
Foundation for supporting the publication of this title in its *Art of
Nature* series.

© 1998 The Natural History Museum, London

First published in 1998 by
Merrell Holberton Publishers Ltd
Willcox House, 42 Southwark Street, London SE1 1UN
and
The Natural History Museum, London

British Library Cataloguing in Publication Data
Jackson, Christine E. (Christine Elisabeth), 1936–
Sarah Stone : natural curiosities from the new world. –
(Art of nature)
1. Stone, Sarah – Criticism and interpretation   2. Natural
history illustration   3. Painting, English   4. Painting, Modern
– 17th–18th centuries – Great Britain
I. Title   II. Stone, Sarah
759.2

ISBN 1 85894 063 x

Designed by Roger Davies

Produced by Merrell Holberton Publishers
Printed and bound in Italy

Front jacket (detail) and frontispiece: The interior of Sir Ashton
Lever's Museum when at Leicester House, London. Sarah Stone
painted and exhibited this picture in 1786. The original is now in
a private collection. This reproduction is of a copy, now in the
Ethnographic Department of the British Museum, purchased with
the assistance of Michael Crawford. It was painted on Whatman
paper watermarked 1835, in watercolour and/or coloured inks.
Reproduced by courtesy of the Trustees of the British Museum.
Back jacket: *The cock of the rock* (plate 59)

Contents

Acknowledgements

The first time I saw a Sarah Stone watercolour was when Hugh T. Fattorini showed me his painting of a spoonbill. I was privileged to be invited to join the team at Christie's preparing the catalogue of the Fattorini sale of British bird books and the Spoonbill painting in 1995, and thank Hugh for introducing me to Sarah with all the pleasure that working on her paintings has brought to me.

The cooperation and permission of many people was required for the compilation of this record of Sarah Stone's work. I am pleased to have this opportunity to thank the owners of private collections, who generously either sent me notes on their watercolours or allowed me to see and list them myself. I owe a great deal to Mrs Sylvia Ackland who gave me much of the biographical information and has generously passed on the results of her research into the Stone family. I am further grateful for help with collections in Australia to Andrew Isles, Peter Willcox, Elizabeth Ellis, Jan Brazier and Barbara Perry; for the collection in Honolulu to Betty Lou Kam and Stuart W.H. Ching; and to Göran Frisk in Stockholm and to Ragnar Insulander in Uppsala. Clemency T. Fisher organized the identification of one of the private collections, and John Thackray oversaw the identification of the species depicted in the first collection of Sarah's drawings in The Natural History Museum, London. Michael Walters of The Natural History Museum, Tring, had the greatest number of drawings to identify and took infinite care in establishing the correct modern scientific names.

To all the scientists who took the time and freely gave of their expertise, a very big thank you. The names of those who identified the species are noted at the beginning of each collection. Michael Graham-Stewart showed me the large painting of *Two eagles and a bronze-winged pigeon* before its sale. Since this was one of Sarah's last dated pictures, I was particularly pleased to see it. Jonathan C.H. King of the British Museum (Department of Ethnography) and E. Charles Nelson shared their researches with me before going into print on some points, which I greatly appreciated.

Christine E. Jackson

The Natural History Museum would like to thank The Hayward Foundation for supporting the publication of this title in its *Art of Nature* series.

The Museum holds three collections of original drawings by Sarah Stone: A collection of watercolour drawings, completed between 1781 and 1785, depicting shells, corals, mammals, fossils and other specimens that were formerly in Sir Ashton Lever's Museum. The drawings were presented to the Museum in 1931 by the Superintendent of the University Museum of Zoology, Cambridge. In 1937 the Museum acquired 13 watercolour drawings of birds as part of Sir Walter Rothschild's bequest of his library. A third collection of 175 watercolour drawings of birds was purchased by the Museum in 1996. These too were probably drawn from specimens in the Lever Museum. This purchase was made possible with assistance from the National Heritage Memorial Fund and National Art Collections Fund.

Introduction

Sarah Stone, like many other 'accomplished' young ladies at the end of the eighteenth century, painted in watercolours. More remarkably, Sarah Stone was both talented and meticulous in her observation and recording of the objects she painted. She began by painting for pleasure, but was soon commissioned to paint the contents of Sir Ashton Lever's museum — one of the most comprehensive and extraordinary of the many collections that were being made in the wake of new scientific discoveries in the Americas and Australasia.

It was an exciting period. Zoological, botanical and ethnographical objects were being brought back to the West for the first time, and Sarah Stone was one of the first artists to paint objects from Australasia and the South Seas. She painted over a thousand watercolours of birds, mammals, fishes, insects, reptiles, shells and minerals, as well as ethnographical artefacts, including many brought back to England from Captain Cook's three round-the-world voyages. Her watercolour paintings form a unique record of the discoveries made by sailors and naturalists on board British survey ships and in the new colonies in the 1780s and 1790s.

Objects from the Leverian Museum were dispersed when the the collection was sold in 1806, and most of the zoological specimens have been lost. Sarah Stone's paintings provide important information for scientists today. They are often the only remaining record of specimens which were used by scientists in the eighteenth century for descriptions of new species (some now extinct) for the first time.

Remarkably, annotated catalogues of the 65-day sale of objects from the Leverian Museum still exist, and, where possible, Sarah Stone's paintings have been linked to the lot descriptions. Catalogues of over 900 known paintings by Sarah Stone, in both public and private collections, are provided and indexed; the illustrations she did for important scientific publications at the time are described; and the eighteenth-century scientific names have been updated by experts in the different fields.

Sarah Stone's work is undoubtedly of historical importance, both scientifically and for what it reveals about exploration and collecting at the time, but the charm of her paintings will appeal to everyone. A remarkable number of her paintings has been preserved; others, unsigned and unrecognized, are waiting to be discovered.

8

Sarah Stone

ca. 1760–1844

1 Samuel Shelley (1750–1808), *Portrait of Sarah
Stone*, engraved for *The Universal Review*, 1890

COLOUR PLATES

Unless otherwise stated, the plates here are from the collections in The
Natural History Museum (NHML). See further pp. 109ff.

PLATE 1 Thorny Oyster *Spondylus ?regius*
The piece of blue paper, realistically painted, under the
shell of a thorny oyster from the West Pacific,
demonstrates Sarah's use of shadows and *trompe l'oeil*
effect.
NHML (1) 71

A letter written in December 1822 by Lewis Allen,
an artist who married Sarah Stone's niece, and
quoted in *The Universal Review* of 1890, tells us
what he thought about this famous lady (here referred
to as Mrs Captain Smith):

"I forgot to tell you that all the guests admired my
sketches exceedingly particularly those of Lambeth and
Westminster; and I was vastly flattered to receive the
approbation of Mrs Captain Smith, who is herself a fine
painter. You remember she was the celebrated Miss Stone,
who was painted by Shelley and who herself, when a
young lady, made a large number of watercolour paintings of some of the curious birds in Sir Ashton Lever's
Museum, in Leicester square. An old newspaper of the
time (some thirty or forty years ago) says of her 'she is
allowed by all artists to have succeeded in this effort
beyond imagination.' Judging from her portrait and herself, (although no longer young), she had all the best
parts of beauty, a fine countenance, a good figure, and
a pleasing address."[1]

Sarah Smith (née Stone) was over sixty years old when
this was written. Some idea as to her share of the "best
parts of beauty" may be judged from the charming portrait (fig. 1) executed by Samuel Shelley before her marriage to Midshipman, later Captain, John Langdale Smith
(see fig. 2), in 1789. By that date, Sarah was well known
in London, both to the public who visited the famous
museum belonging to Sir Ashton Lever, where she
painted the specimens, and to the *cognoscenti* of the day
who were interested in natural history and everything to
do with the discoveries made on three round-the-world
voyages by Captain Cook.

Sarah spent hours in Sir Ashton Lever's museum,
faithfully drawing and painting mounted birds, insects,
mammals, fishes, lizards, fossils, minerals, shells and
corals from all over the world, as well as ethnographical
artefacts brought back from exploratory voyages, including those of Captain Cook. Lever's museum was dispersed in 1806, and the original specimens which formed
the subject of over one thousand of Sarah's paintings are
now scattered or lost. Very few are still preserved in

2 Lionel John Beale (?), *Portrait of John Langdale Smith*, engraved for *The Universal Review*, 1890

as children, the Stones, unable to get proper colours wherewith to paint, fabricated them out of brickdust, and the juice of the leaves and petals of flowers." Fan painting requires fine and accurate colouring skills, and this intricate and delicate job was often done by map colourists. Being able to draw, however, was a different skill, and an inherited talent that Sarah appears to have had in abundant measure. It was not present in her younger sister, Frances Mary Stone (baptized at St Giles, London, in 1769).

During the late 1770s and throughout the 1780s, Sarah painted at Ashton Lever's museum (or the Leverian Museum, as it came to be called) in Leicester House, Leicester Square, London. She may have asked permission to draw some object from this extraordinary collection of natural history specimens, ethnographical artefacts and other curiosities, and so came to the notice of their owner. Ashton Lever soon commissioned her to record the outstanding articles, both zoological and ethnographical, in his collection. Sarah signed her watercolours, and dated some of them, but the signed and dated watercolours are in the minority.

We know the locations today of over 900 watercolours out of the thousand painted by Sarah Stone between 1777 and 1806. During those thirty years, she matured from a teenager painting very simply and painstakingly to an artist who could compose an interesting picture incorporating several subjects. Her watercolours were painted after preliminary pencil sketches had been made. Some of these sketches, on very flimsy tracing paper, are preserved in a private collection and are, on the whole, livelier than her finished paintings. When working on a watercolour of a mounted zoological specimen in the museum, she was concerned, perhaps overconcerned, to record precisely what was in front of her, consequently reproducing all the inadequacies of eighteenth-century taxidermy. Taxidermists made their models compact, both to save space when arranged on shelves, and to

museums in Europe, North America and Australia. The importance of Sarah's drawings lies in the fact that she not only recorded so many new scientific discoveries for the first time, but also so many important items before their dispersal. Lever purchased, or had given to him, the first specimens ever recorded or known to science in several fields. That she was highly regarded, and her work appreciated by the eminent naturalists of the last twenty years of the eighteenth century, is in no doubt; several authors (see pp. 140ff.) requested the use of her drawings for engravings to illustrate their books.

Sarah's baptismal record has not been found, but the same article in *The Universal Review* reported that the drawings of her birds "show a considerable amount of technical skill", adding that this was "not surprising as the artist's father was a fan painter, somewhat in the style of Antoine Watteau. A family legend ... relates that

PLATE 2

Fossil crinoid

The drawing is inscribed on the reverse: *This was the first drawing Miss Stone did for me. Ashton Lever.*

NHML (1) 88

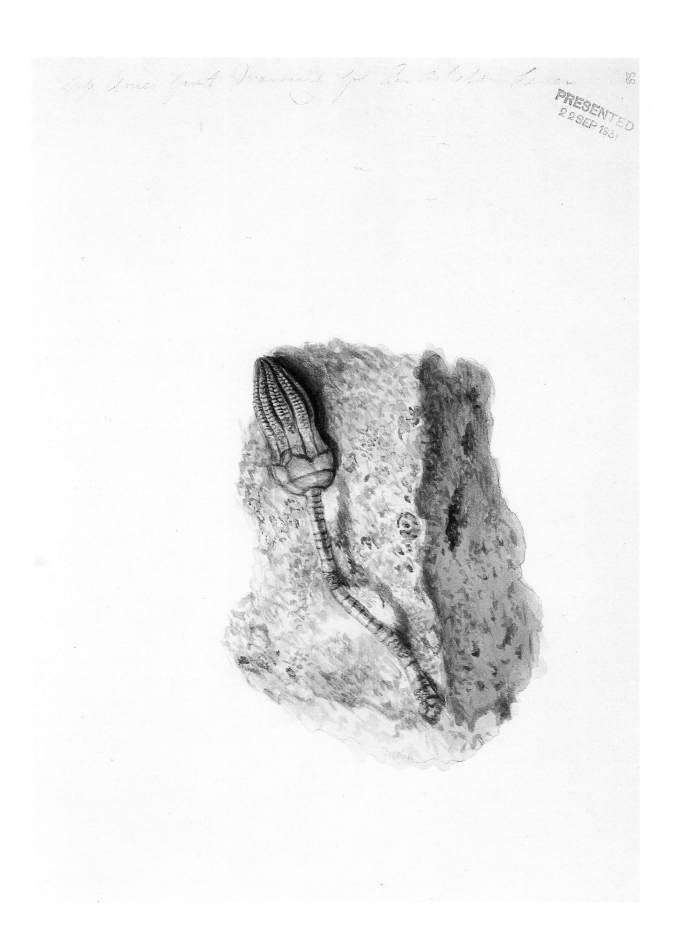

ensure that no part of a specimen, such as a bill, stuck out at an angle, allowing it to be caught in a sleeve and ruined. A painting of a bird with its head turned so that the bill fits neatly along its back is a sure sign that the artist was working from a mounted model. With only a limited understanding of the anatomy of animals, taxidermists stuffed cotton or other material into dried skins, rounding out the shape of the skin regardless of the animal's musculature. Sometimes the dried skin was overstuffed, sometimes understuffed, but the final shape frequently failed to resemble that of the living specimen. Sarah's work may be an interesting, perhaps even important, historical record of eighteenth-century taxidermic practices, but we could legitimately wish that she had had a greater knowledge of animal biology, and had taken a little more artistic licence and used her imagination to set her subjects free from rigor mortis.

Not all her work can be criticized in this way. She was capable of painting more naturally, and did so when her pictures were intended to be framed, and were not done merely for identification and reference purposes. At the time Sarah was painting, her work was highly regarded as being accurate ("faithful", in eighteenth-century terms), beautifully coloured and carefully drawn. Several of her birds are painted with insects, or with other birds, in an attempt to introduce life and movement or inter-action. What we admire today is the delicacy of the brushwork, the sure touch in applying colour, and the skill in being able to paint so many diverse subjects, both zoological and ethnographical.

Birds were Sarah's favourite subjects and her earliest studies of birds, probably done in the Leverian Museum because they are not common British species, are dated 1777, when she was about seventeen years old. At this stage, she did not incorporate backgrounds, but con-centrated all her effort on finely detailed images. If Sarah

had been taught by a father who was a fan painter, this would be consistent with his method of working. Another salient feature of Sarah's technique was her use of sized paper, at a date when this was uncommon. This may be detected not only by the smooth surface on which she painted, but the glazed surface on the reverse side. The materials on which fan painters worked were carefully sized with a substance that was not too stiff to allow the fan to be mounted and folded, and there are printed directions for making this size and applying it – though fan painters often bought pre-sized factory-made paper. The appreciation of the benefits of sized surfaces for very fine brushwork would have been part of her father's professional knowledge. The design was placed on to the fan surface, either with a fine brush or with a tracing. Sarah's pencil sketches are on similar trac-ing paper.

Most of Sarah's watercolours have been preserved in folios and have not been exposed to the light. By the end of the eighteenth century, artists had some knowledge as to which colours were fugitive and which could be con-sidered "safe" or permanent. The more permanent pig-ments were those used by fan painters – and by Sarah: Chinese white, ivory black, burnt sienna, Vandyke brown, yellow ochre, chrome lemon and yellow, light and orange cadmium, vermilion, carmine, madder lake, Veronese green, sap green, cobalt, ultramarine and Prussian blue. Nevertheless, there is evidence that some of her yellows have proved fugitive. The charge of painting parts of zoo-logical specimens in the wrong colours cannot be laid at Sarah's door. Any faulty colouring of legs, eyes and soft parts was a result of these fading soon after death in all zoological species, and is a common factor in most pictorial records of this date. It was not until freshly killed specimens were used consistently in the nineteenth century, combined with notes made of eye colour and

PLATE 3

Two feather god heads

The original feather heads, taken to England by one of Captain Cook's ships in 1780, were in the Leverian Museum by 1781, painted by Sarah *ca.* 1783. They were purchased by Hewitt at the 1806 sale and nearly one hundred years later presented to the British Museum.

Bernice Pauahi Bishop Museum, Honolulu, Hawaii (vol. III, no. 1)

Sarah Stone

13

Great Hook-billed Creeper La. Syn: 2. p. 103   Certhia arcuata La:

122

Sarah Stone: 1781

PLATE 5

Mamo *Drepanis pacifica* (Gmelin 1788)

The last definite sighting of a mamo was in the Kaumau forest in 1898. It was the victim of feather
hunters and firearms introduced to Hawaii. Sarah probably painted the type specimen of this species
in 1781, the same year in which John Latham drew it for his *Synopsis of Birds*.

NHML (3) 50

PLATE 4

Feather cloak (*'ahu'ula*) and 'O'o bird *Moho nobilis* (Merrem)

Sarah painted three Hawaiian chiefs' feather cloaks with the birds from which the colourful green, red
and yellow feathers were taken. The 'O'o, *Moho nobilis*, limited to the island of Hawaii, is now thought
to be extinct, but the *Moho braccatus*, the Kauai species, may still be seen.

Bernice Pauahi Bishop Museum, Honolulu, Hawaii (vol. III, no. 21)

skin tones before the skin was dried, that accurate colouring of soft parts became a regular feature in artwork.

As a child, Sarah had been used to employing any materials that came to hand as painting pigments. To add gum arabic to gouache powders would be a logical progression from using dried, ground-up plant materials. She would also have learned to mix watercolour paint to obtain sufficient depth of colour, and to add white for opacity and highlights long before she began reproducing the colours of zoological specimens and artefacts. Many of her colours have both richness and depth. Some of her blues and yellows are strong, while her browns and reds have considerable depth. She painted flamingos and roseate spoonbills with true rich pinks.

When Sarah provided tree branches as part of her backgrounds, they are distinctive and one of the features by which her paintings may be recognized. Nearly always they are pale grey or silver, like a silver birch bark, with a little lichen very delicately traced. The same delicacy is used to paint wispy twigs and foliage. Tree trunks, with transverse banding and broken ends resulting in jagged surfaces, were highlighted in brown. This convention was followed by other contemporary artists, notably members of the Lewin family who (painting before the Industrial Revolution polluted the atmosphere) also embellished their branches with lichens, a device used less often by Sarah. Her more solid clumps of foliage were drawn in ink and then painted with yellow or pale green wash.

One of the outstanding features of Sarah's work, which again was probably learned from a professional artist such as her father, was her use of heavy shadow to create an illusion of solidity. This was a rare practice in zoological illustration at this period. Shadows appear under the feet of animals, to the side of echinoderms and insects, and under shells, making the object appear more moulded and realistic. She also showed an understanding of *trompe l'oeil*, demonstrating this in two or

three studies where labels attached to specimens were reproduced in her drawing, with vivid effect. She was employing these techniques before the great *trompe l'oeil* expert, Leroy de Barde, painted at the Leverian Museum (see pp. 90ff.), so did not learn this from him.

With such a wide range of subjects, Sarah was inevitably better at painting some species than others. Her insects, shells and echinoderms are exquisite. Her birds, given the limitations of painting from mounted specimens, are important records and, although her mammals are rather more stiff, the fur is sufficiently convincing. She used exceedingly fine brush strokes, probably with brushes containing only two or three hairs for the lightest feathers, and succeeded in giving some life to her animals by the manner in which she painted the eyes.

In the few composite pictures (mainly consisting of a tree with several birds, or a tree with several nests of humming-birds and the birds flying about it), it is noticeable that Sarah balanced her colours with care. The birds were chosen for their warm browns and cool colours, and skilfully arranged so that those with areas of red in their plumage are strategically placed to catch the eye and enliven the whole composition. Several specimens — for example, sea-urchins — are so neatly arranged and positioned according to size and pattern that they form charming compositions despite being painted principally as scientific records of the species.

Paintings which were intended to be framed had more detail in their backgrounds, and Sarah also painted in a sky. However, we have only a few examples of this type of work. Most of her paintings, whether for framing or as scientific records, were neatly finished off with ruled ink or colour-wash borders round them. Many had double ruled borders. All her work speaks of careful, unhurried and conscientious painting, done with skill and care, and well presented.

Sarah's watercolours may be divided into two groups: zoological specimens, with fossils and minerals, and

PLATE 6

Satyr tragopan *Tragopan satyra*

"The Napaul Pheasant", hand-coloured engraving, plate XII facing p. 344 in Thomas Pennant's *A View of Hindoostan*, 2 vols., 1798–1800

Lilian delin.

J. Barlow sculp.

17

3 Ramsay Richard Reinagle, thought to be of "Mr Thomson, animal and bird preserver to the Liverian and British Museums" examining a bird of paradise, oil on canvas, exhibited at the Royal Academy in 1802. The Yale Center for British Art, New Haven

because they were brought back to England from Captain Cook's three voyages (between 1768 and 1780), and represent the first imports from the South Seas and Australasia. However, the original use of some of the objects still remains unknown today and, since they are often difficult to describe in words, relating these items drawn by Sarah to the lots described in the sale catalogue when the Leverian Museum was eventually sold in 1806 must be done with greater caution than relating zoological specimens to her watercolours. Sarah made the first pictorial records and studies of hundreds of artefacts taken to London by British Navy ships in the 1770s, 1780s and 1790s, and her drawings are of great importance, especially where this original material has since been lost or scattered to the four corners of the globe.

The majority of the zoological specimens can be given specific names on the evidence of her drawings; indeed, some of Sarah's drawings of birds and reptiles form the basis of the first descriptions of those species (*i.e.* the 'type' or 'syntype'). The fact that there was a known specimen in the Leverian Museum adds to their verification. A small proportion of the zoological specimens that Sarah painted were not in the Leverian Museum, but in private collections and in the British Museum.

The sheer number of species that were recorded pictorially by Sarah Stone is astonishing, and by far the largest number of her watercolour studies were of birds. Some of these had already been described and illustrated by John Latham, whose drawings in his *General Synopsis of Birds* (1781–85), and scientific names in his *Index Ornithologicus* (1790), were frequently noted on Sarah's paintings. Latham specifies in the text of his *General Synopsis* that he used specimens both from his own extensive collection and from Lever's, so he and Sarah were working from the same specimens for a number of their illustrations. The Latham references on The Natural History

ethnographical objects. She painted specimens from every category represented in the Leverian Museum, other than the grotesques and more bizarre oddities that found a place in an eighteenth-century museum but would not be given shelf-room in a museum today. Among the natural history specimens, she painted quadrupeds, birds, fishes, reptiles, insects, shells, echinoderms, minerals and fossils. When she turned to the ethnographical items, she tackled native costumes, culinary and war implements, jewellery, and musical instruments. Many of these objects are unique. Some were from Europe, North America and Africa, but the most important were subjects from Hawaii and the South Seas.

Many of the ethnographical items are important

PLATE 7

Tahitian lory *Vini peruviana*

These "Parokets of Oteheate" were painted "Natural Size", *i.e.* 18 cm or just under 4 inches long, and signed by Sarah Stone. The Tahitian lory inhabits the Society Islands, western Tuamotu Islands and Aitutaki, Cook Islands.

The Alexander Turnbull Library, Wellington, New Zealand

2

Sarah Stone

PAROKETS of OTEHEATE Natural Size

Museum collection of Sarah's watercolours (NHML (3), see pp. 114–21) appear to be in a hand contemporary with the drawings, but not Sarah's. The scientific names pencilled on the bottom margin of the paintings in a private collection (Private Collection B, see pp. 132–37) were written at a later date. In the lists of her watercolours (see pp. 109ff.), all these inscriptions on her paintings have been reproduced. Sarah's own inscriptions on the watercolours were confined to her signature, and occasionally – but all too rarely – the date on which she made the drawing.

Someone wrote a large number, in pencil, on seventy-one of the known watercolours, all but twenty of which are bird paintings, but no apparent logic or systematic numbering can be discerned from them. Indeed, they are very puzzling, because six numbers on paintings which bear both a signature and a date in Sarah's hand (between the years 1777 and 1783) are duplicated. However, the drawing on which Ashton Lever wrote that it was the first drawing Miss Stone did for him bears the pencilled number 198, suggesting that there was no initial plan for a systematic recording of items in Lever's collection, but rather that someone, at a later date, owned a collection of her drawings and numbered them. The highest number is on an undated painting of a bird; the number on one of the earliest dated paintings, an octopus of 1777, was 22. If more of Sarah's watercolours come to light, the reason for and the pattern of the numbering may perhaps become apparent.

The Leverian Museum had been open for two years when Sarah first painted there. She dated an Angola vulture 27 February 1777, a mantis and other insects 1777, and a spoonbill the same year. It was either in this year, or early in 1778, that she began to paint the museum exhibits for Ashton Lever on commission. She was at work in the early winter months of 1778, painting pieces of marble, butterflies from Jamaica, the Indies, Africa, America and China, and then a buzzard and a heron for a hawking picture. (Advertisements in *The Morning Post and Daily Advertiser* frequently mention that there were good fires in the rooms and galleries of the museum for the comfort of the visitors – and, no doubt, for artists.)

The advertisements until 4 June 1778 were for "Mr Lever's Museum", and from 9 June for "Sir Ashton Lever's Museum". George III bestowed a knighthood on Lever on 5 June 1778, so any of Sarah's watercolours with inscriptions stating the specimen was in the collection of "Ashton Lever Esq" were painted before that date.

In 1779 Sarah was even busier painting at the museum. On 23 February, Sir Ashton notified the public that "a good collection of books on natural history" was kept in the library. Sarah may have had access to these, and gained some ideas from the illustrations. Paintings bearing the date 1779 include *Parrots and a butterfly*, *Three parrots in a tree*, *Two parrots and a butterfly*, and *Studies of exotic birds and an insect*, suggesting that her earlier, simpler compositions had now become more interesting by the addition of butterflies. George Edwards's *A Natural History of Uncommon Birds* (1743–51), and its continuation, *Gleanings of Natural History* (1758–64), were the standard texts of this period, before Latham began publishing in 1781. Edwards said of the design of his plates, "the better to set off the whole I have, in a few plates, where the Birds were very small, added some foreign insects to fill up the naked spaces in the plates".[2] Any "good collection of books on natural history" was bound to include Edwards's titles. Inserted in a collection of Sarah's paintings (NHML (3), no. 162) are two signed watercolours by George Edwards, which were preparations for two plates in his book. It is more than probable that Sarah was aware of his work.

The following year, 1780, Sarah reverted to painting single specimens of birds, and no longer noted the exact day on which she painted them. She continued to record the fossil specimens in the collection. There were very few advertisements in the newspapers this year; the museum was still popular and did not need them. A small

PLATE 8

African grey parrot *Psittacus erithacus*

An unusual colour variation of the African grey parrot, *Psittacus erithacus*.

Yale Center for British Art, New Haven, Paul Mellon Collection

innovation, made in April – "the tutor and governess are included in the family ticket"[3] – probably meant more children running round the museum, a situation not conducive to the concentration of any artists at work there.

Sarah first exhibited a painting in a London exhibition in 1780. The Society of Artists of Great Britain had been founded in 1760 and held exhibitions until 1791. Exhibit no. 326 in 1780 was *Butterflies in Sir Ashton Lever's Museum. Watercolours* and a *Mandarine Duck in ditto* by "Miss Stone (afterwards Mrs Smith) Painter (Honorary Exhibitor)".[4] Far greater prestige was attached to being "hung" at the exhibitions of the Royal Academy, and Sarah achieved this as an honorary exhibitor in 1781, when she showed two pictures entitled *Birds*, another of *A Peacock* and one of *Shells*.[5] She attempted a more ambitious painting of a still life of a partridge, like the old masters, and perhaps made the first attempt at a mammal, a *Goat of Angora*.

In 1781, Sir Ashton Lever acquired thousands of artefacts and natural history specimens from Captain Cook's third voyage (1776–80), from which Sarah painted a great hook-billed creeper, the now extinct mamo of Hawaii. John Latham began publishing his account of the world's birds and visited the museum in order to make drawings of specimens that he himself did not own. Lever and Latham were rival collectors of bird specimens and exchanged letters detailing their latest acquisitions. Sarah would be aware of Latham's activities, even if she did not meet him at the museum at this time. She continued to paint the birds in Lever's collection, also shells and insects, but it was not until 1783 that she really came to grips with the ethnographical items. Later, these paintings were collected into albums which are now in Honolulu, Australia and the British Museum's Ethnographical Department, London (see pp. 122–26). Sarah did not date the ethnographical watercolours, with the exception of the very fine and interesting picture of two feather gods brought to England by one of Cook's ships in 1780 and placed in the Leverian Museum.

The folio of ethnographic watercolours in the Bernice Pauahi Bishop Museum, Honolulu, contains a series of scraps of newspaper discovered between the pages of the two volumes, probably serving as bookmarks. The newspaper was published on or after Thursday 27 March 1783, and before Wednesday 2 April 1783, suggesting that these watercolours were painted in the same year. Apart from the studies of artefacts, Sarah continued to paint birds. Corals also took her fancy, and she painted a series of them on several sheets.

Between 19 January and 25 March 1784, Sir Ashton Lever placed several advertisements in the London newspaper, *The Morning Post and Daily Advertiser*, informing prospective visitors to the museum of an exhibition of over a thousand of Sarah's watercolours (called "transparent drawings in watercolours"):

"Sir Ashton Lever, Holophusicon Is open every Day (Sundays excepted) from ELEVEN till FOUR To which is now added, a large Room of Transparent Drawings in Water Colours, from the most curious specimens in the Collection, consisting of above one thousand different articles, executed by Miss Stone, a young lady, who is allowed by all Artists to have succeeded in the effort beyond all imagination. These will continue to be open for the inspection of the public until they are removed into the country. Admittance HALF-A-CROWN each. Subscriptions as usual. Good Fires in all the Galleries."[6]

The thousand watercolours exhibited and then "removed to the country" appear to have been owned by Sir Ashton Lever and taken to his home at Alkrington. When the contents of the Leverian Museum were disposed of in 1786, under a Lottery Act obtained in 1784, Lever was permitted to retain the watercolours. The Alkrington estate itself was disposed of only in 1845, but some of the watercolours were sold following Lever's death

PLATE 9
Owlet nightjar *Aegotheles cristatus*
The National Library of Australia, Canberra, no. 5

PLATE 10

Saddleback *Creadion carunculatus carunculatus* (Gmelin 1789)

The New Zealand Tieke or Saddleback is an endangered species today. The South Island race survived only on the Cape Islands and the North Island race on Hen Island. Both races have now been transferred elsewhere for safety. Sarah almost certainly painted the first specimen taken to England.

NHML (3) 59

PLATE 11

I'iwi *Vestiaria coccinea* (Forster 1781)

This is one of the species used to make the feather cloaks of Hawaiian chiefs, and still fairly common in Hawaii.

Dixson Library, State Library of New South Wales, Sydney

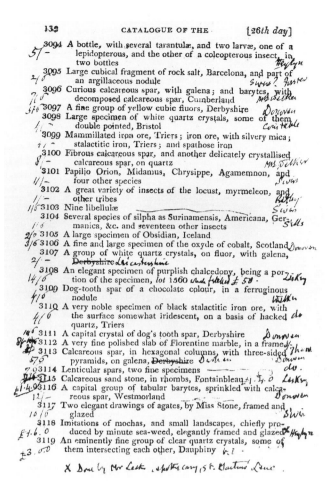

3094 A bottle, with several tarantulæ, and two larvæ, one of a lepidopterous, and the other of a coleopterous insect, in two bottles

3095 Large cubical fragment of rock salt, Barcelona, and part of an argillaceous nodule

3096 Curious calcareous spar, with galena; and barytes, with decomposed calcareous spar, Cumberland

3097 A fine group of yellow cubic fluors, Derbyshire

3098 Large specimen of white quartz crystals, some of them double pointed, Bristol

3099 Mammillated iron ore, Triers; iron ore, with silvery mica; stalactitic iron, Triers; and spathose iron

3100 Fibrous calcareous spar, and another delicately crystallised calcareous spar, on quartz

3101 Papilio Orion, Midamus, Chrysippe, Agamemnon, and four other species

3102 A great variety of insects of the locust, myrmeleon, and other tribes

3103 Nine libellulæ

3104 Several species of silpha as Surinamensis, Americana, Germanica, &c. and seventeen other insects

3105 A large specimen of Obsidian, Iceland

3106 A fine and large specimen of the oxyde of cobalt, Scotland

3107 A group of white quartz crystals, on fluor, with galena, Derbyshire Leicestershire

3108 An elegant specimen of purplish chalcedony, being a portion of the specimen, lot 1560 and fetched £ 50

3109 Dog-tooth spar of a chocolate colour, in a ferruginous nodule

3110 A very noble specimen of black stalactitic iron ore, with the surface somewhat iridescent, on a basis of hacked quartz, Triers

3111 A capital crystal of dog's tooth spar, Derbyshire

3112 A very fine polished slab of Florentine marble, in a frame

3113 Calcareous spar, in hexagonal columns, with three-sided pyramids, on galena, Derbyshire

3114 Lenticular spars, two fine specimens ———

3115 Calcareous sand stone, in rhombs, Fontainbleau

3116 A capital group of tabular barytes, sprinkled with calcareous spar, Westmorland

3117 Two elegant drawings of agates, by Miss Stone, framed and glazed

3118 Imitations of mochas, and small landscapes, chiefly produced by minute sea-weed, elegantly framed and glazed

3119 An eminently fine group of clear quartz crystals, some of them intersecting each other, Dauphiny

X Done by Mr Leek apothecary 15 t. Martins Lane.

4 Page of the sale catalogue of the Leverian Museum recording lot 3117, "Two elegant drawings of agates, by Miss Stone, framed and glazed"

in 1788. Matthew Gregson of Liverpool wrote to Sir Joseph Banks on 13 August 1791, offering to sell him a collection of nearly 800 drawings of birds, shells, fossils, crab *etc*, most of them being birds painted by Miss Stone and others for Sir Ashton Lever, under his supervision.[7]

A further exhibition of her drawings (date unknown) was reported in an article in the *Universal Review* in 1890 (VI, p. 584) by a descendant of Sarah's, who wrote, "In connection with the account of my great-aunt's drawings, we have a newspaper notice of Sir Ashton Lever's museum as follows":

"TO ADMIRERS OF FINE PAINTING
To be disposed of to 150 subscribers, at one guinea each, a collection of beautiful Water-colour Paintings, the production of the celebrated Miss Stone, consisting of four hundred and forty pieces. Specimens may be seen and particulars known on application to T. Billinge."

In 1784, Lever obtained permission, by means of an Act of Parliament, to hold a lottery in order to dispose of his museum and recoup some of his expenditure. By 22 December 1785, Sir Ashton was urging people to view before the lottery closed.[8] In this unsettling atmosphere, Sarah continued to paint her favourite subject: birds.

The lottery was held on 23 March 1786 and Sir Ashton Lever lost his museum to a law stationer, James Parkinson. Realising that the museum might be broken up, or moved, Sarah painted the interior of the museum at Leicester House in this year, and exhibited the picture at the Royal Academy under the title, *Perspective view of Sir Ashton Lever's Museum*. The painting remained in the museum and was catalogued as no. 887 when the Leverian Museum was sold in 1806; it was bought by a Mrs Oliphant for £2. 10s. 0d. and is now in a private collection. What is believed to be a copy of this watercolour is conserved in the Ethnographic Department of the British Museum (see frontispiece).

Also in the 1806 Leverian Museum sale were "Two elegant drawings of agates, by Miss Stone" (lot 3117), which sold to "Sivers" for 10s. 6d., suggesting that Sarah did not own the watercolours she had executed at the museum (see fig. 4).

Preserved in Spirits. In the Collection of Ashton Lever Esq.

1

PLATE 12
Three-bearded rockling *Gaidropsarus vulgaris* (Cloquet 1824)
Painted before June 1778. The largest of the rocklings, found in the waters around Britain and western
Europe.
NHML (1) 1

Not a single painting of Sarah's from 1787 is known. The museum at Leicester House closed on 1 September and the contents were removed to the Rotunda, south of the Thames in Albion Place, where it opened to the public on 3 December. The following year, Sarah painted a group of thirteen watercolours of birds, now preserved in The Natural History Museum, London, nine of them signed, and dated 1788.

James Parkinson vigorously promoted the museum and encouraged artists to use it. Charles Catton worked at the museum at this period for about a year, and about this time John Walcott and William Lewin visited the museum to draw British bird species that they could not otherwise obtain. Sydenham T. Edwards and Charles Reuben Ryley were also painting museum bird and mammal specimens.

When, in the spring of 1789, Thomas Wilson received a superb cargo of natural history specimens collected by John White in the newly established territory in Australia, Sarah's services were again in demand. She painted from the skins of birds and reptiles to illustrate White's *Journal of a Voyage to New South Wales*, each engraved plate being dated 29 December 1789 (see pp. 140–44). The book went on sale early in 1790, and in advertisements between 26 August and 11 November 1790 Parkinson informed museum visitors that Wilson had presented the skins to the museum.[9]

The Australian skins sent back to England in 1789 included those of previously unknown birds and reptiles. Artefacts arriving from both the Sandwich Islands (Hawaii) and from Australasia were also seen and recorded pictorially for the first time – many of them by Sarah. It was an extraordinary task with which this young woman was entrusted. That she painted such a large number of objects, and accomplished her work with such precision, consistent care and charm, is even more remarkable.

The year 1789 was an eventful one for Sarah. Not only was she kept busy painting, but on 8 September "John Langdale Smith, of the Hamlet of Hammersmith in the County of Middlesex, a Batchelor, and Sarah Stone, a Spinster" were married at St George's, Bloomsbury, "by Licence this Eighth day of September 1789 by me Thomas Ball, Curate ... In the presence of Frances Mary Stone, Ann Stone, etc.", after payment of the licence fee of 4s. 8d. Sarah's midshipman husband was described as being "*exceedingly* handsome and of *excellent* parts".[10] He was a few years younger than Sarah, who was nearly thirty at the time of their marriage, and had already sailed to the West Indies, Jamaica, Barbados and Ascension, America and Africa more than once.

Parkinson began publishing his *Companion to the Museum* this same year, with a text by George Shaw from the British Museum, and a frontispiece that was the joint work of Sarah and Charles Reuben Ryley. Once again Sarah painted the interior of the Leverian Museum, but this time showed the display in the famous Rotunda, or round room, in which the birds were shelved, with several figures of people inspecting the cases and in the foreground. If Sarah had not met Ryley before, she undoubtedly did over this joint venture. Ryley was eventually to take over Sarah's position as recorder of species at the museum, together with other ocasional artists, such as Sydenham T. Edwards who, from 1800 onwards, painted creepers and humming-birds in the museum for the French author Jean Baptiste Audebert to incorporate in his *Histoire naturelle ... colibris, oiseaux-mouches, jacamars, promerops* (2 vols., Paris 1801–02).

Sarah's love of painting was shared by her husband. In 1791 they both exhibited at London shows. He exhibited a portrait at the Royal Academy, and she showed two pictures of birds at the Society of Artists: *The yellowheaded Parrot from the Brazils, drawing* and *The Mandarine Drake: ditto*.[11] Their address was given as Cowley Street, near College Street, Westminster.[12]

In 1791, Parkinson began publishing a more detailed catalogue of the objects in the museum in his *Museum Leverianum*, with a text again by George Shaw, in which two of Sarah's drawings were used, though perhaps not recent ones. We have no dated watercolours preserved from the next three years, and only one in 1795, of a *Blue grosbeak*. This lack of watercolours can be in part explained by a baptismal record on 8 September 1792 of John and Sarah's daughter, Eliza Jane, at St John the Evangelist, Westminster, although the child probably died in infancy, for there is no further record of her; and three years later

PLATE 13

Asian elephant *Elaphus maximus*

The Asian elephant present in the Leverian Museum from 1777, painted again by Sarah (see
frontispiece) in 1786.

NHML (1) 7

5 *Portrait of Henry Stone Smith, 1795–1881* (Sarah and John Langdale Smith's son). House of Lords Records Office

their son, Henry Stone Smith, in May 1881, "This drawing of the Bird 'Topial' (a bird brought from the West Indies by my late dear father Captain John Langdale Smith, then Commander of *H.M. Ship 'Penguin'* about 1806 or 1808) was made by my late dear mother Mrs Smith, while the bird was still living and domesticated with us. (Henry Stone Smith May 1881)." The bird is probably a troupial, *Icterus icterus,* for which natives use the local name *turpial.*

The last year in which Sarah dated work that has survived to the present day, was 1806, when she produced an unusual composition, signed and dated, of an eagle with a bronze-winged pigeon underfoot, and the head of another eagle.

From 1823 until 1827, John Langdale Smith was an out-pensioner of Greenwich Hospital. In November 1827, *The Gentleman's Magazine* reported, "October 30 In Smith-square, Westminster, aged 60, after a tedious illness, much lamented, Captain John Langdale Smith, R.N.".[14]

Sarah had moved to Smith Square to live with her son and his growing family, and was there at the time of the 1841 census, when her age is given as seventy-five. Ages in this census are notoriously inaccurate (they were allowed to be rounded up, or down, to the nearest five) and Sarah's was certainly wrong. When she died, in 1844, her death certificate stated that on "11th January, the widow of John Langdale Smith Capt RN died, aged 82, after suffering from pneumonia for two weeks, at 3 Smith Square, Westminster". She was buried 19 January at St Margaret's, Westminster, by John Jennings, the Rector of St John's, Westminster, when her age was recorded in the parish register as eighty-three.[15] The Reverend John Jennings, later Archdeacon Jennings, was a friend of the family.

Sarah's younger sister survived until 1852, leaving in her will of 1849 a "mourning ring I wear in memory of my late sister, Mrs Smith, with her hair in the centre". Sarah's son, Henry Stone Smith (1795–1881) (fig. 5) was a clerk in the House of Lords from 1819 to 1826, then Clerk of Committees from 1826 to 1840, and was finally promoted Chief Clerk in 1840, a post he retained until 1874 when he retired. Henry played a dramatic part when fire engulfed the Palace of Westminster in 1834. The fire was

a son, Henry Stone Smith, was baptized at the same church on 4 March 1795.[13]

In 1793, Sarah's husband sailed to St Helena, and was away for much of the next few years until finally discharged from the Navy in November 1806, aged "50 years 6 weeks". During that period, Sarah continued to paint, though few pictures have survived from this period. Thomas Pennant included an engraving after one of Sarah's watercolours in his *Views of Hindoostan* (1800), but it was signed "S Stone del" and so must have been executed before 8 September 1789. Sarah seems to have continued to paint birds, for her *Yellow-headed amazon* and *Salmon-crested cockatoo* watercolours, now in a private collection, are dated 1801.

Sarah's husband had been promoted to lieutenant in 1804, and commander in 1806, and he sailed to Jamaica on six occasions during that period, bringing back live birds for his wife. The family still has a note, written by

PLATE 14

Asian tube-nosed bat   *Paranyctimene ?raptor*

NHML (1) 14

the result of a decision to burn a huge quantity of wooden tallies. "Until the Court of Exchequer was abolished in 1826 it had continuously kept records of accounts by a system of tallies and foils, notched elm-wood sticks split in half, one half being retained by the Exchequer, the other half constituting a receipt to those who were required to pay money into the Court."[16] (Charles Dickens made some pithy comments about these sticks and their fate to an audience in Drury Lane: "It would naturally occur to any intelligent person that nothing could be easier than to allow them to be carried away for firewood by the miserable people who live in that neighbourhood. However, they never had been useful, and official routine required that they never should be, and so the order went forth that they should be privately and confidentially burned."[17]) The tallies were burned in the furnace beneath the Lords' chamber and by early the following morning not only the sticks but nearly all the buildings collectively known as the Palace of Westminster lay in smouldering ruins.

While the fire raged, Henry Stone Smith bravely saved many hundreds of bundles of valuable House of Lords records by throwing them out of the blazing windows into Old Palace Yard, where another clerk collected them up and carted them away to temporary resting places, some to St Margaret's Church, just across the road, others to Henry's own house in Queen's Square (later Queen Anne's Gate). Henry's wife and mother probably helped to stack the bundles, while feeling more concern for Henry's safety than that of the dusty old parchments.

Henry Stone Smith had married his step-cousin, Sophia Sheppard (1787–1840), in 1816, and they had nine children, only one of whom, Elizabeth Beale Smith, married. She had one daughter, Florence Sophia Nightingale, born in 1860, the only great-grandchild of Sarah Stone. After the death of his wife, Sophia, on Boxing Day 1840, Henry and his mother and his daughters lived at 3 Smith Square, Westminster. An inscription on a marble tablet in St John's, Westminster, reads, "Susan O'Brian Smith, 1879, Louisa Stone Smith, 1879, and Henry Stone Smith, only son of Capt. John Langdale Smith, R.N., and Sarah, his wife".

NOTES

1 *The Universal Review*, VI, 1890, pp. 583–84. Sarah's sister, Frances Mary Stone (1769–1852) married James Frost Sheppard in 1799 and had a daughter, Frances Smith (1800–1849), who married Lionel John Beale, a surgeon and perhaps the painter of the portrait of John Landale Smith (fig. 2). A second daughter, Louisa Stone (1802–1840), married the artist Lewis Allen, the author of this letter. Letters written by Lewis to his mother, between 1816 and 1831, give valuable information about the life of Sarah and her sister and their families. I am indebted to Mrs Sylvia Ackland, a great-great-great-niece of Sarah, descended through Frances Mary Stone and her husband, for much of the genealogical information in this chapter.

2 George Edwards, *Natural History of Uncommon Birds*, II, p. xix.

3 *The Morning Post and Daily Advertiser*, 10 April 1780, p. 1.

4 Graves (1907), p. 246.

5 Graves (1905–06), Stone, Miss.

6 *The Morning Post and Daily Advertiser*, 25 March 1784, p. 1, col. 3.

7 The original letter is conserved in the library of the Fitzwilliam Museum, Cambridge.

8 *The Morning Post and Daily Advertiser*, 7 April 1785, p. 1; 22 December 1785, p. 1.

9 *The Morning Post and Daily Advertiser*, 26 August–11 November 1790, p. 1.

10 *Universal Review*, VI, 1890, p. 584. John Langdale Smith, the son of John and Mary Smith, was baptized at All Souls, Fulham, on 23 July 1767.

11 Graves (1907), p. 241, and under Smith, John Langdale.

12 No. 3 Cowley Street was situated immediately south of Westminster Abbey precincts, branching out of College Street, where wealthy families and some bishops lived at the end of the eighteenth century. Barton Street and Cowley Street were said to have been built by Barton Booth, an actor. He gave his name to one street, and the other was named after his favourite poet, Abraham Cowley. Cowley Street was built in 1722 and became sought after by Members of Parliament. (Walford and Thornbury, IV, p. 2.)

13 Parish registers of St John the Evangelist, Westminster. Baptisms and Deaths. Local Studies Library, Westminster Public Library, London.

14 *The Gentleman's Magazine*, November 1827, p. 474.

15 St Margaret's parish registers. Deaths 1842–45, p. 142. Muniment Room, Westminster Abbey, London.

16 *The London Encyclopaedia*, edd. Ben Weinreb and Christopher Hibbert, London 1963, p. 576.

17 *Ibid.*

PLATE 15

Pale-throated three-toed sloths *Bradypus tridactylus*

The sloth will never get up this tree to hang upside down. The taxidermist is to blame.

NHML (I) 20

22

PLATE 16

Silky anteater *Cyclops didactylus*

One of four species of anteaters, this has a soft, silky grey-yellow coat with a darker mid-dorsal stripe.
It climbs a tree to rest and in self-defence. The powerful claws are used to rip open ant mounds.

NHML (1) 22

PLATE 17

Domestic goat, angora breed *Capra hircus*

The goat of Angora (= Ankara, Turkey), thought to be the original home of the wild goat, since
domesticated for its long, silky hair, the true 'mohair'.

NHML (1) 21

PLATE 18

Chameleon ?*Chamaeleo bifidus*

This chameleon specimen was carefully prepared to show its long, blue tongue.

NHML (1) 28

Sir Ashton Lever
and his Museum

Ashton Lever (1729–1788) (fig. 6) was educated at Manchester Grammar School and Corpus Christi College, Oxford. He lived at Alkrington Hall, near Manchester, where he formed an aviary of live birds – said to number 4000 – which quickly gained a reputation as the finest in Britain. In 1760, he bought a hogshead of foreign shells in Dunkirk, and these formed the nucleus of a fast-growing collection which eventually included every "curiosious" object on which he could lay his hands. The first published reference to Lever's collection, in *The Gentleman's Magazine* for May 1773, said it consisted of 1300 glass cases, "placed in three rooms besides four sides of rooms shelved from top to bottom with glass doors before them". Lever allowed people to visit the museum, and it was extremely popular, but his expenditure on the collection soon outran his income, forcing him to sell off some land in Lancashire. He determined to remove the whole collection to London, and charge visitors an admission fee.

In 1774, he leased Leicester House in Leicester Fields (now Square), at £600 a year, and displayed the contents of the museum in sixteen rooms, with the intervening corridors all filled with showcases. The house was a vast brick mansion, built in the 1630s for Robert Sidney, 2nd Earl of Leicester (figs. 7 and 9). Lever advertised the museum's opening on 4 February 1775 in *The Morning Post and Daily Advertiser*, "Mr Lever's Museum of Natural and other curiosities, consisting of beasts, birds, fishes, corals, shells, fossils extraneous and native, as well as many miscellaneous articles in high preservation, will be opened on Monday the 13th of February for the inspection of the public ...".[1] Tickets were half a guinea (10s. 6d.) each. A warning was issued: "As Mr Lever has in his collection some very curious monkies and monsters, which might disgust the Ladies, a separate room is appropriated for their exhibition, and the examination of those only who chuse it."

The museum proved to be a great success, despite the enormous entry fee. By the beginning of 1776, a season ticket costing two guineas had been introduced, permitting free admission for one year. The following month Lever advertised to say that so many additional items, gifts and purchases had been added that another room

6 Unknown artist, *Portrait of Sir Ashton Lever*, 1784, engraving

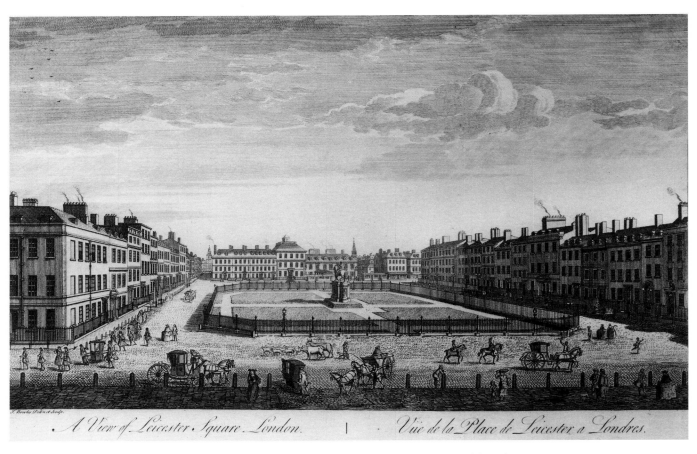

7 Leicester House (at that time the largest house in London) and Leicester Fields in the 1740s, engraving

PLATE 19

A flying (?) snake ?*Chrysopelea* sp.

Flying snakes drop from one branch to another so quickly that they appear to be gliding.

NHML (1) 27

27

8 Thomas Pennant's admission ticket to the Leverian Museum for the year 1780. Copied from the original in the Warwick County Record Office, Pennant papers, CR2017/TP290/2, by permission of the Countess Dowager of Denbigh

had been opened.

On 5 June 1778, Lever was knighted. He had been High Sheriff of Lancashire in 1771, and had fulfilled other obligations as a landowner in Lancashire, while entrusting the running of the museum in London to Thomas Waring, secretary to the museum, in his absence. His knighthood may have been bestowed in connection with his civic duties, rather than his generosity in sharing his museum. In one copy of the 1806 Leverian Museum sale catalogue, a letter written by George Humphrey, 30 December 1812, states, "Sir Ashton Lever came up [to London], with other Gentlemen, to present a Congratulation (I think from the County of Lancashire) to His Majesty on his escape from the knife of Margaret Nicholson, on which Occasion he was Knighted" at St James's Palace.

In this same year, 1778, Susan Burney visited the museum and wrote a letter to her relation Fanny Burney, Madame d'Arblay, which shows the general public's appreciation of the novelties, but also their ignorance about the objects and their importance:

"I wish I was a good Natural Historian, that I might give you some idea of our entertainment in seeing birds, beasts, shells, fossils, &c., but I can scarce remember a dozen names of the thousand I heard that were new to me. The birds of paradise, and the humming-birds, were

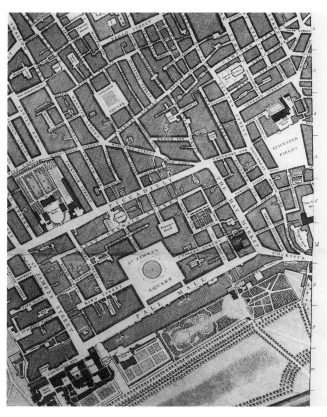

9 From Rocque's map of London, 1746, detail showing Leicester Fields (upper right). Guildhall Library, London

I think, among the most beautiful. There are several pelicans, flamingos, peacocks (one quite white), a penguin. among the beasts, a hippopotamus (sea horse) of an immense size, an elephant, a tyger from the Tower, a Greenland bear and its cub – a wolf – two or three leopards – and Otaheite dog (a very coarse ugly-looking creature) – a camelion – a young crocodile ... Lizzards, bats, toads, frogs, scorpions and other filthy creatures in abundance. There were a great many things from Otaheite, the complete dress of a Chinese Mandarine, made of blue and brown sattin – of an African Prince. A suit of armour that they say belonged to Oliver Cromwell – the Dress worn in Charles 1st's time – etc, – etc – etc."[2]

Serious natural historians were more appreciative, and Gilbert White, Thomas Pennant and John Latham, in particular, visited the museum (see fig. 8) to see newly purchased items from ships which had visited the Americas, the Indies and, most importantly, returned

Sarah Stone · 1784

PLATE 20

Hercules beetle or Horned scarab *Dynastes hercules*

The Hercules beetle from south America can attain six inches in length. The male has a long horn
on the thorax and a smaller one on its head.

NHML (1) 24

from the second and third voyages round the world by Captain Cook (1772–75 and 1776–79). The naturalists must have found the broad grouping of similar animals, with no attempt at a scientific arrangement, frustrating.

Artists, too, visited the museum, to draw and paint the specimens. Sarah Stone was chief among them, and seems to have been unperturbed by the huge variety, calmly settling down in each successive department to draw items of greatest novelty, suggested by Sir Ashton Lever, or subjects requested by authors.

The true significance of the Lever collection, and Sarah's record of it, has only been realised in the twentieth century, when scientists have been obliged to search for scraps of evidence regarding the zoological and ethnographic exhibits from old catalogues of museums and passing references in the few natural history books of the late eighteenth century. Only now do we recognize the full value of Sarah Stone's watercolours, executed in the museum both during the time it was in Lever's ownership, and later when James Parkinson owned it.

Between 9 June and 12 September, the museum opening hours, normally 11 a.m. to 4 p.m., were extended until "7 at night", but by then the original price of admittance had been halved. Advertisements appeared in the London newspaper, *The Morning Post and Daily Advertiser*, similar to the one on 8 June 1778: "Sir Ashton Lever's museum containing many thousand articles, displayed in two galleries, the whole length of Leicester House, is open every day … . Admittance 5s and 3d each person". Initially, crowds had flocked to the museum, but attendance had slackened. Lever nevertheless took about £13,000 in entry fees between February 1775 and February 1784. He continued to place advertisements in the newspaper, sometimes whetting the public's curiosity by ambiguity. On 20 May 1779, for example, he wrote, "Sir Ashton Lever informs his subscribers that a living curiosity is arrived at Leicester House, so particularly charac-

terised as to be worth their early inspection". This advertisement continued to appear until 19 June, and was changed on 24 June. On 10 April 1780, the advertisement noted that "the tutor and governess are included in the family ticket" (costing five guineas). However, Lever was still being so lavish in his expenditure, constantly adding to the collection, that by 1784 he had to face selling the museum in order to recoup his losses.

In 1783, the collection, containing 28,000 articles, was valued (at £53,000) and a report presented to a committee of the House of Commons.[3] Lever offered the collection to the British Museum for a moderate sum, but the trustees declined to buy it. On the basis of the Parliamentary report, Lever obtained an Act of Parliament, allowing him to dispose of the whole by a lottery. The Act was passed in October 1784,[4] and Lever had 36,000 tickets printed, priced at one guinea each (see fig. 10).

On 7 April 1785, Sir Ashton's advertisement in *The Morning Post and Daily Advertiser* informed the public, "This collection is allowed to be infinitely superior to any of the kind in Europe … the average amount [spent on it] for the last three years being £1833 per annum …. No one will hereafter be admitted but by the Lottery Tickets, excepting those who have already annual admission." On 16 January 1786, the notice was published, "The Lottery for Sir Ashton Lever's museum will be drawn in Guildhall, London, one of the days betwixt the 20th and 25th March next …. The first drawn number will be the prize, consisting of the whole of this most invaluable Museum, a schedule of which was laid before Parliament, and is annexed to the act, containing upwards of 26,000 articles."[5]

The lottery took place on 24 March 1786,[6] by which time only 8000 tickets had been sold. Lever decided to go ahead, despite the lack of interest, reckoning that his chance of winning, with 28,000 tickets still in his possession, was high. His gamble failed when lot no. 34,119

PLATE 21

Fossils: two views of the internal cast of a naticid gastropod in white stone; part and counterpart of a fossil leaf in a nodule

Sarah painted these fossils prior to June 1778, very early in her acquaintance with Ashton Lever.

31

1

Buccinites
Thama

2

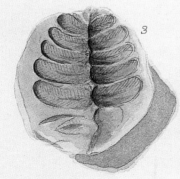

3

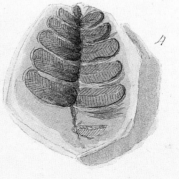

4

Nᵒ 1 }
2 } Buccinites Thama
3 }
4 } Coal Brook Dale

In the Collection of Ashton Lever Esqᵣ

10 Three of Thomas Pennant's six lottery tickets for the Leverian Museum. Copied from the originals in the Warwick County Record Office, Pennant papers, CR2017/TP280/1–4, by permission of the Countess Dowager of Denbigh

was drawn. An agonizing five weeks then elapsed before the prize was claimed.[7]

While visiting London, a German lady, Sophie von La Roche, went to the museum shortly after the draw had taken place, and heard from Sir Ashton himself what had happened when he discovered that he did not hold the winning ticket.

"Through a delegation of his friends, parliament and people gave permission to Sir Ashton to show his collection daily until the beginning of November at a charge, and the latter has been streaming in horde-wise ever since to help pay damages to the poor man thus twice disappointed. Sir Ashton not only did he not sell his lots, but lost a hope cherished for five weeks; for during the period after the draw there was no announcement made, and Sir Ashton himself, and his friends as well, thought

some magnanimous soul had won it and decided not to put in an appearance ... when a barrister turned up with the winning ticket, saying that his late wife had taken part in his lottery unbeknown to him and died before the draw. He was her heir and had found the lot when looking through her papers."

On 11 April, Sir Ashton again used the first page of *The Morning Post and Daily Advertiser* to notify his readers,

"Sir Ashton Lever presents his compliments to his Friends and the Public, and informs them that his late Museum is now open again, and will continue open everyday until further notice, for his sole advantage, at Half-a-Crown each, by permission of James Parkinson, Esq, at the usual hours of Eleven until Four."

Popular sympathy was such that while Lever was allowed to keep the museum open, "some went ten and more times to see it, contributing an equal number of shillings toward his losses". Sophie von La Roche said that James Parkinson, having destroyed the fine ideal of generosity entertained for so many weeks, found that "nearly all showed a certain aversion" to him.

She described having been met at the museum by Lever, who showed her round it.

"In the first entrance stood a number of long, narrow cupboards, on which large crests were painted [where] distinguished officers' uniforms were kept ... ready to hand there for service. Then the big door to the main apartments opened, and we stood in a large marble hall at the foot of a handsome staircase, in the midst of a heap of old armour and guns from every age and corner of the globe, displayed as trophies. The high walls of the well-hole are hung with dried sea-monsters of every description, and at the top of the flight of stairs in front of the first room an excellently stuffed young elephant bids one welcome. On leaving him one enters the room, hung with sea-green damask, curtains of the same, and with sweet little benches by the windows. Lining three walls there are nothing but neat glass cases containing all species of sand, earth, stones, metals, resins and

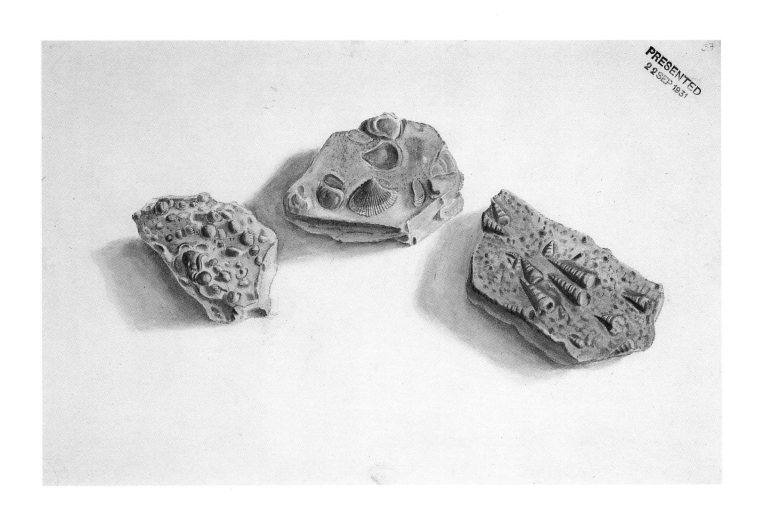

PLATE 22

Three pieces of fossiliferous rock (probably Wenlock limestone) with high-spired Turrilitid gastropods,
with a caritid bivalve and a globose gastropod, and with small brachiopods and a trilobite fragment.

NHML (1) 37

PLATE 23

Honeycomb oyster *Hyotissa hyotis*

From the Caribbean and Indo-Pacific.

NHML (1) 57

PLATE 24

Bear's paw clam *Hippopus hippopus*

This south-west Pacific shell grows to a massive foot in length. There is a great variation of this species. In the Solomon Islands the sculpting on the outside of the valves look like small curled protuberances but the surface of specimens in the Sula Sea of the Philippines are nearly smooth.

NHML (1) 54

fossils. Madrepores come next; after all kinds of birds from every clime, from the ostrich to the humming-bird, whole families of them, old and young, eggs and nests. A room full of fish is equally fine and perfect, another containing various kinds of snake and reptiles; all the rare quadrupeds of the known world; all manner of apes and insects. Another room full of musical instruments of all nations, ancient and modern, and in with these different types of music since the discovery of notes. Of all these sights the most charming and unique was the person of Sir Ashton himself, a good friendly man of some fifty years or so."[8]

An English visitor, the Revd W. Gilpin, was rather more critical. When writing to Mrs Delany, he complained that Lever "had endeavoured to array his birds to the best advantage by placing them in *white* boxes round his rooms, and when you enter you are presented with a succession of rooms, still multiplied by a mirror at the end, everywhere invested with these little white apartments". Gilpin deplored the lightness of the rooms and this whiteness, saying that a display of birds would be much better "if they were set off by some *deep shadow behind*". Gilpin had seen the collection when it was in Alkrington and, although it was not so varied, he thought it had been better displayed there.[9]

Lever evidently felt the loss of his museum keenly. He told Sophie von La Roche, "I come here daily to view these objects which I cherish as old friends; for one day they will be in strange hands .... It was a passion of mine to possess all nature's wonders, no expense was spared; I have spent over a million on it, and now that I am old, I find I have hardly enough to be able to live in comfort."

Lever retired to Alkrington in November 1786, managed what was left of his estate (he had sold most of his property in Manchester in the early 1780s to raise funds for the museum), and fulfilled his duties as a magistrate.

He died suddenly, at the Bull's Head Inn, Manchester, on either 31 January or 1 February 1788.[10] A short notice about Sir Ashton Lever, in *The Annals of Manchester* for 1788, concluded, "It has been surmised that Sir Ashton's death was due to poison self-administered."[11]

On 8 August 1786, the secretary to the Leverian Museum, Thomas Waring, told readers of *The Morning Post and Daily Advertiser* that the museum, "late Sir Ashton Lever's, will continue open ... until Michaelmas Day next At Half a Crown each On which day Mr Parkinson, the holder of the Fortunate Ticket ... takes possession thereof". Waring decided to use the same means to communicate the news (26 September 1786) that "Mr Waring presents his compliments ... and he will remain at Leicester House until the 25th of next March". Waring remained at Leicester House until it was demolished following the death of the 7th and last Earl of Leicester in 1791.[12]

The majority of Sarah Stone's paintings are dated to the 1780s, when Sir Ashton owned the museum, and include the watercolour of the museum at Leicester House (see frontispiece), which she exhibited at the Royal Academy in 1786. This must have been a momentous year for her, too, with the uncertainty about the fate of the museum, and Sir Ashton's unhappiness. What, she must have wondered, would it be like at the museum with a new owner.

James Parkinson and the Leverian Museum

James Parkinson (*ca.* 1730–1813) discovered that he was the new owner of the Leverian Museum some time in May 1786. The unexpected legacy from his wife must have been a considerable shock, and it may have been a little while before he revealed his hand.

According to *The Dictionary of National Biography*, Parkinson was born in Shrewsbury, and was trained in the business of a law stationer.[13] This downplays Sophie

PLATE 25

West African duplex murex *Hexaplex duplex*

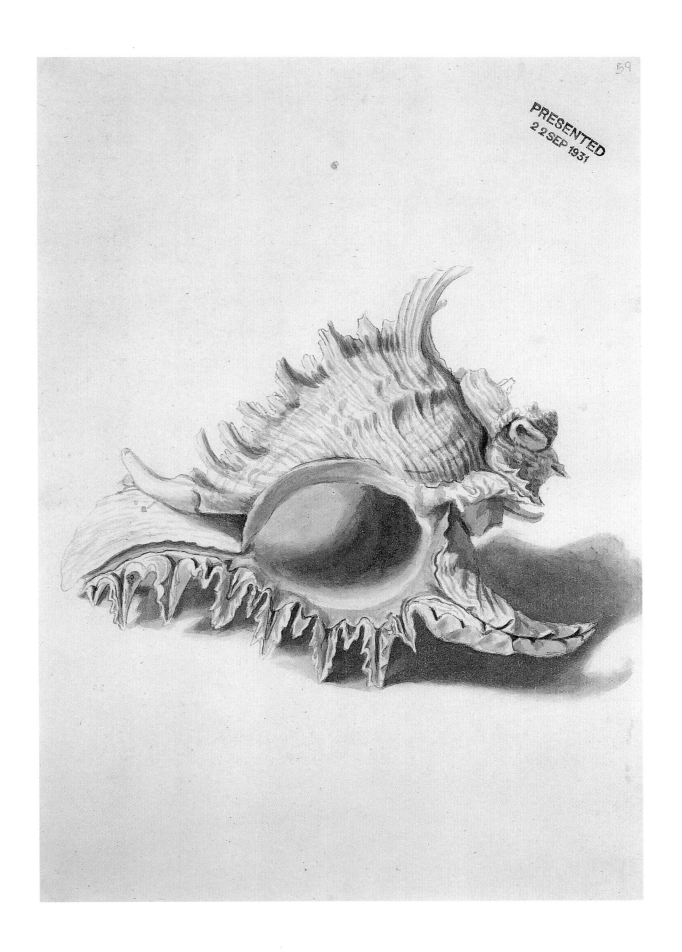

von La Roche and others' reference to him as a "barris-ter", and contradicts Mullens's statement that he was a dentist.[14] In his capacity of law stationer, he became an agent to many noblemen's estates. He was fifty-six when he acquired the museum, and his first instinct was to attempt to sell it. The Queen of Portugal and the Empress of Russia were tempted, but eventually declined to buy it. Parkinson could not afford the high rent of Leicester House, so sought an alternative site. While he deliberated, he permitted Lever to continue to exhibit at Leicester House, until 25 September 1786.

Despite the hesitant start, once he took over, Parkinson became quite entrepreneurial in exploiting the possibilities of the museum. In March 1787, he pro-posed "to introduce a course of Lectures on Natural history, which shall be read at his museum, by a gentle-man of the most respectable character".[15] He was more enterprising in advertising new acquisitions, such as the "Creature of Ape species, strongly impressed with the human similitudes being when living, nearly five feet in height, a Unique", along with "A curious Partridge (variety), A beautiful Ring Pheasant, Also a remarkable fine Blue and Yellow Maccaw, brought from the Havan-nah, by General Keppel, in 1762. Fossils, some very ele-gant varieties of spars, &c."[16] The collection was to be arranged in the "New Building lately constructed for its reception" – the Rotunda in Albion Place, south of Blackfriars Bridge – with 1000 square yards of space in seventeen apartments.[17]

Parkinson owned the Leverian Museum for twenty years, from 1786 until 1806; Lever had shown his collec-tion in London for twelve years, from 1775 to 1786. Despite this discrepancy, it is the name of Sir Ashton Lever that is still known, while Parkinson's is largely for-gotten. Part of the reason for this lies in Parkinson real-ising that advertising his museum as "The Leverian Museum" would not only provide continuity and utilize the kudos gained by Lever, but would also allay some of the animosity towards him for having claimed the museum by declaring he held the winning ticket. When he moved the collection from Leicester House to the Rotunda, he had the words "Leverian Museum" engraved in the headstone over the entrance.[18]

Parkinson closed the museum at Leicester House on 1 September 1787 and spent three months moving all the exhibits to the Rotunda, where he opened the museum on 3 December 1787, charging an admittance fee of 2s. 6d. The new site, however, was on the wrong side of the river for fashionable Londoners, in a district where there was no other attraction, and this always militated against the popularity of the museum.

Parkinson nevertheless proved to be a good show-man, advertised well and published a booklet about the museum in 1790, followed by an illustrated catalogue of the most memorable items, *A Companion to the museum*, which began publication in 1792. He dedicated the first fascicule to George III and Queen Charlotte, and another, in 1796, to Sir Joseph Banks. He also added to the museum, constantly attempting to keep the collection fresh and interesting: for example, an ivory cup from Vienna, "A beautiful male Elk", an alligator, an ape from Mount Tibet, an Impeyan Pheasant.[19] The elk advertise-ment read:

"A beautiful male ELK. This noble creature is the most lofty of all the European quadrupeds, and may be con-sidered as the first ornament of the forest. It is a per-fect, grand, and stately figure, and appears with inexpressible animation. The curious in Natural His-tory will now have an opportunity of determining whether this is of the same species with the American elk figured and described by Mr Pennant. The Natural History of this animal in manuscript by Dr Peter Gustavus Lindroth may be read at the Museum."

This ran in the newspaper until 5 August, and the elk was then included in a list of "many additions" on 19 August, as "A most grand and beautiful ELK".

The collection grew, and Parkinson intimated to his visitors that "several necessary alterations have been made in the arrangement".[20] Some new iron ores from the Electorate of Trier were acquired in May 1789, and more fossils, including aventurine and opals, arrived in 1791.[21] In 1789, Parkinson scooped an exciting natural history specimen:

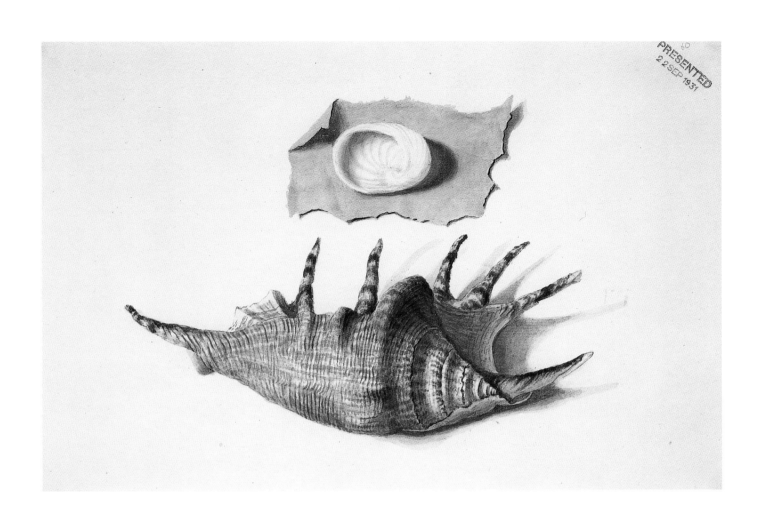

PLATE 26

Fluted clam *Tridacna squamosa* (Lamarck 1819) and Thorny oyster *Spondylus* sp.

Top: The scaly or fluted clam with a thick shell with convex ribs has a greyish-white inside, sometimes tinged with yellow. By placing it on a piece of blue paper, Sarah has given it a three-dimensional effect. It was not described scientifically for another thirty years after she painted it.

Bottom: One of the numerous species of *Spondylus*, thorny oysters, ornamented with spines.

NHML (1) 60

11 *Portrait of George Shaw,* Assistant Keeper and Keeper of Natural History in the British Museum from 1791 to 1813

"A male Kanguru, of the largest species, being one of the most perfect specimens yet arrived from New South Wales. It stands upwards of five feet from the ground, and exceeds in length by twelve inches that described by Mr Pennant ... . One principal variation is its moving in an erect posture on its hind feet and its tail, by means of which, when pursued, it springs over bushes ten feet in height and flies from its pursuer with astonishing swiftness by successive leaps or bounds of as many yards in length."

This was so novel an acquisition that it was advertised from 21 July until 8 October 1789. An "Elastic Stone, from the Brazils" was also procured this year,

culminating in December with:

"A noble and unique specimen of the Condor or great South American vulture, the only Bird of its kind ever brought to Europe. It is the largest of all known Birds that are able to fly, and from its extraordinary strength and size has given rise to many incredible and romantic accounts. It is represented in the act of seizing on another animal of an amphibious nature, most curiously formed. This latter is both a unique and non-descript. The extent of the wings of the Bird, when spread, measured from tip to tip ten feet one inch; but authors of credit affirm wings of Birds of this species have been known to measure six yards from tip to tip."[22]

In an advertisement in March 1790, Parkinson stated, "Recently added to the Museum, a variety of Specimens of the most rare and beautiful Birds from Guayana, in South America". Objects obtained from Captain Cook's last voyage (1776–80), collected at Nootka Sound, off the west of Vancouver Island, were noted in *The World* on 25 June 1790, and Australian specimens sent back to England by John White after he had landed with the First Fleet to colonize Australia were presented to the museum by Thomas Wilson. They were advertised from 26 August until 11 November 1790.

Unlike Lever, Parkinson attempted to record the contents of his museum, room by room, by means of an illustrated catalogue. The *Companion to the Museum* was compiled by George Shaw (fig. 11), from the British Museum, and the frontispiece to the first issue, of 1790, the *Companion to the museum removed to Albion Street, the Surrey end of Black Friars Bridge,* showed the famous round room from which the building got its name, the Rotunda, with a welcoming, proprietorial figure, tricorn hat in hand, at the entrance. This engraving had been copied from a

PLATE 27

Carrier shell *Xenophora ?conchyliophora*

These are sometimes called 'original shell collectors' from their curious habit of cementing other shells, bits of coral and other debris to their shells.

NHML (1) 72

72

Sarah Stone - 1782.

53

12 Sarah Stone and C. Ryley, The interior of the Rotunda where the Leverian Museum
was housed when owned by James Parkinson from 1787 until 1806,
engraving by W. Skelton

The Rotunda.

13 *The Rotunda*, 1805, engraving by S. Porter

joint work, inscribed *Miss Stone & C Ryley delin. W Skelton sculp.* (fig. 12). Which artist was responsible for which section of this illustration is not known. The room was shown lined with display cases containing birds, and some visitors enjoying the museum. The same engraving, with different visitors and without the welcoming figure, appeared in an 1803 description of the museum, signed merely *S Porter sc* (fig. 13). It has not been possible to identify the proprietorial figure. Sir Ashton Lever owned a tricorn hat, similar to the one in the first engraving, but the face is not like any of his portraits, least of all the portrait in which he is wearing a tricorn hat. Nor can the face, which is that of a young man, be that of Parkinson, who was seventy-three at the time. Perhaps it was one of his sons, who is known to have been present at the museum.

Parts I and II of the *Companion* were advertised as being for sale at the museum, price 2s. 6d. each, in November 1794, but by this time the series had been discontinued owing to lack of interest. Shaw had begun by describing the contents of the entrance hall; then of the Sandwich Room, in which the South Seas enthnographical items were displayed; and then the Saloon, where natural curiosities such as pods, plants and roots, fossils, nests and eggs and parts of birds, quadrupeds and fishes were displayed. Zoophytes and minerals followed. The *Companion* ceased before the really colourful and more familiar mammals and birds had been reached. The museum had been carefully arranged in order to take the viewer through what might have been perceived as the 'duller' items, towards the great Rotunda which was full of brightly coloured birds. Shaw's progression in the catalogue might have been logical, but it was not adroit from a commercial point of view.

Parkinson's next publishing venture was far more attractive, and successful. He again employed George Shaw to write the text, but this time got some of the best animal artists to make colourful illustrations, for his *Museum Leverianum*. This was advertised in *The Morning Post and Fashionable World* (30 September and 4 October 1794, among other dates): "Price coloured (to persons subscribing for a second volume) five guineas; plain three Pounds. To be had at the Museum; also parts first and second of a Catalogue to the Museum, price 2s. 6d. each".

Parkinson must have become aware of the value of good drawings about this time, because there was a curious sentence added to the advertisements for the museum at the end of that same year: "Youth subscribing may draw any of the figures for their pleasure or improvement".[22] At this time, good fires were still noted as a feature for the comfort of visitors, with new additions of "The magnificent Bird of Paradise, A Beautiful specimen of Native Gold, and Another of Copper, pronounced to be matchless". More significantly, and ominously, the price of admittance was now down to "One Shilling".

Despite all Parkinson's attempts to revitalize the collection, public interest waned and he was losing money. By 1806, he could no longer afford to support the museum, and was forced to sell it. The story of his attempts to dispose of it are recorded in the diaries of Joseph Farington, an artist and a great London gossip. On 9 July 1806, he wrote that Parkinson had:

"... offered it to the late government & Mr Pitt referred it to Lord Melville, but nothing was done. He offered it to the present administration. Lord Grenville referred it to Lord Henry Petty, who approved the proposal and the conditions offered by Parkinson, viz: £20,000 *not to be exceeded* whatever it might be valued at by persons appointed & *less if it shd. be valued under that Sum.* — But

PLATE 28

Spider conch *Lambis chiragra*

Inside of the shell called Devil's claw in the collection of Ashton Lever Esq

This was painted prior to June 1788. The spider conch has a thick shell with a conical spire and six long projections.

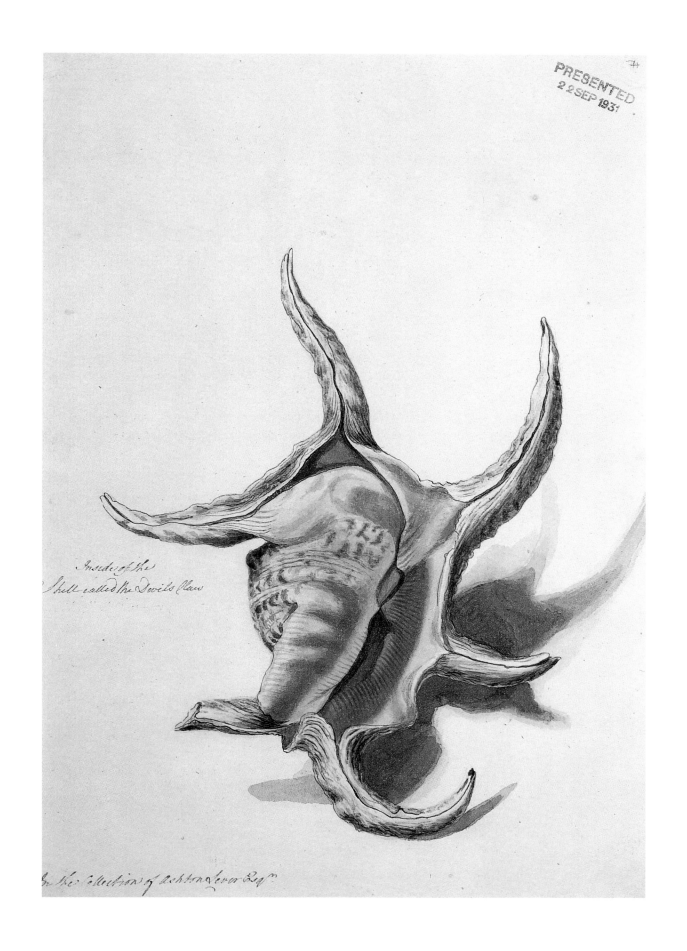

Inside of the
Shell called the Devils Claw

In the Collection of Ashton Lever Esqr.

PLATE 29

Gorgonian coral in the subclass *Octocorallia*

Monochrome drawing of a gorgonia with eight feather-like tentacles.

NHML (1) 77

PLATE 30

Gorgonian coral in the subclass *Octocorallia*

NHML (1) 80

Ministers declined responsiblity & referred it to Sir Joseph Banks *who disapproved purchasing it.* Parkinson says Sir Joseph hated Sir Ashton Lever & therefore hates the collection."[24]

Banks's dislike might well have stemmed from the fact that Lever and Parkinson had arranged objects aesthetically rather than scientifically. They made no attempt to place the zoological specimens in any taxonomic order.

The sale of the Leverian Museum, 1806

Parkinson decided to sell the museum by auction. The sale turned out to be a great social event in London, lasting for sixty-five days, from Monday 5 May to Saturday 19 July, with breaks for the sabbath and the King's birthday. Over the first fifty-seven days, for which there was a printed catalogue, 6840 lots were sold. A further group of 354 lots was sold on the last day but two, the last day but one, and the last day, and still there remained 684 lots, many of which were composite, that were listed in an Appendix for a further five days of auctions. Edward Donovan, a naturalist with a collection of his own, and the author of several natural history books, was asked to prepare the sale catalogue of 7879 lots. The sale netted Parkinson "£6,642. 13. 6d, out of which £1,600 was bought back, and a few of the principal lots passed, as no adequate price was offered". According to a letter written by the officiating auctioneer throughout the entire sale, John Lochée, the sale was well attended, "Indeed there were more people the last than the first Days".[25]

Farington wrote: "Being sold in Lots it has sold very well & will probably produce 10 or £12000, besides the value of valuable things which it is probable will not be purchased. – Charles Greville has purchased, – Lord Ossery, Lord Stanley & others *Birds*; – Lord Tankerville *Shells*. – Hayes is collecting *Minerals."* There was no representative from the British Museum.[26]

There were just over 180 bidders, and a few copies of the catalogue were annotated by people attending the sale. Not every lot was annotated, but a surprising number of the 7878 lots had notes written in by hand. From these annotations we know most of the names of the bidders, which lots they purchased and at what price (see fig. 5). There were three main bidders. Edward Donovan, who had compiled the catalogue and owned a museum open to the public which displayed British natural history items, obtained some 500 lots and was by far the largest purchaser. He was followed by Leopold von Fichtel, who bid for just over 400 lots on behalf of the Imperial Museum in Vienna; during the sale Fichtel stayed at 5 Arundel Street, Strand. Lord Stanley of Knowsley Park was present on many of the days when birds were offered for sale, and up to the fortieth day (20 June 1806) bought birds in his own name; later in the sale, he deputed the task of bidding to T. Thompson,[27] a dealer and taxidermist who was attending the sale. Lord Stanley acquired about 100 bird species, some of which were represented by both the male and female, less often also by the young of the species.

Fewer lots were purchased by William Bullock, owner of another museum which exhibited at the Egyptian Hall in London, following its removal from Liverpool; nineteen Lever items were exhibited in his museum after the sale. A Captain Laskey bought in for the Hunterian Museum, Glasgow.

Thomas Pennant purchased two lots (lot 200, a waxwing, and lot 317, a jackdaw variety and sparrow variety). George Humphrey,[28] another dealer, of 4 Leicester Street, Leicester Square, London, the original owner of the marked-up sale catalogue that was used for the 1979 reprint, made a few purchases and marked them with a cross +.

If Sarah attended the sale, she would have seen hundreds of objects that she had sketched and painted. Two lots would have been of particular interest to her, for they were her own watercolours. Mrs Oliphant paid £2. 10s. od. for Sarah's watercolour of the interior of the Leverian Museum when it was in Leicester Square (lot 887) (and evidently shared Sarah's interest in birds, for she also bought a blue-breasted finch (lot 3502) and a kingfisher from the South Seas (lot 3529)). A second watercolour painting by Miss Stone, lot 3117, "Two elegant drawings of agates", framed and glazed, was bought for 10s. 6d. by Sivers.

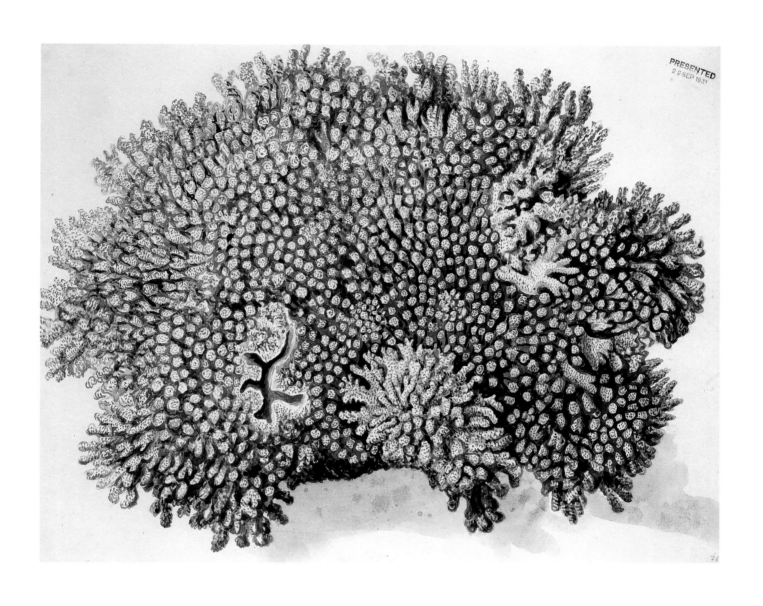

PLATE 31

Scleractinian coral *Acropora* sp.

NHML (1) 76

Most of the animals in the sale were sold in glass cases. They were stuffed, mounted specimens, preserved from dust and insects by being enclosed in this manner. Where the specimens were not encased, this is noted in the catalogue. Fragile specimens, such as worms, snakes, fishes, were kept in stoppered jars and bottles.

Where possible, the watercolours of specimens and species by Sarah Stone that are listed in this book have been linked to the Leverian Museum sale catalogue lots. We know that she painted in the museum (for example, among the watercolours in a private collection, one sheet bears the inscription, unfortunately undated, "Ab^r this time I was in London & saw Miss Stone at Museum"), and it is reasonable to assume that many of the objects in the sale – both zoological specimens and ethnographical articles – had been painted by her. In some instances there is direct evidence by which the paintings can be linked to sale lots; in many, however, this is not possible, and the notes on the sale catalogue descriptions merely indicate the possibility that an object may have been one painted by her. Unfortunately, very few of the museums owning paintings also own the complementary physical articles.

The dispersal of the Leverian exhibits

During the time that the zoological specimens and ethnographical artefacts were in the museum (under the proprietorship of Sir Ashton Lever to 1786, and of Parkinson from 1786 to 1806), several catalogues and guides were published. Only the 1790 *Companion*, however, described the collection in detail, and that was left incomplete owing to lack of public support for the publication. It was not until 1806, when the sale catalogue of the museum's possessions was drawn up, that a full list of the museum contents was published.

The 7879 lots itemized by Edward Donovan in the sale catalogue had for the most part single-line entries, and Donovan had the use of Lever's original labels to guide him. Sophie von La Roche recorded that "Good Sir Ashton had labelled and named even the smallest trifles, or attached little pieces of cardboard, so that the curious might find information about everything, complete". This was important, especially as "Captain Cook so much admired this good Ashton's intellect, he gave him a complete collection of all kinds of South Sea curiosities which to me seems much vaster even than the one in the British Museum."[29] However, there were deficiencies: many entries in the catalogue were of groups of items, such as "Glass case with 6 species of pigeon", which are of no use now when trying to trace the locations of items from the museum. There were hundreds of composite lots, which occur most frequently, as one would expect, with small insects and similar exhibits that were difficult to label. Donovan's own purchases appear in the catalogue for the sale of his museum in 1818, and others in the sale catalogue of the Bullock Museum in the same year.

Fortunately, the sale was attended by at least four buyers with sufficient interest to mark up their catalogues with the names of some the successful bidders, and the prices they paid for each lot. Several attempts have been made, on the basis of the annotated sale catalogues, to identify the Leverian Museum specimens now conserved in public museums, and papers detailing extant specimens have been published. But two centuries have passed, and only a small portion of the original exhibits has survived either the passage of time or the recataloguing and relabelling that have taken place. Original labels, also, were often either lost or wrongly transferred to specimens when they were taken out of their glass cases, dismounted and converted into skins for storage in drawers.

Two buyers who bought a large number of items subsequently deposited them in museums where some of the items may still be found: Leopold von Fichtel's items for

PLATE 32

Sea fan *Isis* sp.

NHML (1) 78

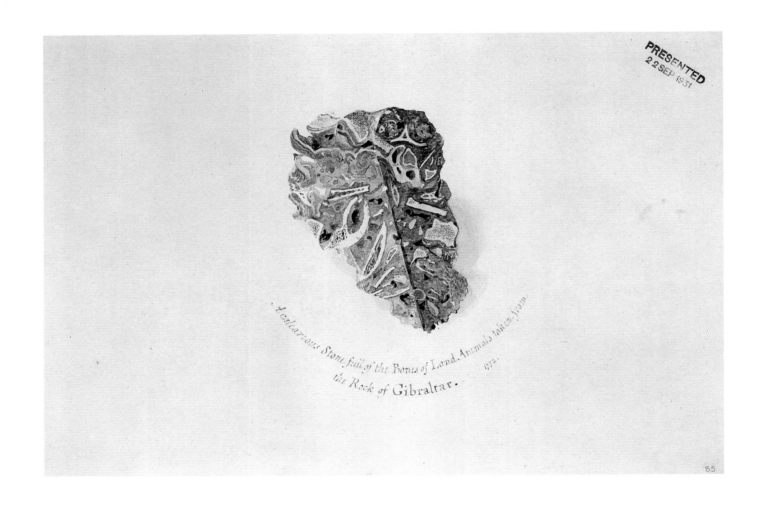

PLATE 33

Quaternary fissure breccia with mammalian bones, probably from Rosia Bay, Gibraltar

Gibraltar was ceded to Britain by Spain in 1713. It contains extensive limestone caves.

NHML (1) 85

PLATE 34

Fossil fish or reptile teeth

Mass of Fishes teeth found in the Blue Lodge Quarry, near Bath.

NHML (1) 87

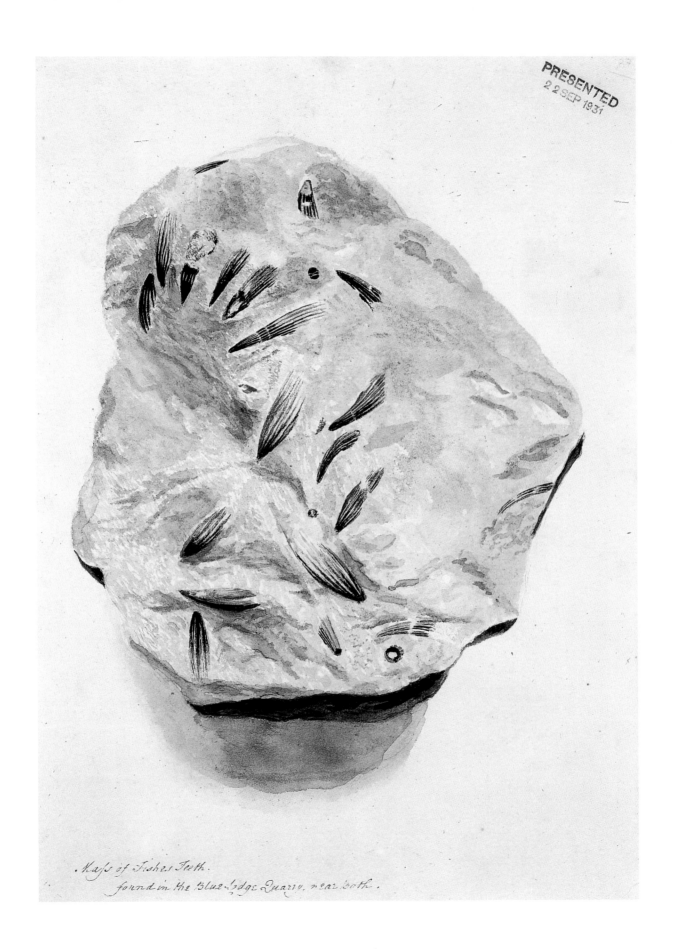

Mass of Fishes Teeth.
found in the Blue Lodge Quarry, near Both.

65

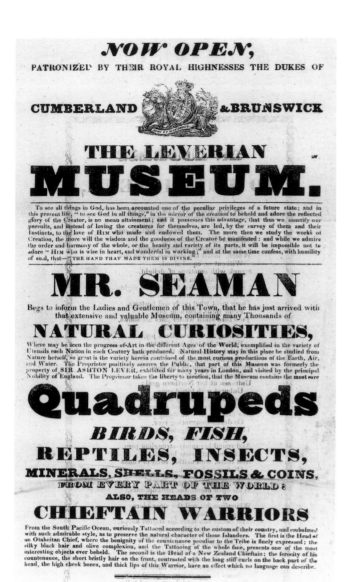

14 Mr Seaman's advertisement using the name 'The Leverian Museum'. The Archives Department of The Natural History Museum, London

the Imperial Museum in Vienna,[30] and Lord Stanley's purchases which were later deposited in the Liverpool Museum, where some remain.[31]

Eleven bird specimens survive in the Swedish Museum of Natural History in Stockholm. In 1788, sixty-one birds, valued at 200 guineas, were given by Lever to the Museum Grillianum, a private museum at Söderfors, in exchange for the Swedish elk brought over to England by Pehr Gustaf Lindroth (1758–1809), a Swedish ornithologist and surgeon major in the Uppland regiment. Twenty-four of the birds were later transferred to Stockholm, of which eleven remain, and eight of these are represented by Sarah's watercolour drawings. The birds were all duplicates, other specimens having remained in the Leverian Museum up to the date of the sale.[32]

A certain amount of confusion ensued when buyers of lots from the Leverian Museum sale for their own collections then described these as being "Leverian".[33] A travelling museum owner, Simpson Seaman, for example, advertised in Ely by means of a broadsheet: "Now open ... The Leverian Museum". A poem, dated 30 October 1824, addressed to the owner by the Revd. W. Harrison, was printed on the reverse of one of these broadsheets and directed to Mr Seaman, Leverian Museum, Ely (see fig. 14).

"A Mr Simpson Seaman of Ipswich had a museum of natural history, presumably in that city, and issued a catalogue without indication of place or date. It was named the Leverian Museum, possibly from its proprietor having made extensive purchases at the dispersal of Parkinson's Leverian Musum. Or was he a recognized successor to the exhibition originally established by Sir Ashton Lever."[34]

This, however, was a faulty surmise; Seaman does not

PLATE 35

Four calcareous sponges   *Callyspongia* sp. or *Aplysina* sp.; *Niphates ?digitalis*; *Ianthella ?basta*;

Dactylochaliia sp.

NHML (1) 79

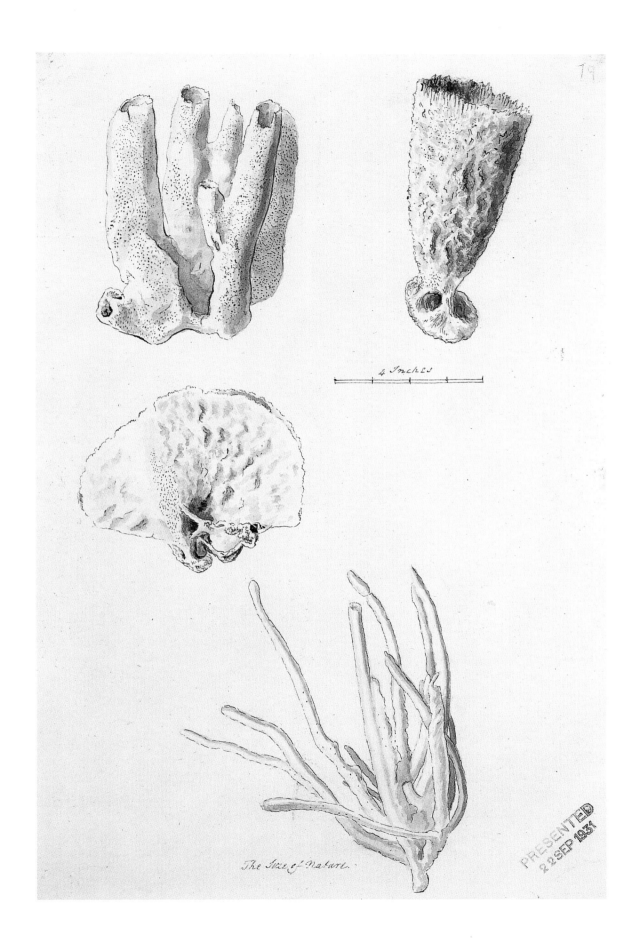

4 Inches

The Size of Nature.

figure as a purchaser at the Leverian Museum sale of 1806 in any of the annotated sale catalogues.

James Parkinson died at Somers Town, London, on 25 February 1813, aged eighty-three, leaving two sons and a daughter. One of the sons, Joseph (1783–1855), was an architect, and when the Rotunda was altered after the Leverian Museum left, he designed the library for the Surrey Institution in 1809. He was surveyor to the Union Assurance Society, subsequently housed there, until 1854.

The second son, James, was frequently seen at the museum. Robert Jameson, the Scottish naturalist, later a professor at the University of Edinburgh, met him there in 1793 and thought him "a very polite and agreable young man".[35] After the sale, James Parkinson was employed as a diplomat in Brazil and France. William Clift (1775–1849), who was employed by John Hunter at his museum, annotated his own copy of the Leverian Museum sale catalogue, and there is a note in the endpapers which reads:

"Mr Parkinson married some relative of the Duke of Devonshire (a natural daughter?) and was sent I think to Bahia as Consul, or something of that kind. I saw him in Paris in Novr. 1819 covered with Gold Epaulettes going to pay his respect to Louis XVIII, in sword & bag & buckles & white silk stockings. I was surprized at his recollecting me and the Leverian Museum, & his then dirty face and hands."[36]

The fame of Sir Ashton Lever's museum has lingered on, despite its dispersal, and Sarah Stone's drawings are now "often the only extant record or means of authenticating objects in that museum, particularly those from the Cook voyages".[37] Today, we should appreciate having all the "thousand transparent drawings in watercolours", advertised in *The Morning Post and Daily Advertiser*, 25 March 1784, but must recognize that it is remarkable that we still have over 740 in public ownership, with a further 117 plus known to be in private collections. A few more have gone through the sale rooms and their present location is unknown; they are probably in private homes, unrecognized because they bear no signature. More may well be discovered and identified in the future.

NOTES

1 Ashton Lever (Sir Ashton Lever after 1778) advertised his museum in *The Morning Post and Daily Advertiser* from 1775–86, the advertisement appearing on every occasion on p. 1.

2 *The Early Diary of Frances Burney, 1768–1778*: letter from Miss Susan Burney, 16 July 1778, following a visit on Saturday morning to the museum.

3 *Gentleman's Magazine*, 1812, 1, vol. LXXXII, p. 516. John Church (born *ca.* 1740), a friend of Lever's, whom he visited both at home and at the Leverian Museum in Leicester House, made the report to the Committee of the House of Commons. Church said that he himself was a collector and had seen all other collections of note in England, and that "the whole of them put together, would not form one so rare and valuable as that at Leicester House; that the Articles there are in complete beauty and Perfection; that he had taken great Pains to form an Estimate of their value, ascertained by the Prices he had known similar Articles sell for at Public Sales, or otherwise; and that, according to his Calculation, the Value of the whole to be sold, is upwards of 53,000*l.*" Church knew the contents of the Museum well, and enjoyed a special relationship with their owner, being allowed to play with the live animals Sir Ashton Lever owned at various times. Church was especially interested in mammals, and wrote *A Cabinet of Quadrupeds*, 2 vols., 84 pls., London [1795]–1805, while Parkinson owned the museum. There are references to mammals owned by Sir Ashton Lever, who had died seven years before publication began, but the use of Leverian specimens is only implied, not stated. Church was described as a Fellow of the Medical Society of London in his book.

4 A full list of the contents of the Museum as they were in 1784 was appended to Act 24 George III 2 Sess. c. 24.

5 *The Morning Post and Daily Advertiser*, 16 January 1786.

6 The advertisement in *The Morning Post and Daily Advertiser*, 21 March 1786, read: "Admittance will be given at Nine o'Clock This and To-Morrow Morning and until one on Thursday next, and no longer, as the Lottery will be drawn at Two o'Clock in Guildhall on that day." Signed Leicester House, 21 March 1786.

7 The winning ticket became lot no. 4681 in the Museum sale of 1806, and was sold, with a letter from Hyder Alley, for 11*s.* 6*d.* to Lord Weymouth.

8 La Roche (1933), pp. 111–15. Sophie took in England on a tour of the Continent with her husband during 1784, 1785 and 1786. She landed at Harwich on 4 September 1786 and proceeded to London, where she lodged in Suffolk Street. Her diary describing visits to exhibitions, museums and all the sights of London was first published in 1933. Sophie's sympathetic attitude to Lever over the loss of his museum would have been fully understood and shared by Sarah.

9 Delany (1862), 8 May 1786, vol. III, pp. 349–50.

10 *The Gentleman's Magazine*, 1812, 1, vol. LXXXIII, p. 516: "Last Thursday, 31 January 1788, died in Lancashire, Sir Ashton Lever, collector of the Museum, which, while his property, bore his name, and a monument of his name it will be to all posterity. He died while sitting on the bed of justice with his brother magistrates."

11 The full text of the notice in William Edward Armitage Axon's *The Annals of Manchester: a chronological record from the earliest times to the end of 1885*, Manchester 1886, pp. 114–15, reads: "Sir Ashton Lever, Knt., of Alkrington, died at the Bull's Head Inn, Manchester, February 1. Having as a young man shot a 'white sparrow', it formed the starting point of an important but very miscellaneous collection of objects of natural history and archaeology, known as the Leverian Museum. Financial difficulties induced Sir Ashton to part with this collection, and Parliament authorised a lottery for the purpose in 1785. The winner afterwards disposed of it by public auction in 1806, when the sale occupied 65 days. It has been surmised that Sir Ashton's death was due to poison self-administered."

PLATE 36

A radish with intertwined growth, and a carrot also intertwined

Eighteenth-century collectors loved 'curiosities' like this.

NHML (1) 81

90

PLATE 37

A group of fragments of fossil crinoids (feather-stars or sea-lilies)

These are typical of the unidentified specimens jumbled together in some of the sale lots of the
Leverian Museum.

NHML (1) 90

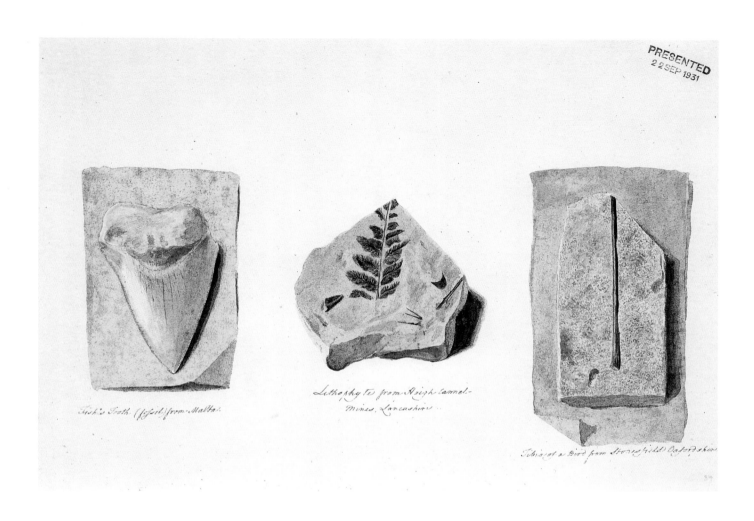

Fish's Tooth. (fossil) from Malta.

Lithophyte from High Cannel-Mines. Lancashire.

Skeleton a Bird from Stonesfield Oxfordshire

PLATE 38

Left: Fossilized shark tooth *Carcharodon* sp., Miocene

Middle: Frond of a fossilized fern from the Coal Measures, Lancashire

Right: Phalange of a pterodactyl from the Stonesfield Slates, Oxfordshire

Joshua Platt's important finds of fossil vertebrates in the Stonesfield Slates in 1758 stimulated the study of fossils in England.

NHML (1) 84

12 *Notes and Queries* (VIII), XVIII, 16 May 1896, p. 383. Under the heading 'Leicester Square', a quotation from *St James's Gazette* of 4 April was printed: "An hotel is to be built on the north side of Leicester Square, a purchase having been effected of the property now lying between the Empire Theatre and Leicester Street, and having a return along the west side of the latter. This (says the *Builder*) is the site of Leicester House, erected for Robert Sidney, second earl of Leicester, upon a piece of lammas-land which adjoined the Military Yard of Henry, Prince of Wales – afterwards used for Major Foubert's riding academy. In Newcourt's map, engraved by Faithorn in 1658, Leicester House appears as standing upon open ground, nor was Leicester Field surrounded with houses until about fifteen years later. The house faced southwards, with a spacious carriage-yard in front; the south elevation showed two stories and an attic, with rows of nine windows." It was for many years the largest house in London. The hotel was built and Lisle Street was laid out over the garden-ground in 1791.

Thomas Waring looked after the Museum from the day Lever moved it to London and opened it to the public on Monday 13 February 1775, until it closed, 1 September 1787. In *The Morning Post and Daily Advertiser*, 26 September 1786 (the day after James Parkinson took possession of the museum), an advertisement read: "To the Nobility, Gentry and Public at Large Notice is hereby given that the museum, late Sir Ashton Lever's, will continue open every Day (Sunday excepted), from Ten o'clock in the Morning to Six in the evening, until Michaelmas Day next at Half a Crown Each On which day Mr Parkinson, the holder of the furtunate Ticket in Sir Ashton's Lottery, takes possession thereof. Thomas Waring, Secretary, Aug. 8 1786." In his capacity as secretary, Thomas Waring probably issued Sarah Stone with a pass or special ticket, enabling her to enter the museum whenever she wished to paint there.

Pennant (MS, Warwick County Record Office, TP5/590/1) stated, "Thomas Waring was manager and superintendant of the collection ... ever since it was brought to London 1775."

13 *Dictionary of National Biography*, London 1895, vol. XLIII, pp. 313–14.

14 Mullens (1915), p. 128.

15 *The Morning Post and Daily Advertiser*, 6 March 1787.

16 *Ibid.*, 20 February 1787.

17 *Ibid.*, 30 August 1787, and 1 December 1787.

18 *The Dictionary of National Biography* (under 'Parkinson') states that Parkinson "bought a piece of land on which he erected for its display the building known as The Rotunda". According to William J. Smith ('A museum for a guinea', *Country Life*, 10 March 1960, pp. 494–95), the Rotunda was "designed by James Burton in 1786", but Mullens (1915), p. 162, said it was "only adapted by Parkinson for exhibition purposes, although it has been frequently and incorrectly stated that it was built by him when he acquired the Leverian collection."

19 *The Morning Post and Daily Advertiser*, 7 May 1789. Ivory cup 20 May 1788, elk 26 June 1788, ape and Impeyan pheasant 19 August 1788.

20 *Ibid.*, 25 November 1788–21 April 1789.

21 *Ibid.*, 3 March 1791.

22 *Ibid.*, 10 December 1789–25 February 1790.

23 *The Morning Post and Fashionable World*, 27 November–23 December 1794.

24 Farington (1922–23), III, 9 July 1806, p. 273.

25 John Lochée, letter to W. Bury, undated, from the Authors' Club, 2 Whitehall Court, W.W., reproduced in the reprint of the sale catalogue (*Leverian Museum sale catalogue*, Johnson and Hewett 1979).

26 Alfred Newton, at the Museum Association meeting of 1891, described the omission by the British Museum authorities as "Disgraceful as Lever's Museum contained the greater part of the specimens collected on three voyages of Captain Cook – their present custodians are the curators of the museums of Liverpool and Vienna". This is not quite accurate. For the disposal of collections from Cook's voyages, see note 37.

27 Robert Jameson (Sweet (1965), pp. 104, 113) went to the Museum on 10 October 1793, "when I got into conversation with a man that preserves & sells stuffed Birds &c. Address T. Thomson N.5 Little Martin's Lane where I promised to call." On 22 October, Jameson "Went this morning to the Leverian Museum where I met with Thomson the Bird Preserver. He engaged to get for me a specimen of the Spoonbill for £1.11.6, and the variety of the Banksian Cockatoo for 24s. Enquired of him the price of the following Birds etc. ..." (these were then listed with their prices). Thom(p)son is probably the dealer who bid for birds for Lord Stanley, and whose portrait was painted by R.R. Reinagle (fig. 3).

28 The reprint copy of the sale catalogue (Johnson and Hewett 1979) was the one marked up by George Humphrey (1730–1826), a London dealer in natural history specimens and ethnographical objects who had a fine collection of shells. He lived at 48 Long Acre, before moving to 30 St Martin's Lane where his museum was housed until it was sold in 1779. About 1786, he moved to 4 Leicester Street, near Leicester Square and the Museum. He bought shells from sailors on Cook's three voyages. When Robert Jameson met him at the Museum in 1793, he wrote afterwards (Sweet (1965), pp. 113–14), "Mr Humphreys seems to be very well versed in the Conchology for he has not one shell in his collection but what he names at first sight, in a scientific manner. He has also a very great knowledge of Corals, Insects and fossils." Humphrey was consequently in demand as a cataloguer of collections about to be sold. He took such a close interest in the Museum sale in 1806, that he marked up his own catalogue with the names of purchasers and the prices they had paid for some eighty per cent of the lots. He also wrote out, by hand, the 684 lots (apart from lots 1–15) in the Appendix following the "Last day of the sale". This, the best marked-up copy, was used for the reprint.

29 La Roche (1933), p. 115.

30 Pelzehn listed the birds still at Vienna in *Ibis*, 1873, pp. 14–54, and 1874, 3rd series (4), pp. 461–62. Fichtel purchased 82 mammals, 200+ birds, 60 reptiles, 73 fishes.

31 Largen and Fisher (1986), pp. 225–72, and Largen (1987), pp. 265–88. Edward Smith, Lord Stanley, 13th Earl of Derby (1775–1851) was interested in birds and mammals from an early age, and when he succeeded his father in 1834, he maintained a huge menagerie, covering some one hundred acres of land and seventy of water, in the park at Knowsley Hall, near Liverpool. Birds were housed on lakes and in plantations, as well as in aviaries. Lord Stanley employed collectors all over the world to supply new and little known species, and financed several expeditions to Europe, the west coast of Africa, Honduras and Hudson Bay. The skin of any animal that died was transferred to his museum.

Lord Stanley corresponded with John Latham, among other naturalists (Wagstaffe and Rutherford (1954), pp. 173–83), and occasionally sent him drawings of birds for identification or for Latham to etch for inclusion in his *General Synopsis of Birds*. (Several of his drawings are conserved among the 888 original watercolours of the Latham folio in The Natural History Museum, London.) Lord Stanley visited the Leverian Museum and bought birds at the sale in 1806. His sale catalogue was annotated with a few names of purchasers and prices, and on several days, when he was not present at the sale, a dealer, Thom(p)son bid on his behalf (see note 27). He also owned albums and portfolios of watercolours of birds by many artists, including Sarah Stone. On his death, the living birds were auctioned 6–11 October 1851, in 650 lots; they numbered 1,272 birds, representing 318 species, of which 756 individual birds had been bred in his own menagerie. There were also ninety-four species and 345 heads of mammals, principally antelopes. The 14th Earl of Derby presented the City of Liverpool with 20,000 specimens of quadrupeds, birds, eggs, reptiles and fishes, including many type specimens from the museum. During the bombing of Liverpool in 1941, some mammals were destroyed, but the birds survived. For details of the birds in the Stanley sale, see Sir William Jardine, *Contributions to Ornithology*, 1852, pp. 5–6, and *A Catalogue of the Menagerie & Aviary at Knowsley*, Liverpool 1851.

PLATE 39

Giant toucanet *Selindra culik*

The Guyanan or Culik toucanet was originally called *Ramphastos piperivorus* (= pepper-eater) because
it was said to feed principally on peppers when first imported from Cayenne or French Guyana.

NHML (3) 16

32 Göran Frisk of the Swedish Museum of Natural History notified the author of the list of sixty-one birds acquired by the Grill Museum, marking those that had been transferred from Söderfors to Stockholm, and the eleven still in the Stockholm collection, *viz. Strix scops, Phasianus pictus, Phasianus colchicus, Columba coronata, Crax alector, Ardea pavonina, Ardea virgo, Anas galericulata, Mergus cucullatus, Psittacus macao* and *Sturnus ludovicianus*. Ragnar Insulander has written an article "recently published in the yearbook of the Swedish Linnaeus Society" (information in an undated letter, received 9 January 1997), 'Pehr Gustaf Lindroth – an unknown Linnean', and is preparing a biography of Lindroth.

33 Churchill Babington, *Catalogue of the birds of Suffolk*, London 1884–86, reprinted from *Proceedings of the Suffolk Institute of Archaeology*, Natural History, vol. V.

34 *Notes and Queries* (11), X, August 1914, p. 170.

35 Sweet (1965), p. 102; also p. 116, "Entries in Jameson's letter-books show that he kept up a correspondence with Dr Shaw, Dr Crichton, Mr James Parkinson and also his son, young James Parkinson, the Leverian Museum."

36 Quoted King (1996), pp. 167–68.

37 Whitehead (1978), p. 84, who also noted that in 1893 a number of specimens from the Leverian Museum were still in the Syer Cuming collection in Kennington, Surrey. The natural history specimens and artefacts which were brought back from Cook's voyages went to several different collections and persons. Sir Joseph Banks had many items of his own from the first voyage (1768–71), and he received birds in alcohol, among other things, from the second voyage (1772–75). Solander wrote of these to Banks on 22 August 1775: "Captain Cook has sent all his curiosities to my apartements at the [British] Museum. All his shells is to go to Lord Bristol – 4 Casks have your name on them and I understand they contain Birds & fish &c the Box D° with Plants from the Cape" (Beaglehole (1961), 2., the Calendar of Documents, p. 961).

The Museum apparently received little or nothing from the first voyage, but Cook sent six birds from the Cape to Leicester Fields (*i.e.* to the LM), and a shell, from the second voyage (Beaglehole (1967), p. 1558). Ethnographical material from the third voyage was sent to the Museum (Kaeppler (1978), p. 46, citing a newspaper article of 31 January 1781). Cook was well aware that his crew collected on their own account, either out of curiosity or to make extra money by selling objects when they returned home. In order to keep this under control, he issued orders to the sailors before they disembarked in Vaitepiha Bay, 17 August 1773. The private journal of James Burney, 2nd Lieutenant of the *Adventure*, was published in 1975, and the text of Cook's orders appears on pp. 62–63. In September 1774, Cook commented in his journal on what happened to the items collected by his crew in New Caledonia: some had "brought with them some arms such as Clubs, darts &c which they exchanged away, indeed these things generally found the best Market with us, such was the prevailing Passion for curiosities, or what appeared new .... the reader will think the Ship must be full of such articles by this time, he will be misstaken, for nothing is more Common than to give away what has been collected on one Island for any thing new at a Nother, even if it is less curious, this together with which is distroyed on board after the owners tired with looking at them, prevents any considerable increase" (Beaglehole (1961), 2., pp. 531–32).

PLATE 40

Waxwing *Bombycilla garrulus* ; Cardinal *Cardinalis cardinalis*

The Waxwing was called a 'chatterer' in the 18th century, hence *garrulus*; the Cardinal was then called a 'Virginian nightingale', and both were thought desirable as vocal cage-birds.

NHML (2) 59

Other Artists and Illustrators painting in the Leverian Museum

It is evident that while Sir Ashton Lever owned his museum in London, he regarded Sarah as the main, or official, artist. His friends John Latham and Thomas Pennant were permitted to use the zoological specimens for their books, and the artists employed by W.F. Martyn also had access to all the zoological specimens. Lady (Eleanor) Fenn's illustrator drew insects at the museum in Lever's time. After 1786, more artists took advantage of the specimens in the Leverian Museum, painting birds, mammals, shells, insects in oils or watercolours, and in gouaches for composite pictures. Some of these were exhibited in London galleries such as the Royal Academy. They provide further information about the contents of the Leverian Museum.

Authors of natural history books at the end of the eighteenth and beginning of the nineteenth centuries were keen to include all new discoveries in their texts. They also aspired to portray any new, or rare, species, and sought permission from the owners of such specimens to draw and paint them.

A search through the zoological books published in the 1780s and up to 1806, revealed that many specimens from the Leverian Museum were being drawn for illustration purposes, most of them during the period that Parkinson owned the museum. Some had already been painted by Sarah, others were newly illustrated.

Charles Catton

Charles Catton junior (1756–1819) was born in London in 1756, and went to America in 1804, where he died in 1819. His father, Charles Catton (Norwich 1728–London 1798), was a founder member of the Royal Academy, and exhibited pictures of animals from 1760 until his death. He probably gave his son some preliminary lessons before sending him to be trained at the Royal Academy school. Charles junior exhibited at the Royal Academy from 1776 until 1800. He painted animals, especially species that were the subject of hunting (*e.g. Portrait of spaniels and a bittern*, exhibited 1800), and he engraved *Shooting woodcock* and *Shooting partridge*, after G.H. Morland.

With this background, it was natural that he should be entrusted, in 1789, with the depiction of three of the animals sent home by John White from Australia: the Kangaroo, *Macropus giganteus*, Spotted tapoa tafa, *Dasyurus quoll*, and a Hepoona roo, *Potaurus australis*, Yellow-bellied glider. Similar watercolours for the last two are now in the National Library of Australia, and other watercolours of a kangaroo are in a private collection in Australia. The specimens for these figures were not in the Leverian Museum, but had been given to John Hunter. Waterhouse (1841, p. 27) discovered the original specimen of the Hepoona roo in the museum of the Royal College of Surgeons, founded in 1800 to accommodate John Hunter's collections. Some stuffed birds and mammals from the Hunterian Museum were subsequently transferred to the British Museum.

Charles Catton went to the Leverian Museum to paint the elk that caused such a stir in 1788 when it was given to the museum, and his painting was auctioned at the Leverian Museum sale in 1806 (lot 893): "Water colour drawing of the Elk, by Catton, framed & glazed". It was bought by Mrs Oliphant, the same lady who bought Sarah's drawing of the Leverian Museum. The elk specimen was sold on the last day of the sale, as lot 22: "The Swedish elk *Cervus alces*, a capital and finely preserved specimen".

Edward Donovan

A collector, from a young age and apparently as indulged by his parents as Sir Ashton Lever had been, Donovan (1768–1837) also grew up to form a huge collection of natural history objects, but collected mostly British species.

Unlike Sir Ashton Lever, Donovan wrote, and illustrated, many books about the species in which he took such pleasure. A book on botany, written when he was fifteen years old, was the first of numerous books on shells, insects, fishes, and birds. For these, he drew, etched and then coloured the illustrations by hand.

Donovan was not a good draughtsman, but his colouring was beautiful and he spared no expense in getting the correct pigment for the accurate shading, using gold, where necessary, for his jewel-like insects and shimmering fishes and the sheen on the plumage of birds. He

used the Leverian Museum specimens *in situ* up to 1806, but after his purchase of 500 lots at the 1806 dispersal sale many of the birds and shells were removed to his own museum. By 1807, Donovan's entire collection of birds consisted of "317 species and above 50 interesting varieties" (for a notice of Donovan's museum, see *European Magazine*, LII, December 1807). The additional items from the Leverian Museum boosted his flagging effort to record all British species in his *Natural History of British Birds*: vols. I–V had appeared 1794–98; vol. VI appeared in 1809; vol. VII in 1816; vol. VIII in 1817; vol. IX in 1818; and the final volume, vol. X, in 1819. This was one year after his own museum had been sold. In vol. VI, Donovan claimed to have purchased "the entire collection of the British series in the late Leverian Museum", but this was not strictly true. He probably bought a representative of every species, but did not buy every example of each species.

Donovan specifically itemized Leverian Museum subjects that he had drawn either at Leicester House or in the Rotunda before 1806, as well as those he purchased. Several of the subjects he drew were also drawn by Sarah Stone. Having prepared the Leverian Museum sale catalogue, Donovan knew exactly what he wished to purchase before the first day of the sale. Birds purchased from the Leverian Museum and figured in *The Natural History of Birds*, included: vol. I, pl. x, *Sylvia Dartfordiensis*, pl. xi, the Hoopoe; vol. III, pl. lxv, *Mergus merganser*; vol. VI, *Motacilla simplex*; vol. VII, pl. clxii, *Fringilla linaria*, Twite; vol. VIII, pl. clxxvii, *Tringa nigricans*, Purple sandpiper, pl. ccxliii, Great Auk, *Alca impennis* ("Our figure of this scarce and interesting bird is copied from the well known specimen, originally in the collection of Sir Ashton Lever, and which we obtained by purchase, for our own Museum, at a price not very inconsiderable (ten guineas) that example being at the time alluded to the only one we believe known. Since that period a few of these birds have been killed in the Orknies ...").

Donovan had published books on shells, insects and fishes, and in 1822 began issuing in London *The Naturalist's Repository, or (monthly) miscellany of exotic natural history exhibiting rare and beautiful specimens of foreign birds, insects, shells, quadrupeds, fishes and marine productions*, to bring his other

PLATE 42

Crowned pigeon *Goura cristata*

Goura cristata is one of three crowned pigeons inhabiting New Guinea. The crest feathers have long separated barbs that give them an attractive lace-like appearance. The crest is fan-shaped and laterally compressed.

NHML (2) 52

PLATE 43

Green-tailed jacamar *Galbula galbula*

Sarah attempted to show the metallic green and bronze on this Green-tailed jacamar, without using
gold or bronze leaf.

NHML (3) 38

PLATE 44

Mandarin duck *Aix galericulata*

The drake mandarin raises the fan-shaped, cinnamon innermost pair of secondaries of his back like
sails in the courting gesture.

NHML (2) 54

Mandarin Drake

books up to date. Five volumes, containing 180 finely hand-coloured etchings were published. This publication clearly distinguishes sixteen Leverian items, a number of which Donovan had purchased at the Leverian Museum sale, and reflected his greatest natural history interest – shells. The prices he had paid for some of these was considerable: Vol. I, pl. i, *Conus ammarialis*, Amboyna high-spiral admiral shells [LM Last day but one 90 Five and a half guineas]; pl. iv, *Voluta scapha* var. *nobilis*; pl. viii, *Buccinum harpa* var. *testudo*; pl. xi, *Trochus imperialis* var. *roseus*, given by Captain Cook to Lever, "It was estimated at 100 guineas for the Lottery. Subsequently, it was on view at the residence of the Duke de Bourbon, and sold there, immediately after the Duke's departure for France, early in 1815." [LM Last day 81 An elegant and unique pink variety of the imperial sun, drawn up with the anchor of a ship, from the depth of 60 fathoms, in Cook's straits, New Zealand £24.3.0]; pl. xvi, *Murex scorpio* var. *minor*, Least stag's horn murex; pl. xvii, *Voluta pyrum* [LM Last day 77 The reverse variety of the high-spired turnip, from Madagascar, extremely rare, Donovan Seven guineas]; pl. xxxiv, *Terebratula sanguinea* [LM Last day 74 A large and fine anomia sanguinea, or sanguineous lamp cockle, from New Zealand, extremely scarce, allowed to be the largest specimen known, Donovan 5 guineas]. Vol. II, pl. xlvi, *Voluta scapha*, Noble volute (Donovan drew this from a Leverian specimen purchased for eight guineas); pl. xlix, *Helix reversa*, Reverse Helix (from Prince's Island, brought back by Sir Joseph Banks); pl. li, *Strombus lesbia*, Broad-winged strombus (for which he paid eight guineas); pl. lxvi, *Ostracion tobinii*, Tobin's striped trunk fish (collected by Captain Cook and presented to Sir Ashton Lever). Vol. III, pl. lxxxiv, *Voluta Japonica*, Japanese crown melon shell [LM sale 3 guineas]; pl. lxxxix *Echinus lamarckii*, Lamarck's echinus or Chinese sea urchin (Lever received this lavender-coloured echinus from China: "The only specimen we have seen was that preserved in

the late Leverian Museum ... it realised at the sale of that museum a considerable price, and has, we understand, been since broken, a circumstance by no means unanticipated, the shell being of the most fragile kind. The destruction of the specimen, will probably render the delineation the more acceptable, this being, as we are informed, the only drawing that has been taken of it, excepting one by Chevalier de Barde, a French gentleman ... during exile in this country ... & was carried by him with is other drawings into France & still remains unpublished"). Vol. V, pl. clxxx, *Voluta scabriuscula*, Scabrous volute.

In the *Repository*, Donovan also noted that he had bought the specimens for pl. xcii, *Psittacus pennantii*, Pennantian parrot, and pl. xcvi, egg of Grey parrot, formerly in the Leverian Museum.

As a result of high expenditure, trouble with his booksellers, insufficient interest on the part of the public, who failed to pay their entrance fees in sufficient numbers, Donovan was forced to sell his collection, and died a dispirited, disillusioned and impoverished man.[1]

Sydenham T. Edwards

A Welshman, Edwards (1768–1819) trained as a botanical artist and later also drew animals. He prepared a watercolour of the Andean condor (now in McGill University, Blacker Wood Library, Montreal) for inclusion in George Shaw's *Museum Leverianum*, but it was not used – that by Charles Reuben Ryley being preferred. Several watercolours of birds by him, that must have been painted from specimens in a museum at the time, probably the Leverian, were sold by Christie's, London, in 1994, including a Black swan, Bustard, Ostrich and a Dodo.

S.T. Edwards's signature appeared on two of the mammal plates in George Shaw's *Museum Leverianum*. He

PLATE 45

Flamingo *Phoenicopterus ruber*

A flamingo alarmed by a very small snake. Sarah painted a flamingo on at least three occasions.

NHML (2) 60

West India Flamingo

both painted and etched the picture of the *Fox-tailed monkey* (published 7 March 1790), and that of the *Kangaroo* (two of the Giant kangaroo, *"Macropus giganteus"*) (published 8 June 1795).

Edwards either drew and engraved, or just engraved, a Blue crane, Wattled bee-eater, Red-tailed black cockatoo, Kookaburra and a Laced lizard in 1789 for Arthur Phillip's account of his *Voyage to Botany Bay* with the First Fleet (London 1789). The location of these species was not made clear by Phillip, but some of them were painted by Sarah in the Leverian Museum the same year.

When Parkinson owned the museum, he allowed Edwards to paint eleven creepers (Hook-billed green, Scarlet, Cardinal, Black-capped, Great hook-billed, Red hook-billed, Mocking, Brown, Olive-green, Black and African), and a Black-capped humming-bird for the engravers to copy for the French publication *Histoire naturelle ... colibris, oiseaux-mouches, jacamars, promerops* by Jean Baptiste Audebert (2 vols., Paris 1801–02).

In 1809, the collector Emperor John Woodford's collection of 1800 drawings and prints of birds by "Lewin, S.T. Edwards and R.R. Reinagle" was bought by a dealer, Dent, for £378. These included "drawings from Bankes Museum, Capt. Cook and Lever Museum".

Lady (Eleanor) Fenn

With an unnamed artist, Lady Fenn (died 1813) produced two small (12mo) books: *A Short History of Insects ... designed as an Introduction to that Branch of Natural History, and as a Pocket Companion to those who visit the Leverian Museum,* with seven plates containing ninety-three coloured figures (Norwich 1780), and *A Short History of Quadrupeds extracted from works of credit, designed as an introduction to the Study of that Branch of Natural history and as a pocket Companion to those who visit the Leverian Museum* (2 vols., 54 pls.), which follows

John Church's book on quadrupeds (see p. 88) very closely. The books are undated but one edition of the *Short History of Quadrupeds* refers to a Kangaroo opossum having been "lately added to the collection in Mr Parkinson's museum", so that edition must post-date 1786. G. Quinton engraved the insects. There were several later editions, amended to include new material and specimens from Cook's last voyage, and update the text when Parkinson took over the museum.

Lady Fenn's husband was also an author, and an antiquary. Sir John Fenn (1739–1794) was born at Norwich and educated at Caius College, Cambridge. After editing three manuscript volumes of the Paston letters, he had them richly bound and presented them to George III, who knighted him in honour of his gift on 23 May 1787. He married Eleanor, a daughter of Sheppard Frere of Roydon, Suffolk, in 1766, attracted to her on account of a shared literary interest.

Besides the two guides to the Leverian Museum's quadrupeds and insects, Lady Fenn wrote several small books of an educational kind under the name of Mrs Lovechild and Mrs Teachwell. She died 1 November 1813, having had no children of her own.

Moses Griffith and Peter Brown

Griffith (1747–1819) and Brown (*fl.* 1766–91)[2] were artists who worked on Thomas Pennant's *A History of Quadrupeds* (London 1781). In the Preface (p. viii), Pennant wrote, "From the matchless collection of animals, collected by the indefatigable industry of that public-spirited Gentleman, Sir Ashton Lever, I have every opportunity, not only of correcting the descriptions of the last edition, but of adding several Animals hitherto imperfectly known."

Among the quadrupeds in this book, portraits of

PLATE 46

Golden pheasant *Chrysolophus pictus*

The Golden pheasant was first reported as present in Britain by Eleazar Albin in 1738, and soon became a favourite species with artists.

NHML (2) 49

121

PLATE 47

Tui *Prosthemadera novaeseelandiae*

New Zealanders consider the Tui to be one of their finest forest songbirds.

NHML (3) 47

PLATE 48

Hawaiian akioloa *Hemignathus obscurus*

Four subspecies of the Hawaiian akioloa are now extinct. There were three specimens of "green certhia" in the Leverian Museum, but which subspecies they represented is uncertain. They were taken to England from the Sandwich Islands (Hawaii) on Captain Cook's ships.

NHML (3) 51

which were taken from specimens in the Leverian Museum, were: *Capra sylvestris africana*, Smooth-horned antelope, to which Pennant added the information that in the museum there were "weapons formed of the horns of" this species; an Antelope pygargus; Cape Verd hog, *Sanglier de Cap Verd* (of which De Buffon wrote, "I believe that the only entire specimen now in Europe, is in possession of Sir Ashton Lever, which he received from the Cape"); Great baboon, described from a stuffed specimen in Sir Ashton Lever's Museum, with a stick in its hand; and some members of the dog and cat families. In vol. II, Pennant had some pictures of sloths, of which a Three-toed was in the Leverian Museum (the Two-toed was in the British Museum); Six-banded and Nine-banded armadillos (in the Leverian); an Arctic and a Pinnated walrus, Common and Little seals, and some bats, including the Great and Leaf bats.

In his *Arctic Zoology*, Pennant's artists Moses Griffith, Peter Brown and Mercatti almost certainly used Leverian Museum specimens, but in his account of each species Pennant merely listed "Lev. Mus" among the synonyms, indicating the presence of a specimen in that collection, although in the advertisement for the book he had stated that "To Sir Ashton Lever, Knight, I am highly indebted, for the more intimate and closer examination of his treasures than was allowed to the common visitors to his most magnificent museum".

Moses Griffith was a protégé of Thomas Pennant, who had him trained as a draughtsman. Peter Brown was a Dane by birth, and worked on drawings for Pennant and for his own publication, *New Illustrations of Zoology* (1776).

Moses Griffith and James Heath

Moses Griffith and James Heath (1757–1834),[3] the artists and engravers of the plates that illustrated George Shaw's *General Zoology, or Systematic Natural History* (14 vols., London 1800–26) probably worked on their drawings at the Leverian Museum in the early stages of the book's production, or until 1806. However, the birds (vols. VII–XIV, 501 engravings) were principally engraved by "Mrs Griffith" from 1809. The insects were engraved by M.

Griffith. Some species were noted as having been in the Leverian Museum, and "our figure was taken from the same specimen". In a few cases, Shaw corrected any faulty information in earlier publications.

Julius Caesar Ibbetson

Ibbetson (1759–1817) drew the mammals for John Church to have engraved for his *A Cabinet of Quadrupeds* (1795 and 1805). Church did not specifically state that the plates had been sketched at the Leverian Museum, but the illustrations in Lady Fenn's *A Short History of Quadrupeds* (see p. 84) very closely resemble Church's illustrations, although they are on a smaller scale and the Church plates lack the backgrounds of Fenn's artist or engraver. Since Lady Fenn's book contained "extracts from works of credit", John Church's *Quadrupeds* and Ibbetson's illustrations probably formed the basis for her book's pictures.

Ibbetson was a Yorkshireman, born at Farnley Moor, Leeds; he died at Masham, North Yorkshire. Ibbetson ran away to London in 1777, and worked as a picture restorer until 1784. He first exhibited at the Royal Academy in 1785, continuing to send paintings, mainly of mammals, until 1815. In 1788, he sailed as draughtsman to the British Embassy in China, but only got as far as Java, where the ambassador died. Ibbetson then sailed home, going first to Wales and then moving to London, where he married. His visits to the Leverian Museum for the purpose of painting the mammals must have occurred during the short period that he was in London in the 1780s. He was devastated by the death of his wife in 1794, and did little painting for some time, but the mammals painted for John Church's *Cabinet of Quadrupeds* (1795 and 1805) were done at this time. Perhaps the long delay between the two volumes appearing in print was occasioned by the artist's incapacity or reluctance to paint. Ibbetson married again in 1801 and took commissions in the provinces, finally moving to Masham when crippled with rheumatism.

PLATE 49

Black-capped mockingthrush *Donacobius atricapillus*

This is a Neotropical species. Sarah may have painted this in the British Museum, either for Lever
or for another patron.

NHML (3) 61

John Latham

A remarkable collector of information and a systematic recorder of birds for fifty years. Latham (1740–1837) was the son of John Latham of Eltham, Kent, who practised as a surgeon, and died 23 August 1788. John Latham junior studied with the Hunters in London before qualifying as a doctor and setting up in practice at Dartford, Kent, where he made his fortune. Latham bought many foreign bird skins for his own museum.

Between 1781 and 1785, Latham published his *General Synopsis of Birds* in three volumes, later adding to it by supplements, and corrected his omission of scientific names by publishing an *Index Ornithologicus* in 1790. He retired from Kent in 1796, when most of his own large collection of birds was dispersed, and went to live in Romsey, Hampshire. He lost a lot of money, and recouped some by revising his work, adding new species discovered since he had finished the *Synopsis*; the new book was called *General History of Birds* and was published 1821–24, when he was eighty years old. He lived for another nearly fourteen years.

Latham acknowledged his indebtedness to Sir Ashton Lever for allowing him access to the birds in his museum in order to sketch them. He painted watercolours from the drawings, and etched and hand-coloured plates from these, as illustrations for his *A General Synopsis of Birds*, which included 106 coloured etchings and, where appropriate, the abbreviation "Lev. Mus" in the synonymy in the text. He added two supplements between 1787 and 1801. On several occasions, Latham noted that the only specimen known to science was in the Leverian Museum, making it certain where he had drawn the species. However, he also had a collection of his own, and where a specimen existed in both his own and Lever's collection, would make the drawing from his own – though doubtless checking with the Leverian specimen. In his text, Latham mentioned a handful of other collections where he had seen bird specimens, including that in the British Museum.

Latham was much honoured in both the medical and ornithological fields. In 1787, he claimed to have described between five and six hundred new forms, and by the time he finished his work this was increased by at least another two hundred birds, mostly from Australia.

Latham was a great correspondent, keeping in close contact with Lever, with whom he shared a collector's enthusiasm, and with Thomas Pennant, the Revd John White, brother of Gilbert, and many others. He was taught by the anatomist William Hunter and knew the Hunter brothers in London. They formed a small coterie of collectors, authors and compilers who shared specimens, notes and books. Latham was a genial companion and welcomed when he went to see novelties in Lever's and Sir Joseph Banks's collections. He supported James Edward Smith in creating the Linnean Society.

Latham was the most talented, industrious and extraordinary of this group, in terms of moving forward the knowledge of ornithology. He knew some 3000 birds by the turn of the century; Linnaeus had named 444 in 1758, and this number had been increased to 933 by Johann Friedrich Gmelin (1748–1804) by the time the thirteenth edition of Linnaeus's *Systema Naturae* came out (1788–93). Latham's *General Synopsis* was the standard work, and it is from this that the names of the birds drawn by Sarah at the Leverian Museum were later written on to her drawing sheets. "Gen Syn" or "Syn" in the inscriptions on her drawings referred to Latham's book.

Vicomte Alexandre Isidore Leroy de Barde

A French nobleman, Leroy de Barde (1777–1828) took refuge in London in 1792 following the French Revolution, remaining until the Bourbon restoration in 1814. He was a skilled artist, especially in *trompe l'oeil*, which he demonstrated in six very large gouache paintings (4.5 × 2.5 ft, 1.26 × 0.90 m) that have been conserved in the Cabinet des Dessins, the Louvre, Paris

Unlike Sarah, who was commissioned to paint individual studies of the full range of bird species, including the sombrely coloured species, Leroy de Barde was a free agent. He visited several cabinets and museums, beginning with the Leverian Museum in 1803, then the British Museum and Bullock's Museum, and selected the most colourful and unusual species to paint. He also painted specimens in private cabinets. In 1814, William Bullock

PLATE 50

Hawfinch *Coccothraustes coccothraustes*

There were only two specimens of this shy and elusive British species in the Leverian Museum.

NHML (3) 72

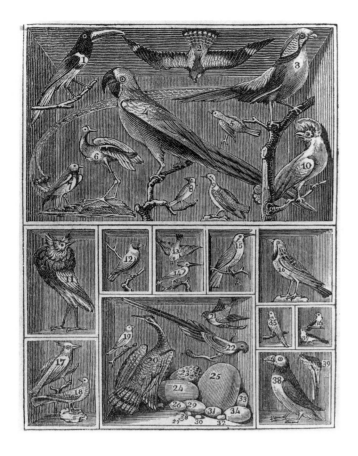 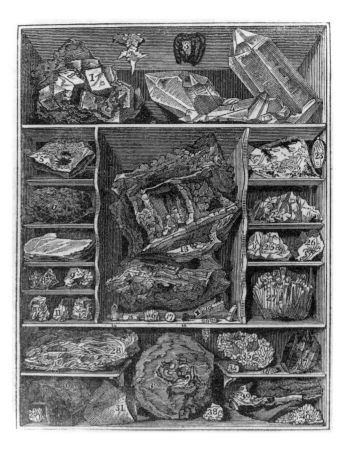

15 Leroy de Barde painted six gouaches at the Leverian Museum and Bullock's Museum, of which four are shown here:

No. 1 Birds. All the birds, numbered 1–10, on the top shelf were drawn at the Leverian Museum

No. 2 Minerals: 7 quartz mixed with aventurine; 10 crystallized iron ore; 13 oriental amber coloured calcedony or sardonyx; 26 stalagmitical calcareous deposition and 39 rose coloured calcareous spar, both from the cobalt mines at Richelsdorf in Hesse. Many of these were drawn at the Leverian Museum.

No. 4 "This Drawing was executed at the Leverian Museum, and some of the specimens are particularly beautiful, such as the Mandarin Duck, the Owl &c. &c."

No. 6 "This Drawing was executed at the Leverian Museum, and gives an exact idea of the manner in which the Shells and Corals were arranged." All the shells were claimed to be items brought back from Captain Cook's voyages.

arranged with Leroy de Barde to exhibit six large paintings at his museum, and issued a *Descriptive Catalogue of the Different Subjects represented in the Large Water Colour Drawings, by the Chevalier de Barde; now exhibiting at Mr Bullock's Museum, The Egyptian Hall, Piccadilly, London*. The admittance to this special exhibition was 1s., and a copy of the catalogue cost 1s. 6d. When Napoleon was defeated, Leroy de Barde returned home to France and exhibited at the Salon in 1817, "*Caisses contenant des oiseaux. Réunion d'oiseaux étrangers placés dans différentes caisses (les tableaux appartiennent à Sa Majesté)*". After their appearance at the exhibition, they became the property of Louis XVIII, who conferred on Leroy de Barde the title of *premier peintre d'histoire naturelle*.

Each painting was dated, and all the objects numbered for identification purposes in the catalogue. A note of the location of the original specimen means that we can trace exactly which items were in the Leverian Museum.

The objects were painted resting on shelves in a cabinet, with deep shadows throwing them into relief, in order to create the illusion that they were physically, three-dimensionally present (see fig. 15). *Trompe l'oeil* pictures of shelves laden with precious objects were a popular art form or genre at the time.

No. 1. A cabinet showing a collection of foreign birds was dated 1811, but the catalogue explained that "This Drawing was begun at the Leverian Museum; all the upper part, as far as the centre bar, has been executed at that place; the lower part, at Mr Bullock's Museum, and from live birds". The ten Leverian birds were: Aracari toucan, Virginia goatsucker or Night jar, Painted or golden pheasant, Hyacinthine macaw (which had been presented to Mr Parkinson by Lord Orford, who had it when living, and was sold as lot 6288, Ultramarine macaw, and went to the Vienna Imperial Museum), Spotted tanager, Spur-winged water-hen common at St Domingo, Ringed plover, Taylor bird (the Leverian Museum displayed this bird with its nest of leaves sewn together with a coarse thread and lined with grass, feathers *etc.*), Grey phalarope and Rock manakin (the eighteenth-century name for Cock of the rock).

No. 2. A cabinet with shelves on which are displayed forty mineral specimens. The text of the catalogue states, "This Drawing was begun with some of the most valu-

able specimens in Mr Parkinson's possession and terminated at the British Museum". Some of the mineral specimens dispersed from the Leverian Museum in the sale of 1806 are still in the British Museum and Hunterian Museum. This gouache is dated 1813. The five Leverian Museum items include no. 7, a specimen of red-coloured quartz, mixed with mica or true avanturine, weighing nearly 5 lb, found in the ruins of the triumphal arch of Julius Caesar in the valley of Suse, in Piedmont, in 1788, by Francis Ludwig of Mayence who was paid 200 guineas for it. It was sold on the last day but one of the 1806 sale, lot 120. No. 10 was a fine specimen of crystallized iron ore from Elbe; no. 13, a most beautiful mass of rich oriental amber-coloured chalcedony or sardonyx, weighing more than 220 lb.; no. 26 was a globose specimen of stalagmitical calcareous deposition from the cobalt mines at Richelsdorf, in Hesse, where several mineral specimens in the Leverian Museum originated; no. 39 was a rose-colour calcareous spar, in primitive rhomba, again from Hesse.

No. 3. A cabinet with ancient vases arranged on the shelves.

No. 4. Another cabinet, with twenty-three birds arranged on its shelves, dated 1804, of which the text said, "This Drawing was executed at the Leverian Museum, and some of the specimens are particularly beautiful, such as the Mandarin Duck, the Owl, &c. &c.". Some of the birds would have been quite common to visitors to the museum (*e.g.* the Jay, Ring ouzel, Bearded titmouse, Goldcrest, Partridge, and perhaps a Great eagle owl). The other birds in this cabinet were chosen for their brilliant colours or interesting physical forms. Sarah Stone had shared Leroy de Barde's enthusiasm for the Mandarin duck, painting it more than once, and she also painted the Black and blue tanager, Blue-bellied parrot, Blue-bellied finch, Pompadour chatterer or Cotinga, Tufted-necked humming-bird, and Fire finch. Leroy de Barde's painting shows us how Lever's specimens of some other birds were mounted (*e.g.* the Leverian trogon that George Shaw named for Sir Ashton, both the Molucca and Java grosbeaks, a Collared creeper from the Cape of Good Hope, a Crested green humming-bird and its nest, the Red-headed Guinea parraket, Purple-breasted

PLATE 51
Cape longclaw *Macronyx capensis*
Sarah frequently painted a neat border around her watercolours, sometimes double-ruled borders.
NHML (3) 95

PLATE 52

Paradise tanager *Tangara chilensis*

This is now found from Colombia to Brazil and Bolivia, not in Chile as its name implies.

NHML (3) 86

PLATE 53

Cirl bunting *Emberiza cirlus*

The Cirl bunting now breeds in the south and west of England.

NHML (3) 80

chatterer, and a Spotted gallinule which had been "shot in England".

No. 5. A very dramatic gouache of *A Tiger crushed to death against a tree, by a large serpent, the Boa Constrictor*, dated 1814. The Bullock Museum exhibited the tiger and boa constrictor, painted by Leroy de Barde, and this exhibit was sold in the Bullock sale of 1819 (lot 98) and bought by Cross. The exhibit was noted as being in the Rawtenstall Museum in 1978.[4]

No. 6. A cabinet crowded with seventy-one land and sea shells, and sea urchins, signed and dated "The Chev. de Barde, delt 1803". The catalogue claimed that "This Drawing was executed at the Leverian Museum, and gives an exact idea of the manner in which the Shells and Corals were arranged". In this, as in the other *trompe l'oeil* paintings, the shells look real enough for the viewer to be able to lift them off the shelf in order to inspect them more closely.

The catalogue stated that all the shells were Cook items. Specifically mentioned as having been collected in the South Seas were nos. 1, a clouded Persian crown melon from New South Wales; 2, an umbilicated sailor shell or Nautilus from Endeavour Straits; 25, a variety of the Imperial sun shells, drawn up by the cable of the *Adventure*, which Lever purchased from George Humphrey for ten guineas and which was sold in 1806 on the last day of the sale (lot 81) to Fillingham for 23 guineas, finally coming to rest in the British Museum (now in The Natural History Museum); 69, Neptune's trumpet shell from Tahiti. Several of the rare shells were purchased at the 1806 sale by Henry Constant Jennings (1732–1819), including a "violet-ringed and stellated sea urchin" brought back to England by Robert Anderson, gunner of the *Resolution* on Cook's second voyage. No. 28 was a Nippled turban sea-urchin from New South Wales, and there were also shells from the Friendly Islands and Society Islands.

In his *Naturalist's Repository*,[5] Edward Donovan recorded a piece of good fortune where the Lamarck's or Chinese sea urchin was concerned. He said that his was the only drawing taken of this Leverian Museum specimen before it got broken, apart from a drawing by "Chevalier de Barde, a French gentleman, during exile in this country".

A piece of true red coral on its native rock, from Sicily, formed another item in this cabinet, with some blush or rose-coloured coral from the Island of Providence, and lace coral formed on a "Lampas Columbiana or Pigeon's Egg Lamp Coral, from the Island of Minorca". Sarah delighted in painting coral on several occasions, and Leroy de Barde used these beautiful pieces to enliven and decorate the shelves of shells.

A Supplement at the end of the catalogue listed some other, small drawings, and included yet more shells considered then to be "very scarce and valuable; the largest is the many-ridged Harp; the small one is a reverse of the Chersirigenus; and the lower shell is a very curious spindal, which was brought up by the ship's anchor (a few years ago) in the Straits of Java". A few butterflies and moths from the Leverian Museum also formed one small picture.

The six large paintings form a most effective display of Leverian Museum specimens, and convey some idea of the manner in which objects in the museum that Sarah Stone chose or was commissioned to paint were arranged.

William Lewin

Trained as a pattern drawer, Lewin (1747–1795) was attracted to flowers, insects and birds, all of which flourished at that time in the area of east London where he was born and brought up: Mile End, Bethnal Green and Stepney. This area also had strong maritime connections, and William's father was a rate mariner. Some of Lewin's watercolours of birds figured in an account of a *Voyage round the World* (1789), by Captain George Dixon.

Lewin was living in Darenth, Kent, near John Latham, when he painted the original watercolours for his own book, *The Birds of Great Britain, with their Eggs* (60 copies of 7 vols., London 1789–94). Robert Jameson said that Lewin's birds "are first traced thro oil paper and then painted ...".[6]

Lewin used Latham's collection of bird specimens, but had recourse to the Leverian Museum for two species, for the watercolours for his *Birds of Great Britain* (London 1789), saying in the Preface, p. vi, "The arduous undertaking I have engaged in, has been rendered more

PLATE 54

Zenaida dove *Zenaida aurita*

The Zenaida dove of the West Indian Islands was not scientifically named and described until painted
by Pauline Knip for Temminck's *Les Pigeons* in 1810.

NHML (3) 110

easy to me, by the assistance I have met with from various Gentlemen, particularly Mr Latham and Mr Parkinson, whose Museum I have not only had the liberty of inspecting, but likewise that of making drawings from some of the birds in their possession". Of the Glossy ibis, *Plegadis falcinellus* (now Purple heron) (vol. IV, pl. clii), he said, "In Mr Parkinson's Museum is one of these, which was shot in Cornwall", and of the African heron, *Ardea caspica* (now *Ardea purpurata*) (vol. IV, pl. cli), "This is an African bird, but has twice been met with in England. The specimen from which this description is taken, was shot in Ashdown Park, near Lambourn, in Berkshire, and is now in Mr Parkinson's Museum".

Lewin's sons helped him prepare a second edition of his book, but he only lived to see the figures for the first four volumes etched, before he died early in December 1795. His son John William Lewin (1770–1819) wrote and etched the figures for the first account of Australian birds to be published in Australia, in 1813.

William Lewin also painted five birds, two crab studies and two shell studies for Captain George Dixon's account of his *Voyage round the World*, 1785–88 (London 1789), but the original drawings were not done from Lever specimens.

When Emperor John Woodforde's collection of 1800 bird drawings and prints was sold in 1809 to the dealer, Dent, for £378, "drawings from the Bankes Museum, Capt. Cook and Lever Museum" by "Lewin, S.T. Edwards and R. R. Reinagle" were included.

Thomas Martyn

Martyn (1735–1825) published *The Universal Conchologist* (2 vols. (originally planned as 4 vols.), London 1784–87) with a text in English and French. In his Preface, he said that many shells had been collected by officers of ships under the command of Captains Byron, Wallace, Cook and others, in the different voyages to the South Seas, and he was aware of about 120 different species. He planned to present forty shell drawings and eighty figures in each of the four volumes, and had seen various cabinets of shells, including those in "Sir Ashton Lever's Holophusicon (Leicester House)". The plates of figures were

numbered, and a list of them given at the beginning of the volume, saying where the specimen was preserved, but no reference to the Leverian Museum occurred in the two volumes published. The eighty-eight sheets of watercolours for *The Universal Conchologist* are conserved in The Natural History Museum, London, with a letter explaining their provenance, and stating that they were the original drawings by Martyn.

Martyn was a dealer in shells, and claimed to have bought two thirds of the shells he acquired from Captain Cook's third voyage, paying the crews of *Resolution* and *Discovery* 400 guineas for them.[7] Martyn was also a Fellow of the Royal Society and a botanist, and author of *The Language of Botany: being a dictionary* (London 1793).

William Frederick Martyn

W.F. Martyn's artists used the full range of natural history specimens in the Leverian Museum for 100 plates in his *A New Dictionary of Natural History: or Compleat Universal Display of Animated Nature with accurate Representations of the most curious and Beautiful Animals, elegantly coloured* (2 vols., London 1785). The plates are signed only by the engraver, Moses Harris, and the specimens gathered into alphabetical order on the plates. Many species are collected onto each plate, and the publication date of each plate (between 1784 and 1786) is noted in the caption; 344 of the illustrations are of birds, including forty of parrots, which were strongly represented in the Leverian Museum. The Leverian dodo was included in pl. xli. Although the figures are small, the mixture of birds, mammals, fishes and butterflies on each plate is attractive.

PLATE 55

Black-fronted piping guan *Aburria jacutinga*

This species was not distinguished from other guans until 1825 by Spix.

NHML (3) 115

Mortimer

An artist in London in the 1780s, whose work was used sparingly, and who has remained in obscurity, Mortimer contributed two plates to White's *Journal of a Voyage to New South Wales*: that of the *Wha tapoua roo* (now *Tricholsurus vulpecula*, Brush-tailed possum) and the *Dog of New South Wales*, a dingo, *Canis dingo* (Meyer 1793), both drawn from specimens sent to Dr John Hunter to describe.

Mortimer used the Leverian specimen to make the original drawing of a chameleon for pl. 194 of George Shaw's *Museum Leverianum*, dated 1 May 1790.

Frederick Polydore Nodder

Nodder (1751–*ca.* 1801) was an artist and engraver and was employed as botanic painter to Queen Charlotte. He associated with the artists and engraver who worked on John White's *Journal of a Voyage to New South Wales*, and painted plants for five of the plates.

Robert Jameson, visiting London in 1793, recorded in his journal for Thursday 26 October, "Went this day and breakfasted with Dr Shaw and Dr Crichton. During breakfast Mr Nodder, Dr Shaws engraver came in. He appeared a very acquard and strange looking man."[8]

Nodder drew fishes, birds and other animals for George Shaw's *Vivarium Naturae, or The Naturalists' Miscellany* (1789–1813). The plates bore the date on which they were published by "F. P. Nodder & Co. No.15 Brewer Street" and Nodder was responsible for the illustrations up to and including plate 988, dated 1801; subsequent ones were done by his wife, Elizabeth.[9] They were finely engraved and very well coloured, accompanying a text in Latin and English.

The plates in *The Naturalists' Miscellany*, bearing illustrations of specimens said to be in the Leverian Museum, are scattered throughout vols. I–XVII, and cover a wide range of species. Of some interest were two "new" species, illustrated in vols. VII and VIII. The first was a Chordated stylephorus, "the only specimen yet known in Europe" (vol. VIII), and a Dilated phasma, with the information "John Parkinson first described it in the 4th volume of the *Transactions of the Linnaean Society*" (vol.

IX). Another interesting reference occurred in vol. XIV (text with pl. 573) to a specimen of the Little bustard, *Otis tetrax*, which was not in the Leverian Museum: "the elegant specimen represented on the present plate, and which was lately shot in our own country, was communicated by Mr Thompson, preparer of birds &c to the British and Leverian Museums".

Philip Reinagle

Reinagle (1749–1833) was of Hungarian origin, his family having emigrated to Scotland in 1745. He learned his art in the studio of Allan Ramsay, until he wearied of portraiture (saying he was fed up with producing "50 pairs of Kings and Queens" at ten guineas apiece), went up to London, and painted horses, dogs, hunting scenes and birds. After 1794 he preferred to paint landscapes. He exhibited at the Royal Academy (120 paintings between 1773 and 1811) and at the British Institution (140 pictures between 1806 and 1829). Two of his exhibits were painted at the Leverian Museum: *Hummingbirds from Sir Ashton Lever's Collection* and *Portraits of macaws and parrots*, in 1786.

Reinagle painted three huge oils on canvas, which were in the collection of George, 3rd Earl of Orford. Each was an evocative habitat scene: birds in a tropical forest; birds in a wooded landscape with a lot of butterflies and insects; and birds on a seashore with corals and seashells in abundance. All the items were in the Leverian Museum, and were painted lifelike in glowing colours.

Despite working from the same stuffed specimens in the white boxes in the museum, Reinagle put life and movement into the birds in his canvases,[10] and his skill at placing birds in a landscape was demonstrated in the first plate in George Shaw's *Museum Leverianum*, published in 1792: the magnificent Magellanic vulture or Condor was provided with a mountainous background, the sea and a small dead seal. In 1793, Reinagle painted the Ground parrot for pl. 219, and also provided the watercolours for the engravings of the Elk (pl. 34), the Ichneumon or Indian weasel (pl. 163), and both a Nine-banded and Twelve-banded armadillo (pl. 247).

PLATE 56

Corncrake *Crex crex*

The corncrake was much more common in 18th-century Britain than today.

NHML (3) 142

white Sheathbill. *La. Syn. 5. p. 268*   *Chionis lactea. La.*

PLATE 57

Snowy sheathbill *Chionis alba*

This painting is an important record of one of only two specimens ever found.

NHML (3) 146

PLATE 58

Purple gallinule *Porphyrula martinica*

This species was first brought to Europe from the island of Martinique in the windward group of
the Lesser Antilles, East Caribbean, a French colony since 1635. The distribution of the Purple gallinule
is now known to be Nearctic, Neotropical and Ethiopian.

NHML (3) 143

570

Ramsay Richard Reinagle

Ramsay Reinagle (1775–1862) studied with his father Philip and then went to Italy and Holland. He was an accomplished landscape painter and included cattle and horses in his scenes, but did far fewer paintings of animals than his father. Though some writers attribute the illustrations for George Shaw's *Museum Leverianum* to R.R. Reinagle, he was only a teenager when they were painted in 1790 to 1793, and it is far more probable that Philip was the illustrator.

In a sale in 1809, Emperor John Woodforde's collection of 1800 drawings and prints of birds by "Lewin, S.T. Edwards and R.R. Reinagle" (= Philip?) were bought for £378 by a dealer, Dent. These included "drawings from Bankes Museum, Captain Cooke & Lever Museum".

The Yale Center for British Art has a portrait of a gentleman examining the feathers of a Greater bird of paradise, *Paradisea apoda*, in a studio with other dead birds, painted by Ramsay Richard Reinagle (see fig. 3, p. 18). The other birds are a superb Lyre bird, *Menura superba* (first described and illustrated by Thomas Davies in 1802), and an Argus pheasant, *Argusianus argus*, with some smaller birds on a table. Two bound volumes on the table are titled *Linnaeus Zoology* and *Latham.* It is thought that the subject of the portrait is Thom(p)son, largely because Reinagle exhibited a portrait of "Mr Thomson, animal and bird preserver to the Liverian and British Museums" at the Royal Academy in 1802.

Charles Reuben Ryley

A brilliant illustrator, engraver and history painter, Ryley (1752–1798) won a Royal Academy gold medal in 1780 and decorated Goodwood House for the Duke of Richmond. He enjoyed his success, but acquired a taste for good living that diverted his attention from applying his talents and the necessary hard work to sustain his career. He consequently resorted to book illustration and teaching.

Ryley took over Sarah Stone's work at the museum when James Parkinson decided to ask George Shaw to publish an account of the *Museum Leverianum containing select Specimens from the Museum of Sir Ashton Lever with descriptions in Latin and English.* Plates for this publication were dated 7 March 1790 through to the time the publication ended, with part of the second volume, in 1796.

Ryley painted twenty-one mammals and thirty-eight birds in the museum.[11] Unlike most of the other artists who worked there, Ryley enjoyed doing the scenic background for these plates. The showiest and most brilliantly plumaged birds were chosen for this work, including an Argus, Golden and Peacock pheasants, the only specimen of the Hyacinthine macaw in Europe, a Blue-backed manakin, King and Greater birds of paradise, a Mandarin duck which was then imported live but had not become feral, a Trogon, Flamingo, parrots and penguins. Some of these were also painted by Sarah, but not all. One interesting specimen that they both drew was the Cinerous wattlebird, the origin of Latham's description (1781, I, p. 364, pl. xiv), collected at Queen Charlotte Sound, South Island, New Zealand, and still in the Liverpool Museum[12]

Ryley's mammals included many primates, with which the museum was well endowed, besides the more unusual Armadillo, Sloth, Giant ant-eater, Angora goat, and a

PLATE 59

Cock of the rock *Rupicola rupicola*

This bird inhabits the Guyanas and northern Brazil.

NHML (2) 53

Cock of the Rock

splendid Polar bear. Sarah painted a few of the same specimens.

One drawing (fig. 12) on which Ryley worked alongside Sarah Stone was used as the frontispiece to *The Companion to the museum removed to Albion Street*, 1790, captioned, "Miss Stone & C. Ryley del." and "W. Skelton sculp.". It shows the Rotunda, where the birds were displayed, and one would expect Sarah to have painted the birds in their cases, several of which could be identified. In 1805, this engraving was copied by S. Porter, the people in the foreground were removed, and a much flatter appearance given to the Rotunda (fig. 13).

John Walcott

Walcott (1754/55–1831) used bird specimens for his illustrations from two hundred specimens in his own collection, and "... from others in a state of high preservation in the Museums of Mr Parkinson and Mr Latham" (Preface to his *Synopsis of British Birds*, 1789–92). He used Rough-legged falcons, *Buteo lagopus*, in both museums, and the Purple heron, *Ardea purpurata*, and Glossy ibis, *Plegadis falcinellus*, shot in Cornwall, that Lewin had also used. The Rough-legged falcon, shot near London, was the specimen from which John Latham inserted it in the English list of birds.[13]

NOTES

1 Jackson (1985), pp. 181–89.

2 Jackson (1985), 'Moses Griffith', pp. 111–15, 'Peter Brown', pp. 110–11.

3 James Heath was an engraver who worked in London where he was born and died (Claus Nissen, *Die Illustrierte Vogelbücher*, Stuttgart 1953, p. 190).

4 Whitehead (1978), (2), 1, p. 81.

5 Edward Donovan, *The Naturalist's Repository* III, 1825, pl. lxxxix of *Echinus lamarckii*, and see p. 66.

6 Sweet (1965), 19 (2), p. 87.

7 Whitehead (1978), (2), 1, p. 78.

8 Sweet (1965), 19 (2), pp. 115–16.

9 Baptismal registers, St Mary in the Field, Westminster, record the baptisms of six children of Frederick Polydore and Elizabeth Nodder (including Richard Polydore in 1774, who also drew and engraved botanical plates) between 1773 and 1783.

10 Jackson (1994), pp. 104–07.

11 He also copied an original drawing "in Mons D'Orcy's collection" of the *Coracias militaris* for pl. 63.

12 Largen (1987), p. 277.

13 Jackson (1985), pp. 148–56.

Watercolour Drawings
by Sarah Stone in Public and Private Institutions

NOTE

Inscriptions on the watercolours or drawings are reproduced here in italics. Present day scientific names, in italic, with present-day common names, follow the headings. References in other contemporary sources to that species or object follow.

LM = Leverian Museum sale catalogue entries, with annotations from the few known annotated catalogues, giving the purchaser and pricce.

1. THE NATURAL HISTORY MUSEUM, LONDON

The Museum holds three collections of original drawings by Sarah Stone: a collection of watercolour drawings, completed between 1781 and 1785, depicting shells, corals, mammals, fossils and other specimens that were formerly in Sir Ashton Lever's Museum. The drawings were presented to the Museum in 1931 by the Superintendent of the University Museum of Zoology, Cambridge. In 1937 the Museum acquired thirteen watercolour drawings of birds as part of Sir Walter Rothschild's bequest of his library. A third collection of 175 watercolour drawings of birds was purchased by the Museum in 1996. These, too, were probably drawn from specimens in the Leverian Museum. This purchase was made possible with assistance from the National Heritage Memorial Fund and National Art Collections Fund.

The Library of The Natural History Museum, London (NHML) has three collections of watercolour drawings by Sarah Stone:

NHML (1) Portfolio of ninety-three watercolours of items in Sir Ashton Lever's Museum;

NHML (2) Thirteen watercolour drawings of birds;

NHML (3) An album of watercolours of birds, containing 175 sheets on 168 mounts.

The library also has one other drawing by Sarah Stone, among 888 original watercolours in portfolios of Latham drawings.

NHML (1) PORTFOLIO OF NINETY-THREE WATERCOLOURS OF ITEMS IN SIR ASHTON LEVER'S MUSEUM, PRESENTED 22 SEPTEMBER 1931 BY THE ZOOLOGICAL MUSEUM, CAMBRIDGE

Fossils were identified by John Thackray; fossil plants by Tiffany Foster; fossil shells by Noel Morris; fossil teeth and bones by Andrew Currant, Sally Young and Sandra Chapman; living mammals by Daphne Hills; fish by Alwynne Wheeler; modern shells by Kathie Way; reptiles by Colin McCarthy; corals by Brian Rosen and Jill Darrell; sponges by Clare Valentine; and a Gorgonian by Paul Cornelius.

1. *Preserved in Spirits in the Collection of Ashton Lever Esq*
   = *Gaidropsarus vulgaris* (Cloquet 1824), Three-bearded rockling, a northern European species that might be British.

PLATE 12

2. *Hippocampus* sp.
   A dried Seahorse. [LM 772 Gobius minutus, Sygnathus Hippocampus; a small Exocaetus, another fish, and two lizards, Laskey 13/-] Other seahorse specimens sold LM were in bottles and therefore not dried.

3. *Raccoon*
   = *Nasua narica* (Linnaeus 1766), White-nosed coati from central America. [LM 657 Coati-mondi Viverra nasua, Smith 13/-; 976 Coati mondi, viverra nasua, Cole 16/6; Last day 17 Coati mondi, young, 2 specimens,

Viverra nasua]

4. *Sarah Stone 191*

= *Castor fiber*, Kerr 1792, or *Castor canadensis*, Kuhl 1820, an abnormal colour variety, semi-albino Beaver. [LM 662 Beaver, Castor Fiber, Donovan 6/6; 1266 Beaver, young, Castor fiber, Jones £3.3.0; 1899 Beaver, N. America, Donovan £2.18.0.] Lady Fenn (1796, 2, pl. 36) wrote that trees "are gnawed all round in as regular a manner as a cutter cuts in felling a tree, bringing the bottom of the wood to a point (specimens of which may be seen in the Leverian Museum [LM 1451 Trunk of tree, gnawed down by beavers, Jones 4/-]

5. *Ibex, Alps*

= *Capra ibex*, Linnaeus 1758, Ibex, Eurasia. [LM Last day 20 Steinbock, Capra ibex, extremely rare]

6. *Musk of Thibet 186*

= *Moschus* sp., the Musk deer of Asia. (John Church included "The Tibetan Musk Capreolus moschi Gesner Moschus moschiferus Linn" in his book, *A Cabinet of Quadrupeds*, 2 vols., 1795–1805).

7. *Elephant*

= *Elaphus maximus*, Linnaeus 1758, the Asian elephant, male. [LM Last day but one 74 Elephant, Elephas maximus.]
PLATE 13
Sarah also painted this stuffed elephant at the entrance to the first Leicester House gallery in her painting of the Leverian Museum, 1786 (FRONTISPIECE). In the advertisements 6–19 January 1778, in the *Morning Post and Daily Advertiser*, a letter from Mr Lever dated 3 November 1777 was incorporated in the advertisement for LEICESTER HOUSE, Mr Lever's Museum of natural Curiosities, stating, "within these few days, many most rare and superb articles added to the collection; among

which are the Elephant most graciously presented to him by his Majesty ...".

8. *Zibet*
Sarah's drawing was of *Potos flavus* (Schreber 1774), the Kinkajou from South and Central America.

9. *188*
= *Didelphis virginiana*, Kerr 1792, the Virginian opossum, from the southern US and Central America. [LM 69 Opossum – Didelphis Virginianus (handwritten note "Bad sp.") Money & Lady 8.6; 2294 Virginian opossum, fem. Didelphis Virginiana, b.i. (*i.e.* "bought in") £2.12.6; 2795 Virginian opossum, Didelphis Virginiana, Sivers 5.6] (See also no. 23.)

10. *Pteropus* sp.
(Probably) Fruit bat from Asia and Australasia.

11. *Herpestes* sp.
Mongoose from Asia and also Africa. [LM 3629 Lemur mongooz, Heslop 10/6; 6534 Lemur mongooz]

12. = *Felis (Leptailurus) serval*, Müller 1776, Serval, Africa.

13. *190* (on reverse)
= *Nandinia binotata* (Reinw.) (J.E. Gray 1843), African palm civet.

14. *34* (on reverse)
Paranyctimene ?raptor, the tube-nosed bat from Asia.
PLATE 14

15. *Gnu Hottentot*
= *Connochaetes gnou* (Zimmerman 1780), White-tailed gnu from South Africa.

16. Perhaps *Tragelaphus scriptus*, female Bush-buck.

17. = *Loris tardigradus*, E. Geoffroy 1796, Slender loris from Asia. [LM 1897 Tailless macauco Lemur tardigradus; 6532 A fine specimen of Lemur tardigradus, Carrudes 11/-]

18. *Mus. Lev. p. 48*
= *Cuon alpinus*, Dhole or Indian red dog, or more likely *Canis*

aureus, Linnaeus 1758, Golden jackal of Africa and Asia.

19. *Sarah Stone*
= *Monodon monoceros*, Linnaeus 1758, skull of the Narwal with double tusks. [LM 1450 Tusk of the Narwal whale. monodon monceros, £1.7.0.]

20. *Mus. Lev. II. p. 13*
= *Bradypus tridactylus*, Linnaeus 1758, Three-toed sloth (two drawings) from South America. [LM 71 5693 Bradypus tridactylus, young (without case) Thompson 4/-; 5777 Bradypus tridactylus, young; Last day 18 Bradypus tridactylus, extremely rare]
PLATE 15

21. *Goat of Angora Sarah Stone 1781 Mus. lev. I. p. 47*
'Capri hirci' = *Capra hircus*, Linnaeus 1758, Domestic goat, angora breed. [LM 5703 Capra Angorensis, very fine, Jennings £10.0.0.]
PLATE 17

22. = *Cyclops didactylus*, Linnaeus 1758, Silky anteater, Pigmy anteater. [LM perhaps 2201 Small anteater, Hislop 11/-]
PLATE 16

23. = *Didelphis virginiana*, Kerr 1792, Virginian opossum, female. [LM (see no. 9)]

24. *Sarah Stone 1784*
= *Dynastes hercules*, Linnaeus 1758, Horned scarab from South and Central America and the West Indies. [LM 4055 Scarabaeus Hercules, a large and perfect specimen]
PLATE 20

25. A dynastine beetle, a horned scarab. (See also no. 24.)

26. *192*
Two lizards, unidentifiable green lizard, with *Gekko vittatus* (Houttuyn 1782) from Madagascar. [LM 3620 Banded snake, a gecko lizard, and another; 3624 Lettered tortoise, testudo scripta, gecko lizard, and a snake, Fichtel £1.1.0; 3673 Gecko lizard, speckled lizard,

and another; 3676 Lacerta gecko, a well-preserved specimen, Fenton 5/-; 4157 Two lizards of the gecko tribe and another lizard, Segelkin 6/-; 4159 A lizard of the gecko family, and another, Smith 4/6]

27. Snake, uncertain, possibly the flying snake *Chrysopelea* sp.
PLATE 19

28. Chameleon, probably *Chamaeleo bifidus*, Brongniart 1800, from Madagascar [LM 2289 Lacerta chamelion, Sivers £1.0.0.; A small chameleon, frog, fish, and another, Donovan 5/-; Last day but one 67 A large and fine specimen of Lacerta Chamaleon].
PLATE 18

29. *Large Pecten Fossil In the collection of Ashton Lever Esq*, and in the middle of the drawing of the fossil, *1768*.
117
A single mass of stone with three embedded fossils, one bivalve *Plagiostoma gigantea*, one *Pecten*-type bivalve, and one ribbed ammonite. Specimens look Liassic (Lower Jurassic).

30. *202*
Three fossils. Three specimens, two being different views of a fragment of white shell, the third being an impressed pattern in reddish stone:
(a) *Part of the Shell call'd the Devil's Claw Fossil RD delin* (Dorning Rasbotham? See no. 38).
(b) no caption
(c) *Part of Devil's Claw Fossill In the collection of Ashton Lever Esq*
Devil's claw is part of the lip of a living stromboidean gastropod, *Lambis* sp.; impression is a bark impression of *Lepidodendron* sp. from the Coal Measures.

31. *In the Collection of Ashton Lever Esq.*
Four fossils:
1 and 2. *Buccinites Thama*
3 and 4. *Coal Brook Dale*
There is a picture of a museum label attached to one of the

fossils, *Buccinites Thama*. Two views of internal cast of a naticid gastropod in white stone; part and counterpart of a fossil leaf in a nodule. "Buccinites" is a Gesner 1758 name, "Thama" is unknown.

PLATE 21

32. Single tubular dark specimen. Rootstock of a tree, *Stigmaria ficoides*, Sternberg, the Coal Measures.

33. Two specimens of fossils, one a grey bivalve, the other a roughly drawn piece of rock, incompletely coloured. Bivalve *Gryphaea arcuata*, Lamarck 1819, from the Lower Lias (Lower Jurassic). The other specimen, may be fossil wood.

34. *Large Pecten Fossil In the Collection of Ashton Lever Esqr.* The single large shell backed by white stone might be *Plagiostoma* sp.

35. Two fossil bivalves, one with a ribbed shell, *Spondylus* sp., the other a smooth internal cast, *Ceratomya* sp.

36. A fossil bivalve, plus an echinoid embedded in chalk, placed on a fascicule of a book. Fossil bivalve, possibly *Inoperna scalprum*; echinoid, *Phymostoma* sp. from the Chalk. The lettering on the book, partly obscured by the shell, reads: "Le Diable ... eux Second Partie, A Amsterdam Chez Henrik Vander Tromp in de Kalverstraat".

37. Three pieces of fossiliferous rock, probably Wenlock limestone from Shropshire or Dudley, with embedded shells:
(a) high-spired Turrilitid gastropods
(b) a caritid bivalve and a globose gastropod
(c) small brachiopods and a trilobite fragment

PLATE 22

38. Single triangular piece of pale pink rock, cut and polished to show fossil section through an

orthoconic nautiloid, Palaeozoic, not British. On the reverse there is a closely similar outline of the rock shape, *by Dorning Rasbotham Esq.*

39. 207 (on reverse). Single black tubular specimen, part of the rootstock of a fossil tree, *Stigmaria ficoides*, Sternberg, the Coal Measures.

40. Two irregular stony specimens with fragments of an ammonite, showing the inside of the whorl.

41–43. Three specimens mounted on one sheet:

41. Single bark impression of *Lepidodendron* sp. on reddish rock, from the Coal Measures.

42. *7 Inches* and a separate scale. Part of a tubular specimen (probably *Lepidodendron* sp.) with spiral marking.

43. *Lithophyte from Colebrooke Dale, Shropshire* Single specimen with impression of a leafy branch tip of *Lepidodendron* sp. in reddish rock, from the Coal Measures.

44. Single tubular ribbed specimen of cast of branch or stem of *Calamites* sp., from the Coal Measures.

45. Two specimens of black stone with diamond impressions: bark impressions of *Lepidodendron* cf. *aculeatum* or *Lepidodendron mannabachense*, from the Coal Measures.

46. Single black specimen with diamond impression: bark impression of *Lepidodendron aculeatum*, Sternberg, the Coal Measures.

47. *Ichthyomorphite from Dudley on the Borders of Shropshire* Single black shaly specimen with trilobite. *Dalmanites* from Wenlock.

48. Single elongated reddish specimen with bark impression: *Lepidodendron* sp., from the Coal Measures.

49. *In the Collection of Ashton Lever Esqr* Single specimen with fossil

bark impression, *Lepidodendron* sp., from the Coal Measures.

50. Three fossil teeth:
(a) *Fossil Grinder, probably of the River Horse dug up two hundred miles distant from the Sea, near Rocky River in North America* Part of a molar of the Mastodon, *Mammut americanum*, from the Salt Lick, on the banks of the Ohio (see John C. Greene, *Death of Adam: evolution and its impact on western thought*, Iowa 1959, p. 105) [LM Last day 60 A large fossil grinder of the mammoth, from the banks of the river Ohio, North America]
(b) *Fossil Tooth of an Horse from Shotover Hill, Oxfordshire Equus* sp. tooth from superficial deposit at Shotover.
(c) Fossil Horses Tooth from North America *Equus* sp. tooth.

51. 206 Two views of the cast of an ammonite in brown rock: inner whorls of (probably) *Cadoceras* sp., Mid-Jurassic.

52. *Fossil Nautilus from Dorset 1759 In the Collection of Ashton Lever Esqr* Two views of a single internal cast of a nautiloid in brown rock, cut and polished.

53. *Fossil from Wiltshire 220* (on reverse) Cut section through a large ammonite, calcite in the inner chambers.

54. *Hippopus hippopus* (Linnaeus 1758), Bear's paw clam, south-west Pacific. [LM 2583 A large and fine bear's paw clamp (Chama hippopus Linn) E. Indies, W Cumming 10/-; another 2941 P Jackson 8/-; a small one 4903 and 5038; 3412 A young leopard porcelain, the bellied variety of the occidental argus porcelain, Providence and a bear's paw clamp, P. Jackson 16/-; 3551 A large and fine chama hippopus, Linn or bear's paw clamp, E. Indies, Sivers

11/-; 3704 A very large tridachna ursina, or bear's paw clamp, E. Indies, Thane 9/-; 4610 A fine tridachna ursina, or bear's paw clamp, from the E. Indies, G Humphrey10/-; 4919 Fine bear's paw clamp, having its foliations very protuberant, and otherwise complete, from Amboyna, G Humphrey £1.9.0. Appendix 368 Chama hippopus, Fillingham 6/-. Another drawing 75]

PLATE 24

55. Four shells: = *Lambis scorpio* (Linnaeus 1758), Scorpion conch from the west Pacific. [LM Last day but two 80 The white scorpion purpura (Murex Scorpio var. Linn) extremely scarce]

56. = *Hexaplex duplex* (Röding 1798), Duplex murex from West Africa.

57. *Sarah Stone* Two shells, both *Hyotissa hyotis* (Linnaeus 1758), Honeycomb oyster from the Caribbean and Indo-Pacific.

PLATE 23

58. Ironstone concretion containing fossil frond of *Neuropteris* sp., a Coal Measures plant.

59. = *Hexaplex duplex* (Röding, 1798), Duplex murex from West Africa.

PLATE 25

60. A large shell with a small one resting on blue paper:
(a) = *Tridacna squamosa* (Lamarck 1819), Fluted giant clam from the Indo-Pacific. [LM 2704 A large chama gigas Linn or giant clamp, from Ceylon, Blackman £5.5.0.; Last day but two 68 A single valve of the chama gigas, from Borneo, in length forty-one inches]
(b) *Spondylus* sp., Thorny oyster

PLATE 26

61. Freshwater bivalve, one of the Unionacea.

62. *Sarah Stone 1780* Horseshoe covered with calcareous encrustation.

63. *Bottle found in the sea covered with wormtubes*
[LM 567 A bottle which having lain some time in the Sea, is overrun with serpulae, Birchell 9/-]

64. Green wine bottle with worm tubes.

65. Three shells: top, *Spondylus* sp., Thorny oyster; bottom, *Tridacna squamosa*, Lamarck 1819, Fluted giant clam from the Indo-Pacific. [LM (see no. 60 (b))]

66. Two shells: *Busycon contrarium* (Conrad 1840), Lightning whelk from south-east USA.

67. Two shells, both *Tibia delicatula* (Nevill 1881), delicate tibia from the Arabian sea.

68. Two shells:
(a) *Hippopus hippopus* (Linnaeus 1758), Bear's paw clam, south-west Pacific. [For LM see no. 54]
(b) *Pecten* sp., Scallop

69. Five shells:
(a) top, *Clanculus pharaonis* (Linnaeus 1758), Strawberry top from Indian Ocean.
(b) middle left, *Drupa* sp., Rock shell.
(c) middle right, *Thais* sp., Rock shell.
(d) and (e) bottom, unidentified.

70. Four shells:
(a) and (d), top and bottom, *Lambis lambis* (Linnaeus 1758), Common spider conch from the Indo-Pacific [LM spider strombus – 291 from Madagascar; 430; 813; 925 Two spider strombi, Madagascar; 2716 fine from China; 4611 from Madagascar 5/6; appendix 363 spider strombus (*Venus literata*]
(b) middle, *Mitra papalis* (Linnaeus 1758), Papal mitre, Indo-Pacific. [LM 1777 A small papal mitre, a bishop's mitre, a scarce white tower from Martinique, and two rare needles, Rowe 7/-; 2446 The papal mitre, of an uncommon

size, from Amboyna; and the great swamp club, from China, both rare, Carrudes 9/-]

71. One shell: *Spondylus ?regius* (Linnaeus 1758), Regal thorny oyster from the west Pacific.

72. *Sarah Stone: 1783*
Two shells: *Xenophora ?conchyliophora* (Born, 1780), Carrier shell from North Carolina, West Indies, Brazil. [LM 2445 A fine onustus maximus, or great carrier, loaded with shells and corals, from Martinique, very rare, Carrudes £1.12.0.; 2713 A fine onustus maximus, or great carrier, loaded with shells, from Martinique, very rare, G Humphrey 9/-]
PLATE 27

73. Oyster, *Crassostrea* sp.

74. *Inside of the Shell called the Devils Claw In the collection of Ashton Lever Esq*
= *Lambis chiragra* (Linnaeus 1758), Spider conch from the eastern Indian Ocean to Polynesia. [LM 211 A young devil's claw with the epidermis, a spider strombus ditto, Madagascar, and an iris ear, New Zealand, 5/-; other young devil's claws 1247 1375, 1521, 1536; 690 A group of the odd valves of the purple oyster, South Seas, and a devil's claw Strombus, Vardon £1.2.0; Last day but two 83 A large and fine devil's claw Strombus, Madagascar; Appendix 506 Devil's Claw strombus shell, 7/6]
PLATE 28

75. = *Hippopus hippopus* (Linnaeus 1758), Bear's paw clam, south-west Pacific. [For LM, see no. 54]

76. Monochrome black ink painting of scleractinian coral, *Acropora* sp.
PLATE 31

77. Monochrome purple/red ink painting of a Gorgonian, of the subclass Octocorallia.

PLATE 29
78. Monochrome painting of a Gorgonian (coelenterate) of the genus *Isis*.
PLATE 32
79. *The size of nature*
Four calcareous sponges with a measured scale of 4 in.:
(a) *Callyspongia* sp. or *Aplysina* sp.
(b) *Niphates ?digitalis*
(c) *Ianthella ?basta*
(d) *Dactylochaliia* sp. or *Chalinopsilla* sp.;
and fish on block of white stone with ?other fossils not readily identifiable. If from Lebanon (where preservation is similar), it would be *Spandion* sp.
PLATE 35
80. *Sarah Stone: 1783 178*
A Gorgonian, of the subclass Octocorallia.
PLATE 30
81. S2 (bottom left corner) Malformed radish and two malformed, intertwined carrots.
PLATE 36
82. Design for a tin or snuff-box? lid with a fish drawn on the lid.

83. Three small fossil teeth:
(a) Crushing fish tooth with parallel ridges, *Ptychodus* sp. from Upper Cretaceous
(b) small block with rows of crushing teeth, from a ray of the order Pycnodontida.
(c) fossil tooth of an unknown reptile in a piece of limestone.

84. Three fossils specimens, two resting on blue paper:
(a) *Fishes tooth (fossil) from Malta* Tooth of fossil shark, *Carcharodon* sp., Miocene [LM 218 Impression of a fish in black slate, Isleben; skeleton of a fish, Papenheim; large fossil tooth of a shark, Malta; and the head of a fish, Sheppey Island, Money 14/-; 3658 Large shark tooth, Malta; various bufonites, parts of palates, &c, 9/6; Last day but two 60 Head of the lily encrinus, Brunwick; part of another, Derbyshire; and large shark's tooth, Malta; Appendix

647 Fossil shark's tooth Malta, and six others, 6/6]
(b) *Lithophyte from High Carmel Mines, Lancashire*
Frond of an unidentifiable fossil fern from the Coal Measures.
(c) *Tibia of a Bird from Stonesfield, Osfordshire*
(on reverse) 206
Phalange of a pterodactyl from the Stonesfield Slate, Bathonian, Jurassic.
PLATE 38
85. *A calcarious Stone full of the Bones of Land Animals taken from the Rock of Gibraltar 1772*
A cut piece of reddish stone containing bone fragments: Quaternary fissure breccia of mammalian bones, probably from Rosia Bay, Gibraltar. (See W. Hunter, 'Account of some bones found in the Rock of Gibraltar ...', *Philosophical Transactions of the Royal Society*, 60, 1770, pp. 414-16.) [LM 2723 Fragments of bones especially teeth imbedded in calcareous spar, Gibraltar – a very interesting specimen, bought in £2. 0. 0.; 3071 Part of a very large pecten, and bones in spar, from Gibraltar, (sold the last to Retley for a 1/-) bought by G Humphrey for 1/6; Appendix 301 Bones in spar, two varieties, Gibraltar, and other petrifactions, Harrison 2/-]
PLATE 33
86. Single fossil bone, vertebra of an ichthyosaur, Lower Jurassic.

87. *Mass of Fishes Teeth found in the Blue Lodge Quarry, near Bath*
A single, pale brown specimen with disassociated teeth of either a fish or a reptile, Jurassic. [LM 220 A mass of limestone, with several teeth of a large species of lacerta, Bath, Donovan 11/-]
PLATE 34
88. *Miss Stones sent drawing for Sir Ashton Lever* A single specimen of a fossil crinoid.; *This was the first drawing Miss Stone did for me.*

Ashton Lever 198 (on reverse), and some partly erased lists and ?prices

89. Single grey stone with an impression, part of an unidentifiable fossil bony fish.

90. Fifteen small fossil specimens,

fragments of the stems of fossil crinoids, probably silicified. Three with a five-rayed section are *Isocrinus* sp. from the Jurassic, the remainder look Carboniferous.

PLATE 37

91. Ten drawings of five species of brachiopod: (a) *Pugnax acuminata*, Carboniferous limestone; (b) *Overtonia fimbriata*, Carboniferous limestone; (c) terebratulid; (d and e) terebratulid.

92. *196*
Single large mass of scleractinian coral, *Turbinaria* sp.

93. Scleractinian coral, *Diploria* sp.

NHML (2) THIRTEEN WATERCOLOUR DRAWINGS OF BIRDS, BY SARAH STONE, ACQUIRED WITH THE ROTHSCHILD BEQUEST

The birds were identified and named by Michael P. Walters.

48. *S. Stone 1788 Hoopoe found in England sometimes*
= *Upupa epops*, Linnaeus 1758. [LM 4923 Common hooppoe, Kirkpatrick 14/-; 3290 Common hoopoe Davis? Prayter 18/; 5837 Hoopoe male]

49. *Golden Pheasant S. Stone 1788*
= *Chrysolophus pictus* (Linnaeus 1758). A specimen of the golden pheasant was given to Lindroth in part exchange for the elk in 1783, and is now in the Swedish Natural History Museum [LM 1832 Gold pheasant, m. and fem. China, Kirkpatrick £2.3.0; 1936 Golden pheasant, China, without case, Smith £1.1.0; 3392 Gold pheasant, m. fem. and two young, Phasianus pictus, Bostock £2.2.0; 4948 Gold pheasant, female 10/6; 5135 Phasianus pictus].
PLATE 46

50. *Peacock Pheasant*; (on reverse) *S. Stone 1788; The Peacock pheasant from China*
= *Polyplectron bicalcaratum* (Linnaeus 1758), Grey peacock pheasant [LM Last day but one 50 Phasianus bicalcaratus, peacock pheasant, China, a most beautiful specimen, very rare.]
PLATE 41

51. *Tawny Owls Sarah Stone 1788*
= *Strix aluco* (Linnaeus 1758). [LM 528 White-fronted parrot, Wood Owl, hen; and Woodcock variety, three cases, Sedelisen 15/-; 1049 White

variety of the rook, and a wood-owl, G Walker £1.3.0; 1752 Wood owl, water hen, and common crow, Heslop 4.6; 3910 Wood owl, Donovan 9/-; 5899 Wood owl, nest and eggs]

52. *Crowned Pigeon S Stone 1788*
= *Goura cristata* (Pallas 1764). [LM 2430 Great crowned pigeon, Columba coronata, Lord Stanley £1.18.0; 4949 A very fine specimen of the Columba coronata, Bullock £1.17.0.]
At the sale of Bullock's Museum in 1818, George Shaw bought several birds for the BM, among them a crowned pigeon, *Goura coronata*, which Bullock had bought from the LM and which "when living was many years in the possession of her present Majesty, who presented it to the Leverian Museum" (Edward Miller, *That noble cabinet: a history of the British Museum*, London 1973, p. 39). A specimen of the crowned pigeon was given to Lindroth in part exchange for the elk in 1783, and is now in the Swedish Natural History Museum.
PLATE 42

53. *Cock of the Rock S Stone 1788*
= *Rupicola rupicola* (Linnaeus 1766). [LM 52 Pipra rupicola, cock of the rock, male, South America, Vaughan £3.15.0; 4784 A very fine specimen of the rock manakin, Pipra rupicola,

Burchell £3.3.0.]
PLATE 59

54. *The Mandarin Drake from China S Stone 1788*
= *Aix galericulata* (Linnaeus 1758). A specimen of the mandarin from the LM was given to Lindroth in part exchange for the elk in 1783, and is now in the Swedish Natural History Museum. [LM 6600 Mandarine duck, female, Donovan 7/6; Last day 30 Mandarine Duck, Anas galericulata, Linn.]
PLATE 44

55. *Cockatoo S. Stone 1788*
= *Cacatua moluccensis*, Gmelin 1788, Salmon-crested cockatoo.

56. *Indian Roller (The roller or Blue jay from America) S Stone 1788*
= *Coracias benghalensis indica* (Linnaeus 1766). [LM 4254 A most beautiful specimen of the Indian roller, Coracias Indica, Brogden £4.13.0.]

57. *Zebra Curassow*
The bird depicted is an unusual plumage phase of *Crax rubra*, Linnaeus 1758, Great curassow. [LM 1931 A beautiful specimen of the zebra curasso bird, Crax alector, var. C. £6.0.0.]

58. *Wydah Bird*
= *Vidua paradisaea* (Linnaeus 1758), Paradise whydah. [LM 3575 Long-tailed whidah bird, m. and fem. (two specimens of the male in different stages of plumage) Kirkpatrick £2.3.0; 1042 Long-tailed Whidah bird,

Africa, m. and fem. Fichtel 7/6]

59. *Cardinal and Waxwing*
= *Cardinalis cardinalis* (Linnaeus 1758), and *Bombycilla garrulus* (Linnaeus 1758) [LM 3572 Loxia cardinalis, m. and fem. Sivers 8/6; 4922 Virginian nightingale, Loxia cardinalis, fem. 2/6; 5123 Loxia cardinalis, mas. Smith 5/6; 5898 Virginian nightingale] and [LM 200 Bohemian chatterer, Ampelis garrulus, in a mahogany case, Pennant 10/6; 544 Nuthatch, grey wagtail, Bohemian Chatterer, Ampelis garrulus, female, and bullfinch, 4 cases, T. Walker £1.4.0; 3122 Bohemian chatterer, Pellaby 7/-; 5492 Waxen chatterer, ampelis garulus, m. and fem., Sivers £1.3.0.].
PLATE 40

60. *West Indian Flamingo*
= *Phoenicopterus ruber* (Linnaeus 1758) Flamingo. [LM 377 Red flamingo, Phoenicopterus ruber, Jamaica, 4/-; 2053 A most beautiful specimen of the flamingo, Phoenicopterus ruber, with red and white variegations, Butt £4.5.0; Last day but one, 60 Flamingo, a singularly fine and high coloured specimen, Phoenicopterus ruber].
PLATE 45

Containing 175 sheets on 168 mounts; the majority of the watercolours approx 25 × 35cm, bound in marble boards edged with brown morocco, the spine stamped "Drawings". Sotheby's, London Topographical drawings, 2 November 1988, lot 77; Property of British Rail Pension Fund on loan to the Department of Library Service (July 1991); sold to The Natural History Museum, 1996.

The inscriptions in italics include the bird's Linnean or Latham's scientific name, and the reference in John Latham's *A General Synopsis of Birds*, London 1781–85 (in six parts with 106 hand-coloured etchings;

usually, later, bound into three vols.). This work is variously referred to as "La. Syn." or "Gen. Syn.". The scientific names were added to the drawings at a later date, in a hand other than Sarah's. Some of the drawings were signed by Sarah Stone, as indicated. On the right hand side, a number was occasionally written in large figures, the significance of which is as yet unknown.

The birds were identified and named by Michael P. Walters and Robert Prys-Jones.

1. *Lark variety Sarah Stone* (sp. unidentifiable)

2. *Vultur percnopterus Alpine vulture La. Syn. 1 Pg 12* 97
An incorrect naming; this species is of the genus *Gyps*. Latham referred to a specimen in the Leverian Museum. [LM Last day but one, 56 Alpine vulture, C. of Good Hope, vultur percnopterus]

3. *Golden Eagle This wants further investigation Falco albicilla junior "non Descript" vol. 1. p. 31* 109
Probably a species of the genus *Aquila*. Latham referred to a specimen in the LM, and [LM Last day but two, 26 Golden eagle, Falco chryaetos, Linn.] might refer.

4. *Honey Buzzard Falco apivorus Gen. Syn. 1 Pg 52*
= *Pernis apivorus* (Linnaeus 1758). [LM 4252 Honey buzzard Falco apivorus, Donovan £1-7-0; 4616 ditto Donovan £8.18.6d.]

5. *Hen harrier Falco cyaneus Lin. Gen. Syn. 1 Pg 68 (sic = 88)* 177
= *Circus cyaneus* (Linnaeus 1758), Hen harrier. [LM 3571 Hen harrier hawk, Falco cyaneus, Donovan £1.1.0; 5122 Hen harrier hawk, P.Walker 10/6]

6. *Merlin Falco Asalon Gen Syn. 1 Pg 106*
A young bird, = *Falco columbarius aesalon*, Tunstall 1771. [LM 4943 Merlin hawk Falco aesalon, Donovan 15/-]

7. *Siberian eared owl Stryx poulchella La. La. Syn 1 Pg 130*
Probably = *Otus scops* (Linnaeus

1758). Latham noted an LM specimen, and a specimen from the LM was given to Lindroth in 1783 in part exchange for an elk, and is now in the Swedish Natural History Museum.

8. *Senegal shrike Lanius senegalus L. La. Syn 1 Pg 162*
= *Tchagra senegala* (Linnaeus 1766), Black-headed bush shrike. Latham did not note a Leverian Museum specimen.

9. *Yellow bellied shrike Lanius sulphuratus L, La Syn 1 Pg 188*
= *Pitangus sulphuratus* (Linnaeus 1766), Great kiskadee. The only specimen of which Latham was aware, was one in the LM. [LM 1109 Lanius sulphuratus, yellow-bellied shrike, Guinea. Sivers 6/-]

10. *Spotted Cayenne shrike La Syn 1 Pg 189 Var. A*
= *Tityra cayanus* (Linnaeus 1766), Black-tailed tityra. [LM 5368 Cayenne shrike, Lanius Cayanensis, 4/6]

11. *Magpie shrike Lanius picatus La La Syn 1 Pg 192* 139
Sarah's watercolour will be the type of *Cissopis leveriana* (Gmelin 1788), Magpie tanager. Latham's name was preoccupied by *Lanius leverianus* (Gmelin 1788, who named the bird after Sir Ashton Lever). Latham knew only of the specimen in the LM, saying in 1781, "This bird is in fine preservation in the Leverian Museum, but from whence it came is not noticed". His was the first description with no other references in

ornithological literature. [LM 5619 The Leverian shrike, Lanius Leverianus, extremely scarce, bought in £1.7.0.]

12. *Otaheitan blue parakeet Psittacus sapphirinus La. La Syn 1 Pg 255 144*
= *Vini peruviana* (P.L.S. Müller 1776), Tahitian or blue lory. Latham owned one specimen and used his, and the one in the LM. Gmelin called it *Psittacus taitiensis*, and both names are predated by *Psittacus peruvianus* (Müller 1776). [LM 4748 Otaheitan blue parroquet, Psittacus taitanus, very fine and rare, Vaughan £3.11.0.]

13. *Ash coloured parrot Psitt: erithacus L. La Syn 1 Pg 261* 74
= *Psittacus erithacus*, Linnaeus 1758, African grey parrot. [LM 187 Psittacus erithacus, Gray parrot, 12/-; 1299 Gray parrot, Africa, Psittacus erithacus, 5/-; 4941 Gray parrot, Sugden 9/-, 5869 Grey parrot]

14. *Red-beaked toucan Ramphastos erythrorhynchos La. La Syn 1 Pg 328?*
= *Ramphastos tucanus* Linnaeus 1758, Red-billed toucan. [LM 53 Ramphastos tucanus, Hall 10/6; 2434 Toucan, Brasil, Rhamphastos rufirostris, Lord Stanley £1.4.0. (Lord Stanley called it *Rhamphastos erythrorhynchus* in the manuscript lists of specimens in his museum (Largen 1987, pp. 282–83)]

15. *Green toucan Ramphastos viridis Lin. La Syn 1 pg 331*

= *Pteroglossus viridis* (Linnaeus 1766), Green aracari. Latham said there was a specimen in the BM and LM in 1781, and there was a specimen in the Vienna Museum in 1873 (Pelzehn 1873, p. 116).

16. *Piperine toucan Ramphastos piperivorus La Syn 1 pg 334*
= *Selindera culik* (Wagler 1827), Giant or Guianan toucanet, known locally as "Culik" from its call, "koo-lik" [LM 3296 Piperine toucan, Ramphastos piperivorus, Brogden £1.2.0; 3921 Piperine toucan Ramphastos piperivorus, Heslop 15/6].

PLATE 39

17. *Rhinoceros hornbill Buceros rhinoceros Lin. La Syn 1 Pg 334*
= *Buceros rhinoceros*, Linnaeus 1758. Sarah's painting has a black, instead of white, belly. [LM 2227 A very capital specimen of the rhinsceros bird, Buceros Rhinosceros, extremely rare, Fichtel £11.0.0. (no longer in the Vienna Museum)]

18. *Cinerous wattle-bird Callaeus cinerea La La Syn 1 Pg 364*
= *Callaeus cinerea* (Gmelin 1788), Kokako. The first description and picture of a specimen taken to England by J. R. Forster from Captain James Cook's second voyage (1772–75, I, p. 148) was given to Latham who quoted, "Mr Forster in his Voy. talks of the shrill notes of Thrushes, the graver pipe of Wattle-Birds, and the

enchanting melody of various Creepers, resounding on all sides", when in New Zealand. [LM 2698 Cinerous wattle bird, S. Seas, Glaucopis cineria, Lord Stanley £1.16.0. A syntype exists in the Liverpool Museum (Largen 1987, pp. 277, 286).]

19. *Nutcracker Corvus caryocatactes L. La Syn 1 Pg 400 138*
= *Nucifraga caryocatactes* (Linnaeus 1758), Nutcracker. [LM 4931 Nutcracker, Corvus caryocatactes, one specimen without case, Donovan £2.15.0; 5126 The nut cracker, Corvus caryocatactes, Foljambe £1.4.0.]

20. *Red-legged crow Corvus graculus L La Syn 1 Pg 401*
= *Pyrrhocorax pyrrhocorax* (Linnaeus 1758), Chough. [LM 4267 Cornish chough, Corvus graculus, Fichtel 8/- (transferred to the duplicates in the Vienna Museum in 1832 (Pelzehn 1873, p. 28)); 5125 A very fine specimen of the Cornish chough, Corvus graculus, P. Walker 15/-]

21. *Lesser Ani Crotophagus Ani Lin La Syn 2 Pg 360 177*
= *Crotophaga ani* (Linnaeus 1758), Smooth-billed ani. [LM 5935 Crotophaga ani; 6165 Lesser ani]

22. *Red winged oriole female Oriolus phoenicurus Lin. Gen Syn 2 Pg. 428*
A young bird of *Agelaius phoeniceus* (Linnaeus 1766), Red-winged blackbird. [LM 365 Red-winged thrush, male and female, with other birds, Money 7/-; and 538 Red-shouldered starling, oriolus phaeniceus, N. America; m. and fem. America, unsold; 4480 Red-winged oriole Oriolus phoeniceus, Fred Swainson 11/; 4090 Red-wing thrush, 7/6; 5846 Red winged thrush]

23. *Lesser bonana oriole This is the Jamaican variety Oriolus xanthorus Lin La Syn 2 Pg 438*
= *Icterus leucopteryx* (Wagler 1827), Jamaican oriole. [LM 1038 Pink breasted oriole,

Heslop 8/-; 6183 Pink-breasted xanthornus, m. and fem.; 5819 Lesser banana bird, and the house sparrow; 6569 Lesser bonana bird, Heslop 5/6]

24. *Lesser black oriole Oriolus nitidus La Syn 2 Pg 446?*
Probably an Icterid, but never certainly identified. Latham said, "I have this very bird in my possession", as that "used for *North American* animals", and Captain Davies had another specimen, but there was not one in the LM.

25. *Climbing oriole Oriolus sundara? [?] La Gen Syn 2 Pg 453*
Probably = *Xiphorhynchus picus* (Gmelin 1788), Straight-billed woodcreeper. The climbing oriole and grackle are given as synonyms in Latham's *General History of Birds*, as *Gracula scandens* in his *Index Ornithologicus* (I, p. 183). [LM 6095 Climbing grackle, Gracula scandens, extremely rare]

26. *Minor grakle Gracula religiosa Lin La Syn 2 Pg 455 153*
= *Gracula religiosa*, Linnaeus 1758. [LM 1757 Mino grakle, Gracula religiosa Stanley 3/-; 2422 Minor grakle, Gracula religiosa, Thompson 12/6; 2688 Minor grakle, E. Indies, Gracula religiosa, Chandler 8/6]

27. *Boat-tailed grakle Gracula barita Lin La Syn 2 Pg 460 131*
Identified from Sarah's painting as *Quiscalus niger crassirostris* (Swainson 1838), Greater Antillean grackle. Largen (1987, p. 283) queried identification as *Quiscalus ?mexicanus* (Gmelin 1788). [LM 2575 Boat-tailed grackle, Graculus barita, Thompson 10–6]

28. *Purple grakle Gracula quiscula Li La Syn 2 Pg 462*
= *Gracula quiscula*, Linnaeus 1758, Common grackle. [LM 4513 Purple grakle, Gracula quiscula, mas. et fem. Jamaica, Fred Swainson 12/-]

29. *Dial grakle Gracula saularis Lin La*

Syn 2 Pg 465
= *Copsychus saularis* (Linnaeus 1758), Magpie robin. A specimen of the male, from Bengal, was in the Vienna Museum (Pelzehn 1873, p. 25). [LM 3917 Dial grakle, gracula saularis, Fichtel 9/6]

30. *Yellow bellied curucui Trogon viridis L. La Syn 2 Pg 488*
= *Trogon strigilatus* (Linnaeus 1766), White-tailed trogon. [LM 4785 Leverian Trogon, Trogon Leverianus, extremely fine and rare, Fichtel £4.4.0.] The male, bought by Fichtel and in the Vienna Museum 1873 (Pelzehn 1873, p. 19), is the type of Shaw's description and plate in *Museum Leverianum*, p. 177, "Leverian trogon, Trogon leverianus (Cayenne) C R Ryley delt.". *Trogon viridis* (Linnaeus 1766) and *Trogon leverianus* (Shaw 1792) are synonyms of *Trogon strigilatus*.

31. *Common cuckow Cuculus canorus L Gen Syn 2 Pg 509 131*
= *Cuculus canorus*, Linnaeus 1758. [LM 3608 Cuckow, m. and fem., 17/-; 4628 A large case containing the common cuckow in its various stages of growth, with the respective birds by which it is fed. W Swainson £.3.3.0.]

32. *Society cuckow Cuculus australis La. La Syn 2 Pg 514*
This specimen should have a long cuneiform tail
Probably = *Urodynamys taitensis* (Sparrman 1787), Long-tailed koel. [LM 1407, Cuckow, S America, Stanley 16-0. Still in the Liverpool Museum (Largen 1987, pp. 276, 286).

33. *Long billed rain cuckow Cuculus vetula Lin La Syn 2 Pg 535 83*
= *Saurothera vetula* (Linnaeus 1758), Jamaican lizard cuckoo. Latham did not indicate that a specimen was in the LM.

34. *Rain cuckow Cuculus vetula Lin La Syn 2 Pg 536*
= *Piaya pluvialis* (Gmelin 1788),

Chestut-bellied cuckoo. The rain cuckoo, bought by Fichtel, was in the Vienna Museum in 1873 (Pelzehn 1873, p. 33). [LM 3066 Cuculus vetula, Fichtel 16/-; Last day but two, 35, Rain cuckoo, Cuculus vetula]

35. *Wryneck Yunx torquilla Lin Gen Syn 2 pg 548*
= *Jynx torquilla*, Linnaeus 1758. [LM 3525 Wryneck, Yunx torquilla, C. D. Burchell 5/-; 4430 A pair of wryneck, Yunx torquilla, Blackman £1.3.0; 5930 Wryneck; last day but one, 42 Wryneck, tunx torquilla m. fem. and young]

36. *Cayenne woodpecker Picus radiatus La La Syn 2 Pg 590*
= *Colaptes puntigula*, Boddaert 1783, Spot-breasted woodpecker. Latham did not give a location of a specimen.

37. *Minute woodpecker Picus minutus La La Syn 2 Pg 596*
= *Picumnus minutissimus*, Pallas 1782, Arrowhead piculet. [LM Appendix 1, lot 92 Little woodpecker, picus minutus, scarce, Heslop 1/-]

38. *Green jacamar Galbula viridus (Alcedo Galbula Lin) La Syn 2 Pg 603*
= *Galbula galbula* (Linnaeus 1766), Green-tailed jacamar. [LM 2423 Long-tailed green jacamar Alcedo galbula var., Thompson 12/-; 6597 Alcedo galbula Sir H. Martin £1.2.0.]
PLATE 43

39. *Black and white kingfisher Alcedo rudis Lin Gen Syn 2 Pg 612*
= *Ceryle rudis* (Linnaeus 1758), Pied kingfisher. Latham did not mention a specimen present in the LM, when he described it in 1782.

40. *Cinerous tody "Sarah Stone" Todus cinereus Lin La Syn 2 Pg 658*
According to Latham, there were specimens in the BM and LM; however, the bird painted by Sarah appears to be *Todirostrum maculatum* (Desmarest 1806), Spotted

tody-flycatcher. [LM 6345
Cinerous tody]

41. *Sacred kingfisher Alcedo sacra La La
Syn 2 pg 621*
Some form of *Halcyon chloris*
(Gmelin 1788), White-collared
kingfisher. [LM 2778 Sacred
kingfisher, Alcedo sacra, from
New Holland, Sivers 8/6; 5612
Alcedo sacra, m. and fem.
Thompson £1.0.0 (identified as
Halcyon tuta (Gmelin 1788) by
Largen (1987, p. 286), so not the
subject of this painting); 6084
A curious kingfisher, South Seas
(stated by Pelzehn (1873, p. 19)
to be the type of Latham's
description), was a young bird,
6590 Alcedo sacra Fenton 5/-]

42. *Blue headed kingfisher Alcedo cyanea
La La Syn 2 Pg 621*
= *Alcedo cristata*, Pallas 1764,
Malachite kingfisher. There was
no specimen in the LM when
Latham described it in 1782.

43. *Nuthatch Sitta europaea Lin Gen Syn
2 Pg 648*
= *Sitta europaeus*, Linnaeus 1758.
[LM 544 Nut hatch Sitta
Europaea, with three other
birds, T. Walker £1.4.0; 743
with three other birds, 8/-;
5854 with three other birds;
5976 Nut hatch]

44. *Spotted nuthatch var? Sitta maculata
L La Syn 2 Pg 654*
A race of *Myrmotherula axillaris*
(Vieillot 1817), White-flanked
ant-wren. Latham makes no
reference to specimens.

45. *Ferruginous-bellied tody Todus
ferrugineus La La Syn 2 Pg 662*
= *Hirundinea ferruginea* (Gmelin
1788), Cliff flycatcher. Latham
knew of two specimens, the LM
specimen "received from South
America", and "I have lately
seen a second of these, which
had the upper part brown
instead of black". [LM 6013
Todus rufiventris, cinnamon-
coloured tody (bought by
Fichtel). Pelzehn (1873, p. 27)
believed the specimen in the
Vienna Museum in 1873 to be

the type of the species.]

46. *Poe bee-eater Merops cincinnatus La
La Syn 2 Pg 682*

47. *Poe bee-eater Merops cincinnatus La
La Syn 2 Pg 682   121*
= *Prosthemadera novaeseelandiae*
(Gmelin 1788), Tui. A male,
purchased by Fichtel, was
present in the Vienna Museum
in 1873 (Pelzehn 1873, p. 109).
Pelzehn referred to this bird in
Cook's *Voyage* (Beaglehole 1955-
67, I, pp. 48, 150). Latham
quoted Cook as saying, "Its
note is sweet, and flesh
delicious, and the greatest
luxury the woods afforded us"
when in New Zealand. [LM
Last day but one, 44 Merops
cincinnatus (m & f)Thompson
£2.12.6. Largen (1987, p. 286)
says two syntypes, male and
female, of this species are at
present in the collection of the
Liverpool Museum.]
PLATE 47

48. *Molucca bee-eater Merops moluccensis
La La Syn 2 Pg 684*
Probably of the genus *Philemon*.
There was a specimen in the
LM in 1782, and Latham said it
came from the Isle of Bouro,
one of the Moluccas.

49. *Cape promerops Upupa promerops Lin
La La Syn 2 Pg 692*
= *Promerops cafer* (Linnaeus
1758), Cape sugarbird. [LM 196
Upupa promerops, C. of Good
Hope – rare, Brogden 7/-;
4266 Cape hoopoe, Upupa
promerops, Thompson for
Stanley £1]

50. *Great hook billed creeper Certhia
arcuata La La Syn 2 Pg 703
Sarah Stone 1781   122*
= *Drepanis pacifica* (Gmelin
1788), the Mamo, which
became extinct *ca.* 1898. Gmelin
named it *Certhia pacifica.* When
Latham included this species in
his *General Synopsis*, 1781, he also
illustrated it (pl. xxxiii) but the
only location he gave was the
LM. Pelzehn stated that two
specimens from Owyhee,

marked no.112 and female no.
113, in the Vienna Museum in
1873, were those of the LM sale
catalogue, lot 2790, and were
the types of Latham's
description. [LM 2790 Great
hook billed creeper, Certhia
pacifica, m.and fem. Sandwich
island, very rare, Latham £1.2.0.]
PLATE 5

51. *Hook'd-billed green creeper Certhia
rostrata Lin La Syn 2 Pg 703*
= *Hemignathus obscurus* (Gmelin
1788), Kauai Akialoa. [LM 4750
Certhia obscura, Thompson for
Stanley £1-2-0. (Largen 1987, p.
277) The Stanley specimen may
no longer be preserved in the
Liverpool Museum.] Also [LM
Appendix 487 Green Certhia,
rare, from Sandwich islands,
Brogden 11/-; 1034 Green
certhia, under a bell glass,
Robinson £1.1.0. When Latham
wrote of this species (*General
Synopsis*, I, p. 703, pl. xxxiii), he
said it was from the Sandwich
Islands, and knew only of a
specimen in the LM.] It was
painted on at least three
occasions by Sarah (see Index:
Akioloa DL and HH).
PLATE 48

52. *Violet headed creeper Certhia violacea
Gen Syn 2 Pg 718   134*
= *Nectarinia violacea* (Linnaus
1766), Orange-breasted sunbird.
Latham knew of only one
specimen, in the LM.

53. *Cinerous creeper La Syn 2 Pg 721 I
believe an imperfect specimen as it has
no elongated Tail feathers*
= *Nectarinia famosa* (Gmelin
1788), Malachite sunbird. In his
General History (IV, p. 216),
Latham gives this as the
Famous Creeper Var. A. He did
not specify that this was in the
LM, and gave no synonymy.

54. *Blue creeper Certhia caerulea Lin La
Syn 2 Pg 725*
= *Cyanerpes caeruleus* (Linnaeus
1758), Purple honeycreeper.
[LM 2683 Blue creepers, S.
America, Blackman £1.7.0; 4618

Certhia caerulea, blue creeper,
Carrudes 17/-; 4743 Blue
creeper, Certhia caerulea,
without case, Blackman £1.2.0;
6580 Certhia caerulea var.,
Smith 8/-; 6593 Certhia caerulea
var. Sir Henry Martin £1.7.0.]

55. *Black capped creeper Certhia spiza Lin
La Syn 2 Pg 727*
= *Chlorophanes spiza* (Linnaeus
1766), Green honeycreeper.
[LM 2786 Black-headed
creeper, Certhia spiza,
Blackman 17/6; 3139 Certhia
spiza, Sivers 8/-; 3294 Certhia
spize, Breedon 9/-]

56. (a) *Finch not yet described*
Sarah's painting almost agrees
with *Pytilia afra* (Gmelin 1788),
Orange-winged pytilia, except
that she painted a grey line
through the eye.
(b) *Orange-bellied creeper La Syn 2
Pg 734*
This species has never certainly
been identified. It was the
Certhia auranti of Gmelin 1788,
and called Orange-breasted
creeper by Latham, who did not
refer to an LM specimen, but
says "from Mr Smeathman".
Latham's description tallies
with Sarah's picture.

57. *Mocking creeper Certhia mimica La
Syn 2 Pg 735*
= *Anthornis melanura* (Sparrman
1786), "Bellbird" from their
beautiful song, of which Sir
Joseph Banks wrote on 17
January 1770 while on board
ship lying off New Zealand,
"This morn I was awakened by
the singing of the birds ashore,
from whence we are distant not
a quarter of a mile, the numbers
of them were certainly very
great who seemd to strain their
throats with emulation perhaps;
their voices were certainly the
most melodious wild musick I
have ever heard, almost
imitating small bells but with
the most tunable silver sound
imaginable, to which maybe the
distance was no small addition.

On enquiring of our people I was told that they had observed them ever since we have been here, and that they begin to sing at about 1 or 2 in the morn and continue till sunrise, after which they are silent all day like our nightingales" (Beaglehole 1962, I, p. 192). Latham (*Gen. Syn.* 1781, I, p. 735) knew of only one specimen, in the LM. Pelzehn (1873, p. 22) said that the Vienna specimen, bought by Fichtel, possibly Latham's type, had been rejected, "being in a bad state".

58. *Ruby-crested humming-bird Trochilus elatus Lin La Syn 2 Pg 780*
= *Chrysolampis mosquitus* (Linnaeus 1758), Ruby topaz hummingbird. Latham refers to a specimen in the LM. [LM 4101 Certhia Sannio, mocking creeper, New Zealand – very rare, 16/-]

59. *Wattled stare Sturnus palearis La La Syn 3 Pg 7 (= p. 9)*
= *Creadion carunculatus carunculatus* (Gmelin 1789), Saddleback. Latham knew only of the LM location for a specimen when he wrote about it and illustrated it (pl. XXXII) in *General Synopsis*, 1783, II, p. 9. Two Leverian birds went to the Vienna Museum, but both specimens bought by Fichtel had been discarded by 1873 (Pelzehn 1873, p. 28). [LM Last day but one 54 Wattled stare, Sturnus carunculatus.]
PLATE 10

60. *Fieldfare Sarah Stone Turus pilaris Linn La Syn 3 Pg 24*
= *Turdus pilaris* (Linnaeus 1758), Fieldfare. [LM 3579 Turdus pilaris, Kirkpatrick 4/6; 5487 Young sparrow hawk, and fieldfare, two cases, Davis 9/-; 5894 Hedge lark, and fieldfare]

61. *Yellow bellied thrush Turdus brasiliensis La La Syn 3 Pg 42*
= *Donacobius atricapillus* (Linnaeus 1758), Black-capped

mockingthrush. According to Latham, this was located not in the LM but in the BM.
PLATE 49

62. *St Domingo thrush Turdus dominicus L La Syn 3 Pg 42*
= *Mimus polyglottos orpheus* (Linnaeus 1758), Northern mockingbird. [LM 418 Mocking thrush-Turdus orpheus, N. America, 11/6 (Largen 1987, pp. 282-83, purchased by Lord Stanley); 3295 Turdus orpheus Mocking thrush, Brogden 4/-; 3603 Mocking thrush, Turdus orpheus, Fichtel 5/6 (Pelzehn 1873, p. 25)]

63. *Blackbird, female La La Syn 3 Pg 43*
The bird painted by Sarah was not the female of the common blackbird, *Turdus merula*, but an Icterid. In very faint pencil, under the image is "? female of Purple Grackle".

64. *Blackbird Turdus merula Lin La Syn 3 Pg 43*
= *Turdus merula*, Linnaeus 1758. [LM 5818 Blackbird, and linnet; 5839 Blackbirds, male and female; 5824 Blackbird, male and female; 5888 Common teal, and blackbird]

65. *Ring ouzel "Sarah Stone" Turdus torquatus Lin La Syn 3 Pg 46 136*
= *Turdus torquatus* (Linnaeus 1758), but poorly drawn.[LM 4088 Ring ouzel, 6/-; 4505 Turdus torquatus, the ring ouzel, with the young, Sivers 17/-; 4407 Rock ouzell, m. and fem. Donovan £1.5.0; 4932 Rock ouzel, male and female, Kirkpatrick 14/-]

66. *Water ouzel Turdus cinclus La La Syn 3 Pg 48*
= *Cinclus cinclus* (Linnaeus 1758), Dipper. [LM 2424 Water ouzel, m. and fem., Kirkpatrick 19/-; 5755 Water ouzel variety; 5805 Water ouzel, male and female]

67. *White-tailed thrush Turdus leucurus La La Syn 3 Pg 49*
Latham only knew of the LM

specimen, from Gibraltar, which was *Oenanthe leucura* (Gmelin 1789), Black wheatear. [LM 5391 White rump'd thrush, Gibraltar, Fenton 3/-]

68. *Shining thrush Turdus nitens Lin La Syn Pg 56 Var. A*
[LM 3399 Turdus nitens, var.A, Angola. Thompson for Stanley £1-19-0 = *Lamprotornis ?chalybaeus* Ehrenberg, 1828. This identification was queried by Largen (1987: 282). Latham knew of specimens in both the LM and British Museum. Sarah's drawing does not assist in identifying the exact species. The Cape glossy starling is implied both by name and the locality, so perhaps *Lamprotornis nitens* (Linnaeus, 1766) Red-shouldered glossy starling.]

69. *Ceylon thrush Turdus ceylonus Lin La Syn Pg 62*
= *Telephorus zeylonus* (Linnaeus 1766), Bokmakierie. According to Latham, there was a specimen in the BM and another in the LM in 1783.

70. *Long tailed thrush "Sarah Stone 1781" Turdus caudatus La La Syn 3 Pg 72*
Drawing of *Copsychus malabaricus* (Scopoli 1788), the Shama. Latham described this bird, and published his illustration of it (*Gen. Syn.* II, pl. XXXIX), two years after Sarah dated her drawing. He said it inhabited Pulo Condore, and he knew of only one specimen, that in the LM. Fichtel purchased a specimen at the LM sale, which Pelzehn named *Cittacincla macroura* (Gmelin 1788), but it was no longer in the Vienna Museum in 1873 (Pelzehn 1873, p. 25).

71. *Waxen chatterer Ampelis garrulus Lin Gen Syn 3 Pg 91*
= *Bombycilla garrulus* (Linnaeus 1758), Waxwing. [LM 200 Bohemian chatterer, Ampelis garrulus, in a mahogany case, T Pennant 10/6; 544 Bohemian

chatterer, Ampelis garrulus, female, with three other birds, in four cases, T. Walker £1.4.0; 3122 Bohemian chatterer, Pellaby 7/-; 5492 Waxen chatterer, Ampelis garrulus, m and f., Sivers £1.3.0.]

72. *Hawfinch Loxia coccothraustes Lin Gen Syn 3 Pg 109*
= *Coccothraustes coccothraustes* (Linnaeus 1758). [LM 2571 Hawfinch and cuckow, young, two cases, Sivers 18/-; 5948 Hawfinch and a snipe.]
PLATE 50

73. *Blue grosbeak Loxia caerulea Lin La Syn 3 Pg 117 Var. B?*
= *Passerina caerulea* (Linnaeus 1758), Blue grosbeak. [LM 5375 Loxia caerulia, Blackman 7/6; 5494 Loxia caerulea m & f, Thompson £1.5.0 (listed by Largen 1987, p. 284); 6036 Blue grosbeak, America; m. and fem.; 6065 Blue grosbeak, America; 3396 Blue grossbeak, S. America, Loxia coerulea, var. B. cyanea, 5/-]

74. *Brimstone grosbeak "Sarah Stone" Loxia sulphurata Lin La Syn 3 Pg 137 13*
An inaccurate drawing of *Serinus sulphuratus* (Linnaeus 1766), Brimstone canary. This bird was not in the LM when Latham described it.

75. *Malacca grosbeak Loxia malacca Lin La Syn 3 Pg 140*
= *Lonchura malacca* (Linnaeus 1766), Chestnut munia. Specimens were in both the BM and LM.

76. *Molucca grosbeak "Sarah Stone" Loxia Molucca Lin La Syn 3 Pg 141*
Like *Lonchura molucca* (Linnaeus 1766), Moluccan munia, but more white on the breast. Not noted as being in the LM by Latham.

77. 1. *Waxbill Loxia astrild Lin La Syn 3 Pg 152*
2. *Waxbill grosbeak Loxia astrild Lin La Syn 3 Pg 152*
= *Estrilda astrild* (Linnaeus 1758), Waxbill. [LM 1499 Bonana bird

and waxbill, E. Indies, 2/-; 5874 Waxbill grosbeak, Loxia astrild Thompson 4-6 (listed by Largen 1987, p. 284); 5911 Waxbill, E. Indies, marsh titmouse, and young duck; 6182 Waxbill]

78. *Fasciated grosbeak Loxia fasciata La La Syn 3 Pg 156*
= *Amadina fasciata* (Gmelin 1788), Cut-throat finch. [LM 4740 Fasciated grosbeak Loxia fasciata, Sivers 8/6; Last day but two 23 Fasciated grosbeak, loxia fasciata, Gmel]

79. *Minute grosbeak Loxia minuta Li La Syn 3 Pg 158*
= *Sporophila minuta* (Linnaeus 1758), Ruddy-breasted seedeater. This specimen was in the BM, not the LM.

80. *Ortolan Emberiza hortulana Lin Gen Syn 3 Pg 166*
There was a specimen of the ortolan *Emberiza hortulana* in the LM, but Sarah's painting is of *Emberiza cirlus*, Linnaeus 1766, Cirl bunting.
PLATE 53

81. *Reed bunting "Sarah Stone" Emberiza schoenibeus Lin La Syn 3 Pg 173*
= *Emberiza schoeniclus* (Linnaeus 1758). This species was represented in both the BM and the LM by 1783.

82. *Familiar bunting "Sarah Stone" Emberiza familiaris Lin La Syn 3 Pg 194*
Latham explained the bird's name, "This was met with at Java by Mr Osbeck, and was exceedingly familiar; for if the cage-door was opened, it would jump upon the first person's hand that was offered." Mr Osbeck named it Motacilla familiaris in his *Observations on a Voyage . . .*, I, p. 157. Sarah's bird does not agree with Osbeck's description.

83. *Painted bunting "Sarah Stone" Emberiza airida Lin La Syn 3 Pg 206*
Probably = *Passerina ciris* (Linnaeus 1758), Painted

bunting. Latham referred to specimens in the BM and LM. [LM 1410 Painted finch, emberiza ciris, America; and sparrow of Paradise, Fichtel 11/-; 1509 Painted finch, Emberiza ciris, America; and canary, variety, Hall, 5/6; 2681 Painted finch, America, m. and fem. Sivers 13/-; 4840 Painted finch, Burton 7/6; 6064 Painted finch, America]

84. *Black and blue tanager Tanagra mexicana Lin La Syn 3 Pg 230*
Approximating nearly to *Tangara mexicana* Linnaeus 1766, Turquoise tanager. Latham did not say that it was in the LM.

85. *Red-headed tanager Tanagra gyrola L. La Syn 3 Pg 233*
= *Tangara gyrola* (Linnaeus 1758), Bay-headed tanager. [LM 2316 Red-headed tanager Tanagra gyrola, Hall 2/-]

86. *Paradise tanager Tanagra tatao Lin La Syn 3 Pg 236*
= *Tangara chilensis* (Vigors 1832), Paradise tanager. [LM 3286 Titmouse of Paradise, Lord Stanley £1.12.0 (Largen 1987, pp. 282–83 *Tangara chilensis*); 5880 tanagra tetao, m. and fem. in fine preservation, Paradise titmouse; 6592 Tanagta tatao, var. Sir Henry Martin £1.7.0; 6589 Tanagra tatao, vr. Sir Henry Martin £1.18.0; Appendix 2, 205 The paradise tanager, and other rare birds, 9/-]
PLATE 52

87. *Negro tanager Tanagra cayana La Syn 3 Pg 240*
Sarah's drawing looks like some manakin. Latham said there was a specimen in the LM as well as the BM.

88. *House sparrow "Sarah Stone" Fringilla domestica Linn La Syn 3 Pg 248*
= *Passer domesticus*, Linnaeus 1758. Sarah's bird had a white superciliary. [LM 3581 House sparrow, both sexes, with the egg, and a Tringa pugnax,

Kirkpatrick 8/-; 5845 House sparrow, and young cuckows; 5819 Lesser Banana bird, house sparrow]

89. *Beautiful finch Fringilla pulcherrima L La Syn 3 Pg 266*
= *Pytilia melba* (Linnaeus 1758), Green-winged pytilia. Both the LM and BM had specimens by 1783.

90. *Orange finch Fringilla zena Lin La Syn 3 Pg 276*
= *Spindalis zena* (Linnaeus 1766), Stripe-headed tanager. An LM specimen, bought by Fichtel, is no longer in the Vienna Museum (Pelzehn 1873, p. 29. [LM 6342 Mountain goldfinch, m. and fem. Jamaica, Thompson for Lord Stanley £1.5.0. (listed by Largen 1987, p. 284)]

91. *Greater redpole "Sarah Stone 1780" La Syn 3 Pg 304 13*
= *Carduelis cannabina* (Linnaeus 1758), Linnet. Latham refers to specimens in the BM and LM. [LM 194 included a brown linnet; 539 included a linnet variety; 5818 Blackbird and linnet]

92. *Amaduvade finch Fringilla amandava Lin La Syn 3 Pg 312*
The drawing approximates most nearly to *Amandava amandava* (Linnaeus 1758), Red avadavat. [LM 2311 Sandpiper, and an avadavad bird – two cases, Thompson 5/6; 3381 Avadavad, three specimens Sivers 5/6; 1849 Avadavad, and three other birds, four cases, G. Robinson 15/-; 5853 Tufted starling, young starling, and avadavad; 5884 Avadavad, titlark and greenfinch]

93. *Blue bellied finch "Sarah Stone" Fring. Angolensis Lin La syn 3 Pg 315*
= *Uraeginthus angolensis* (Linnaeus 1758), Angola cordon bleu. [LM 2576 Blue-bellied finch, two specimens, Hall 16/6]

94. *Black and white flycatcher Muscicapa melanoleuca La La Syn 3 Pg 328*

Var. A
= *Fluvicola pica* (Boddaert 1783), Pied water tyrant. Latham makes no reference to a specimen.

95. *Cape lark Sarah Stone Alauda capensis Lin La Syn 4 Pg 384*
= *Macronyx capensis* (Linnaeus 1766), Cape longclaw. Latham said, "this I described from a specimen in the Leverian Museum, which I took to be a female". Perhaps [LM 5747 Orange-throated lark, Cape of Good Hope].
PLATE 51

96. *Black cap Motacilla atricapilla La Syn 4 Pg 415*
= *Sylvia atricapilla* (Linnaeus 1758), Blackcap. [LM 650 Blackcap, with other birds, four cases, Donovan 19/-; 1298 Jay, blackcap, m./ fem. and young, Kirkpatrick 18/-; 5833 Cowry finch, East Indies; and blackcap, Gibraltar; 5890 Variety of the sparrow, and black-cap, Gibraltar]

97. *Hedge sparrow "S. Stone" Motacilla modularis Lin La Syn 4 Pg 419*
= *Prunella modularis* (Linnaeus 1758), Dunnock or Hedge sparrow. [LM Lot 193 Two wrens, hedge sparrow, jacksnipe, and greater butcher-bird, 4 cases Beddell 4/-; 638 Wood-lark, Reed Sparrow, Hedge Sparrow, Sparrow (white variety) and House martin – five cases, 11/-]

98. *Sedge warbler "Sarah Stone" Motacilla salicaria Lin La Syn 4 Pg 430*
The drawing approximates to *Acrocephalus schoenobaenus* (Linnaeus 1758), Sedge warbler. A specimen was in the LM in 1783.

99. *Blue headed warbler La Syn 4 Pg 503*
Drawing of the female *Dacnis cayana* (Gmelin 1788) Blue dacnis. A specimen was in the BM when Latham included it in his *Gen. Syn.*, 1784.

100. *Cayenne warbler Motacilla cayana Linn La Syn 4 Pg 503 Var. A* Drawing of male *Dacnis cayana* (Linnaeus 1766), Blue dacnis. Latham knew of a specimen in the BM but not in the LM.

101. *Common wren "Sarah Stone" Motacilla troglodytis Lin La Syn 4 Pg 506* = *Troglodytes troglodytes* (Linnaeus 1758). [LM 193 Two wrens, Hedge Sparrow, jacksnipe, and great butcher-bird, four cases, Beddell 4/-; 195 Black-headed finch, South America, 2 wrens, and white variety of linnet – 3 cases, T. Walker 10/6; 1498 Least grebe, common wren, and ditto robins, three cases, Sedliken 4/6; 4481 Common wren, with nest and young, Fred. Swainson 8/-; 5474 Wren, white variety and Common wren, Thompson 3/6]

102. *Yellow wren, Var. A Motacilla acredula B Linn La Syn 4 Pg 513* Identification uncertain. [LM 2419 Yellow wren, America, Thompson 2/6]

103. *Blue-backed manakin Pipra pareola La Syn 4 Pg 520* = *Chiroxiphia pareola* (Linnaeus 1766), Blue-backed manakin. [LM 3292 Blue-backed manakin, m.and fem. Pipra pareola, rare, £1.10.0. (bought in at the LM sale)]

104. *Gold-headed manakin Pipra erythrocephala La Syn 4 Pg 522 27* = *Pipra erythrocephala* (Linnaeus 1758), Golden-headed manakin. [LM 3909 Golden-crowned manakins a pair Smith £1-1-0]

105. *White-capped manakin Pipra leucocilla L La Syn 4 Pg 523* = *Pipra pipra* (Linnaeus 1758), White-crowned manakin. Latham saw two specimens, in the BM and LM.

106. *White-headed manakin Pipra leucocephala Lin La Syn 4 Pg 524* = *Fluvicola leucocephala* (Linnaeus 1766), White-headed marsh tyrant. [LM 543 White-headed manakin, Pipra leucocephala, Surinam, Vaughan 2/6]

107. *Swift Hirundo apus Gen Syn 4 Pg 584* = *Apus apus* (Linnaeus 1758). [LM 3279 Young swift, with house martins, Kirkpatrick 6/-; 5956 Swift, male and female; 5972 Swift and stormfinch]

108. *White-polled warbler Mottacilla varia Lin: Gen Syn 4 Pg 588* = *Mniotilta varia* (Linnaeus 1766), Black-and-white warbler. Latham noted a specimen in the BM but not in the LM.

109. *White crowned pigeon Columba leucocephala La Syn 4 Pg 616* = *Columba leucocephala*, Linnaeus 1758. [LM 4478 Bald pigeons, a pair, Canada, Fichtel 8/6 (in Vienna 1873 (Pelzehn 1873, p. 34)); 4512 White-headed dove, Jamaica, Sivers 10/6]

110. *Martinico pigeon Var A Columba Martinica Lin La Syn 4 Pg 618 97* Latham gave no location of a specimen in Britain, and Sarah's drawing was not of this species but of *Zenaida aurita* (Temminck 1810), Zenaida dove.

PLATE 54

111. *White bellied pigeon Columba jamaicensis Lin Gen Syn 4 Pg 619* = *Leptoptila jamaicensis* (Linnaeus 1766), White-bellied dove.

112. *Lesser crowned pigeon Columba cirrhata La Syn 4 Pg 622* = *Rollulus roulroul* (Scopoli 1786), Roulroul partridge. Latham said, "A specimen of the above is in the Leverian Museum, which was met with by accident at a sale, without the least history annexed". [LM 6100 Lesser crowned pigeon, columba cristata, very rare] was the type of Latham's description and figure, and present in the Vienna Museum in 1873 (Pelzehn 1873, p. 36).

113. *Triangular spotted pigeon Columba guinea Lin La Syn 4 Pg 639* = *Columba guinea*, Linnaeus 1758, Speckled pigeon. [LM 3388 Triangular spotted pigeon,

Kirkpatrick £1.7.0.]

114. *Cape turtle Columba capensis Lin Gen Syn 4 Pg 666* = *Oena capensis* (Linnaeus 1766), Namaqua dove. Latham referred to a specimen in the LM.

115. *Guan turkey Meleagris cristata Lin La Syn 4 Pg 680 79* = *Aburria jacutinga* (Spix 1825), Black-fronted piping guan. [LM 307 Quan, Penelope cristata, W. Indies, hall 12/-; 6285 Quan, S. America; Last day but one 51 Quan, West Indies, Meleagris cristata.]

PLATE 55

116. *Marail turkey – La Syn 4 Pg 683 94* Possibly a painting of *Penelope marail* (Müller 1776), the Marail guan, but the facial skin is the wrong colour and there is no red wattle. Latham gave no location for this specimen.

117. *Cishew = Cushew curassow Crax pauxi Lin La Syn 4 Pg 696* = *Crax pauxi*, Linnaeus 1766, Helmeted curassow. [LM 746 Cushew birds, Crax Pauxi; two fine specimens, male and female, rare, Vaughan £4.7.0.]

118. *Argus pheasant Phasianus argus Lin La Syn 4 Pg 710* May have been intended to be *Argusianus argus* (Linnaeus 1766), Great argus, but some of the colouring is faulty, and the drawing inaccurate. [LM Last day 28 an eminently fine and perfect specimen of the Argus Pheasant, Sumatra, Phasianus argus]

119. *Black cock Tetrao tetrix L Gen Syn 4 Pg 733* = *Lyrurus tetrix* (Linnaeus 1758), Black grouse. [LM 59 Tetrao tetrix, black Grous, Clark 16.0; 5614 Black grous, m. and fem. tetrao tetrix, Fichtel £3.13.6.]

120. *Spotted grous Tetrao canace Lin La Syn 4 Pg 735 79* May be *Dendragapus canadensis* (Linnaeus 1758), Spruce grouse, or *Dendragapus obscurus* (Say

1823), Blue grouse. Latham said there was a specimen in the LM in 1784. [LM 741 Purple water-hen, Fulica porphyrio, S. America; Grous, Hudson's Bay, two cases, Laskey £1.2.0.]

121. *Guernsey partridge Tetrao rufus Lin La Syn 4 Pg 768* = *Alectoris rufa* (Linnaeus 1758), Red-legged partridge, but Sarah's drawing is more closely allied to *Alectoris chukar* (Gray 1830), the Chukar, or to *Alectoris graeca* (Meisner 1804), Rock partridge. Pelzehn (1873, pp. 36–37) refers to a "Greek Partridge, var. A. and a Guernsey Partridge of Latham, *Gen. Syn.* IV, p. 768" (a specimen of which was in the British Museum and the LM), in the Vienna collection. [LM 2784 Red-legged partridge, Solto 12/-; 4614 Red-legged partridge, m. and fem., Kirkpatrick £2.5.0; 5369 Red-legged partridge 9/-; 5804 Red legged partridge, Guernsey; 5861 Red-legged partridge, Barbary; 6011 Red-legged partridge, Portugal]

122. *Mariland partridge Tetrao marilandus Li La Syn 4 Pg 778* Perhaps = *Colinus virginianus* (Linnaeus 1758), Bobwhite, noted by Latham as being "called Bob-White, by New Englanders". A specimen was in the LM in 1784.

123. *Crested quail Tetrao cristatus Lin La Syn 4 Pg 784* = *Colinus cristatus* (Linnaeus 1766), Crested bobwhite. [LM 3919 Perdix cristata Lath. crested quail, Mexico, rare, Fichtel 19/ In the Vienna Museum in 1873 (Pelzehn 1873, p. 36).]

124. *Little bustard Otis tetrax Li Gen Syn 4 Pg 799* = *Otis tetrax*, Linnaeus 1758. [LM 5607 Otis tetrax (handwritten "Barbary Bustard") – Thompson for Lord Stanley 18/-" (mentioned

by Largen 1987, p. 273); 1503 Bustard, Barbary, Latham 17/-; 5490 Little bustard m. and fem. Otis tetrax – rare, Donovan 11/6]

125. *Crowned heron Ardea pavonina Lin Gen Syn 5 Pg 34*
= *Balearica pavonina* (Linnaeus 1758), Crowned crane. A specimen of the crowned crane was given to Lindroth in 1783 from the LM in part exchange for an elk, and is now in the Swedish Natural History Museum. [LM 1406 Crowned African crane, Ardea Pavonina, one specimen without case, Jackson £3.11.0; 5280 Ardea pavonina, in very fine preservation £4.4.0.]

126. *Green heron Ardea virescens Lin Gen Syn 5 Pg 68 95*
Drawing of *Butorides striatus* (Linnaeus 1758), Green heron. The BM and LM each had a specimen of this bird.

127. *Green heron. Var. B – Gen Syn 5 Pg 70 97*
A young *Nycticorax nycticorax* (Linnaeus 1758), Night heron. The LM was given as the only location for this bird. [LM 202 Night heron, Ardea nycticorax, Laskey 31/6; 372 Night heron, Ardea nycticorax, Donovan 39/-; 739 Night raven, Ardea nycticorax, Donovan £2.3.6 (with a Falco ossifragus)]

128. *Dwarf heron Ardea pumila La La Syn 5 Pg 77*
= *Ardeola ralloides* (Scopoli, 1769), Squacco heron. Latham gave no location for a specimen. [LM 5278 Squacco heron, Ardea comata, very rare £1.11.6.]

129. *Bald ibis Tantalus calvus La La Syn 5 Pg 116*
= *Geronticus calvus* (Boddaert 1783), Bald ibis, but Sarah painted the face red (like that of the Waldrapp, *Gerontius eremita*) instead of white. Pelzehn said (1873, pp. 39–40) that one of the birds mentioned by Latham (there was a

specimen in the BM and another in the LM), bought for Vienna, "was in bad condition, and not placed in the collection. [LM 740 Curlew, Cape of Good Hope; Tantalus calvis, rare, Donovan £2.3.0.]

130. *Great snipe Scolopax media Lin La Syn 5 Pg 133 155*
= *Gallinago media* (Latham 1787). [LM 1096 Great snipe, scolopax major, shot in England, without case, Donovan 4.2.0; 3914 Largest snipe, shot in England, one specimen without case, Donovan £2.13.0.]

131. *Common godwit Scolopax aegocephala Lin La Syn 5 Pg 144 33 40*
= *Limosa lapponica* (Linnaeus 1758), Bar-tailed godwit. Latham recorded a specimen in the LM and another in the BM in 1785. In the LM sale, there were several "Red godwits" (lots 1493, 4930, 5124, 5134) and one "Gray godwit" (lot 3602), as well as [5602 Godwit, N. America, Donovan 6/6], but it is not possible to say whether these were bar-tailed or black-tailed godwits.

132. *Cinerous godwit Scolopax crassirostris Lin La Syn 5 Pg 145 33 40*
Possibly = *Tringa nebularia* (Gunnerus 1767), Greenshank, of LM lots 733 and 6599, rather than [LM 3602 Gray godwit, 16/-]

133. *Green sandpiper "Sarah Stone" Tringa ochropus Gen Syn 5 Pg 170 41*
Drawing, probably of *Tringa ochropus*, Linnaeus 1758, a specimen of which was in the LM in 1785.

134. *Spur-winged plover Charadrius spinosis Lin La Syn 5 Pg 213 66*
= *Vanellus chilensis* (Molina 1782), Southern lapwing. [LM Appendix 4, 488 Spur-winged water-hen from Sumatra, very scarce, G Humphrey 10/6; 2690 Spur-winged plover, S. America, W Cumming 13/6]

135. *[Ruff] [vol. V Pg 215] 20*
136. *[Ruff] [vol. V Pg 215] 57*
137. *[Ruff] [vol. V Pg 215]*
= *Philomachus pugnax* (Linnaeus 1758). The references to *Gen. Syn*.V is wrong. [LM 529 Tringa pugnax, green Plover, m. and fem and Perroquet, S. Seas, three cases, 10/-; 3581 House sparrow, both sexes, with the egg, and a Tringa pugnax, Kirkpatrick 8/-; 4260 A case containing 15 specimens of ruffs and reeves curiously preserved in various attitudes, Tringa pugnax, Shaw £5.15.0; 5838 Ruff, male, and the common bullfinch; 5868 Ruff male, and young, of the bustard plovers]

138. *Pied oister catcher – Gen Syn 5 Pg 219 172*
= *Haematopus ostralegus*, Linnaeus 1758, Eurasian pied oystercatcher. Latham described a young bird with a crescent of white on the throat, as in Sarah's picture. [LM 535 Oyster-catcher, Haematopus Ostralegus; and Wood Pigeon, two cases, Money 8/6; 4832 Haematopus Ostralegus, m. and fem., Kirkpatrick 11/-; 5383 Haematopus ostralegus, Fenton 1/6]

139. *Austrian pratincole "S Stone" Hirundo pratincola La Syn 5 Pg 222*
= *Glareola pratincola* (Linnaeus 1758), Collared pratincole. [LM 5279 Austrian pratincole Glareola Austriaca, one specimen without case, 8/6; 5758 Glareola Austriaca, Austrian pratincole, Donovan 2/6]

140. *Variegated rail Rallus maculatus La Syn 5 Pg 237 84*
= *Rallus maculatus*, Boddaert 1783, Spotted rail. The colour of the legs was altered on the specimen drawn by Sarah. A specimen from the LM sale was in the Vienna Museum in 1873 (Pelzehn 1873, p. 122; perhaps [LM 5739 Water rail, Surinam]).

141. *Little rail Rallus minutus La La Syn 5 Pg 240 Var.*
Drawing of a small rail, a *Porzana* of some kind, based on a specimen in the LM, but now unknown.

142. *Crake gallinule Rallus crex Lin La Syn 5 Pg 250*
= *Crex crex* (Linnaeus 1758), Corncrake. [LM 4482 Land rail, m & f with their young, Donovan £1.14.0; 5732 Corn crake; 5934 Young corn crakes.]
PLATE 56

143. *Purple gallinule Fulica porphriors (= porphyrio) Lin La Syn 5 Pg 254 50*
= *Porphyrio porphyrio* (Linnaeus 1758), Purple swamphen. [LM 1505 Purple waterhen, S. America, Fulica porphyrio, Sivers 12/-, Last day 23 Purple water-hen, Fulica porphyrio, S. America]
PLATE 58

144. *Martinico gallinule Fulica martinica Lin La Syn 5 Pg 255*
= *Porphyrula martinica* (Linnaeus 1766), Purple gallinule. [LM 741 Purple Water-hen, Fulica porphyrio, S.America; Grous, Hudson's Bay, two cases Laskey £1.2.0; 2563 Water hen, N. America, Fenton 5/-]

145. *Favourite gallinule Gallinula gratiosa La La Syn 5 Pg 256 154*
= *Porphyrula flavirostra* (Gmelin 1788), Azure gallinule. [LM 1414 Small water hen, S. America, Fichtel £1.7.0 (this specimen went to Vienna and was given to the collection of the Gymnasium at Agram in 1854 (Pelzehn 1873, pp. 44—45, *Porphyrio parvus* (Bodd), Favourite gallinule).]

146. *White sheathbill Chionis lactea La La Syn 5 Pg 268 14*
= *Chionis alba* (Gmelin 1789), Snowy sheathbill. There is also a watercolour of a sheathbill or *Chionis alba* (Gmelin 1789), unsigned, that might have been done by Sarah, in the Dixson Library, Australia. Cook writes in his Journal (1772–75)

(Beaglehole 1955–67, 2, p. 614), Tuesday 3rd January 1775, Staten Land, "Our Naturalists found two new spicies of birds, the one is about the size of a Pigeon, the Plumage as white as milk, they feed a long Shore, probably on shell fish and Carrion, for they have a very disagreeable smell. When we first saw these birds we thought they were the Snow Peterel, but the moment they were in our possession the misstake was discovered, for they resemble them in nothing but size and Colour. These are not web-footed." On Tuesday 17th Jauary 1775, off South Georgia, Cook made a landing; we do not know exactly where, but his naturalists again collected (*op. cit.*, p. 622) "the new White Bird", which was identified as "*Chionis alba* (Gm.)" in the footnotes. [LM 2782 White fulica, Fulica alba, New Holland, bought by Fichtel 14/-] This specimen remains in the Vienna collection (see Pelzehn 1873, pp. 37–38, and pp. 44–45, "This and Lord Derby's at Liverpool, are the only two specimens. Lord Derby's came from the Bullock Museum"). Pelzehn sent a drawing by T.F. Zimmerman (1808–1880) "ad nat. pinx." which was slightly enlarged and lithographed by J. G. Keulemans for pl. X in *Ibis* (1873), opposite p. 295. [LM 4942 White sheathbill, Vaginalis Australis, very fine and extremely rare, Fichtel £4.4.0.]

PLATE 57

147. *American avocet Recurvirostra rufficollis La Syn 5 Pg 295*
= *Recurvirostra americana* (Gmelin 1788). Pelzehn 1873, p. 122, "Perhaps the Vienna specimen number 28 is that mentioned by Latham as being in the Leverian Collection" in 1785.

148. *Pintado pettrel Procellaria capensis*

Lin La Syn 5 Pg 401 151
= *Daption capense* (Linnaeus 1758), Cape or Pintado petrel. [LM Appendix 95 Procellaria capensis, pintado petrel. Isle of Desolation, + (+ was the sign of G Humphrey) 1/-]

149. *Shearwater petrel Procellaria puffinus Lin La Syn 6 Pg 406*
= *Puffinus puffinus* (Brünnich 1764), Manx shearwater. [LM Appendix 213 Shearwater petrel, Scotland, (bracketed with) 214 Thick-kneed plover, Laskey 4/6; 5111 Shear water, Donovan £1.1.0; 5357 The shear-water petrel, Procellaria puffinus, Donovan £1.0.0.]

150. *Stormy petrel Procellaria pelagica La Syn 6 Pg 411*
= *Hydrobates pelagicus* (Linnaeus 1758), Storm petrel.

151, 152. *Broad-billed petrel female and male Procellaria vittata La La Syn 6 Pg 414*
= *Pachyptila vittata*, Forster 1777, Broad-billed prion. Latham gave LM as the only location of a specimen, and quoted the blue peteril of Cook's Voyage, 1777 (I, p. 29).

153. *Gannet Pelicanus basanus Lin La Syn 6 Pg 608*
= *Morus bassanus* (Linnaeus 1758). [LM 315 Soland goose-Pelecanus Bassanus, Hall 10/6; 536 Soland Goose, Pelicanus Bassanus, Hall 9/-; 1494 Soland goose, m & fem., Anas Bassanus, Ellis, Dr Sillers 14/-; 4622 Soland goose, Vaughan 15/-]

154. *Common tropic bird Phaeton aethereus Lin La Syn 6 Pg 615*
= *Phaethon aethereus* (Linnaeus 1758), Red-billed tropicbird. [LM 1396 Tropic bird Phaeton aetherius, Fichtel £1.19.0. Pelzehn (1873, p. 52) did not think the LM purchase was Latham's type specimen, but it was still present in Vienna in 1873.]

155. *African heron Ardea africana La La Appendix*

= *Ardea purpurea*, Linnaeus 1766, Purple heron. [LM 874 Brown heron, Ardea Caspia, Africa, Donovan £5.6.0; 1110 African heron, Ardea Caspica, shot in England, Lochée for Donovan £8.8.0.]

156. *Descript Black bird of paradise* Sarah's painting is unlike *Lophorina superba* (Forster 1781), Superb bird of paradise. [LM 4631 The black bird of paradise, Paradisea superba, very rare, Vaughan £3.7.0.]

157. 1. *Variegated blackbird and 2. Blackbird variety 36* Partial albinos of *Turdus merula*, Linnaeus 1758.

158. 1. *Rusty-crowned oriole — non-descript* = *Loxigilla portoricensis* (Daudin 1800), Puerto Rican bullfinch.
2. *Finch* A partial albino of some species.

159. 1. *Bullfinch variety* A partial albino. Perhaps [LM 544 Nuthatch, grey wagtail, Bohemian chatterer, and Bullfinch variety, four cases, T Walker £1.4.0.]
2. *A linnet species uncertain 60* Probably a female of some species of *Carduelis*.

160. 1. *Small grosbeak species uncertain non descript* Probably a waxbill, female or young.
2. *Mongrele between canary and goldfinch non descript* [LM 526 Mungrel Canary, Red-pole, ditto variety, and Reed-sparrow, four cases, Donovan 10/6; 744 Snipes, two specimens; Java sparrow, Mungrel Canary; brown Water-hen, and another, 5 cases, Donovan 15/-; 6024 Hybrid, goldfinch and canary]

161. 1. *Plumbeous warbler Sylvia plumbea non descript* This bird has never been satisfactorily identified, but is structurally compatible with *Conirostrum*, Conebill.

2. No description
= *Charadrius hiaticula*, Linnaeus 1758, Ringed plover.

162. 1. No description Water bird variety.
2. No description Water bird variety. These two birds in this folio were both by George Edwards, not Sarah. *The Black-breasted Indian Plover* and *The spur-winged water hen* (watercolours, signed by G. Edwards) were done in preparation for pls. 47 and 48 in Edwards's *A Natural history of Uncommon Birds* 1751, I.

163. *Green heron var. or a new species* Probably some form of *Butorides striatus*, but not sufficiently well drawn to identify.

164. *Young ostrich* = *Strutheo camelus*, Linnaeus 1758. [LM Last day 40 A very well preserved specimen of the female ostrich, a young ditto, and the egg, with the instruments used in catching these birds.]

165. No description A sub-adult male *Houbaropsis bengalensis* (Gmelin 1789), Bengal florican, in intermediate plumage.

166. *Variety of partridge 23* An abnormal specimen of some species of grouse or partridge.

167. No description *Sarah Stone 1785* Drawing = *Chlidonias niger* (Linnaeus 1758), Black tern. [LM 1839 Black tern, sterna nigra, m. and fem. Davis 1/-; 2567 Large black tern, N. America, Heslop 4/6]

168. *Diver* Drawing of *Cepphus grylle* (Linnaeus 1758), Black guillemot. [LM 1837 Black guillemot, and gold-winged woodpecker, two cases, Wells £1.1.0; 5117 Black guillemot, Colymbus gryllus, without case, Donovan 7/6; 5390 Black guillemot, Colymbus gryllus, rare, Thompson 3/-]

John Latham, A collection of 888 original watercolour drawings of birds. A single watercolour in vol. II, p. 307, is a painting of a Jacamar, signed *Sarah Stone 1781*, with a reference to *Latham IV, p. 3. 4. p. 3. pl. 60*. Sarah's

painting of the Green jacamar [= *Galbula galbula* (Linnaeus 1766)] has an abnormally long tail [LM 2423 Long-tailed green jacamar, *Alcedo galbula* var. Thompson 12/-].

2. BERNICE PAUAHI BISHOP MUSEUM, HONOLULU, HAWAII

The Sarah Stone watercolours were itemized and described by Roland Wynfield and Maryanne Force in *Art and artifacts of the 18th century: objects in the Leverian Museum, as painted by Sarah Stone*, published in observation of the eightieth anniversary of the founding of Bishop Museum, 1889–1969, Honolulu, 1968.

The museum catalogues them as two sketchbooks of watercolours by Sarah Stone containing 132 drawings. The sketchbooks are the second and third of three volumes (the first being in the Australian Museum (see page 125)). Reference to the Bishop Museum is, more specifically, to the Fuller Collection of Pacific Artefacts. Captain A.W.F. Fuller first saw the volumes in 1932 and purchased them on 15 March 1940, in London. Mrs Estelle W. Fuller donated them to the Bishop Museum.

There is no sign of a signature except on the two feather god-images in vol. 3, no. 1, 31.7 × 22.9 cm (Force and Force 1968, p. 23).

Several items now in the Honolulu collection were illustrated and described by the Bearne's saleroom catalogue, Tuesday 16 March 1971: *Important works of art and artifacts including items which related to the voyages of Captain Cook and the collection of Sir Ashton Lever*. The articles in this sale were part of a group of curiosities purchased by Rowe, Roe, Rose and Rhode at

the LM sale in 1806 (all names of the same person, entered in annotated copies of the sale catalogue). Bearne's illustrated some of the artefacts alongside the Sarah Stone watercolours of the objects from the Bishop Museum, Honolulu.

The following notes on the watercolours were compiled by Stuart W. H. Ching, Archivist of the Bishop Museum, using descriptions from previously compiled lists of the illustrations, supplemented by titles found in Roland Force's book. Particularly notable were Sarah's paintings of fifty-four featherwork items – cloaks and necklaces made from birds' feathers. Few of these have been identified in museums, so that her record is of particular value. Of special interest to ornithologists were items in vol. 3, nos. 11, 20 and 21. These three watercolours were of feather cloaks and the species of bird that had largely contributed the feathers to make those cloaks. It was a brilliant idea, and a piece of ingenuity to link the cloaks and birds in this manner. They were kept, at the Leverian Museum, in the special 'Sandwich Room' (having been brought from the Sandwich Islands, now Hawaii, named by Captain Cook in honour of his patron, Lord Sandwich, in January 1778). The cloaks were conserved in four mahogany, glass-fronted cases.

VOLUME 2
(Accession number 1964.019.001)

1. Two spears (Fiji) and one club (Cook Islands).
2, 3. Each three clubs (New Caledonia).
4. Three clubs (New Caledonia, Fiji-Tonga).
5, 6. Each three clubs (Tonga).
7. One whale-bone pounder and a pestle (both Northwest Coast of America), one *tapa* beater and a food pounder (both Society Islands).
8. Two Maori wooden hand clubs (New Zealand).
Items 9-18 all from Hawaii:
9. Three hatchets or adzes.
10. Four spears.
11. Three carved bowls.

12. Four anthropomorphic carvings.
13. Four shark-tooth implements.
14. Three shark-tooth implements.
15. One dagger with feather and shark-tooth trim, one turtle shell and bone bracelet, and one whale ivory or bone hook ornament (all Hawaii) and a bracelet of unknown origin.
16. One shark-tooth weapon and three whale-tooth ornaments.
17. One bracelet of "end trimmed" boar tusks and turtle shell, a boar-tusk bracelet, and a necklace of braided human hair with hook ornament or *lei niho palaoa*.
18. One cowrie-shell necklace, one

seed necklace and one seed necklace with whale ivory or wood hook.
Items 19-67 all from the Pacific Northwest Coast, unless otherwise stated:
19. One Dentalium shell necklace, one Ni'ihau shell necklace (Hawaii) and one seed *lei* (Hawaii).
20. Three long-bladed daggers (Hawaii).
21. One wooden bowl (probably non-Oceanic), and one coconut container.
22. One pandanus and sennit fan (Hawaii).
23. One mask, "carved in memory

of a dear friend", and a rattle.
24. One wooden dancing mask, and one seal carving.
25. One ceremonial weapon, and one bird rattle.
26, 27. Each a drawing of two basketry hats.
28. Two bird carvings.
29. Two club-shaped carvings and one dagger-shaped carving.
30. One two-headed ceremonial weapon.
31. One head carving with leg extending from mouth, lashed to piece of wood.
32. Two club-shaped carvings.
33. One dagger-shaped stone weapon, and a necklace.

34. Two weapons.
35. One carrier.
36. Four ornaments.
37. One human image, and seven other various objects.
38. Three combs of various designs.
39. One halibut hook and one comb.
40, 41. Each a drawing of two fishing implements.
42. Three fishing lines and hooks, and one spearhead.
43. One fishing/trapping implement.
44. Two articles of clothing.
45. Three fishing and trapping implements.
46. Two hats with beading and feather trim.
47. One headcovering/bonnet.
48. One quiver and one sash.
49. One circular cape and one cloak.
50. One boot and one woven purse(?).

51. One quiver.
52. Two carvings with human images.
53. Two bowls and one horn or wooden scoop.
54. One bowl and two horn or wooden scoops.
55. One tube carrier.
56. One shirt stitched of strips of animal skins.
57. Two bowls/containers.
58. One weapon (Pacific Northwest Coast) and a wooden container (Fiji or Tonga).
59. One weapon and a wooden bowl.
60. One weapon, wood with stone tongue.
61. One cape(?).
62. One article of clothing.
63. One type of snare(?).
64. Three wolf masks.
65. An eagle mask and a seal mask.
66. One head covering/bonnet.

67. Two carvings.
Items 68-75 are from Hawaii, unless otherwise stated:
68. One wooden image, one Nerita shell bracelet and a wooden stick image.
69. Three game stones or 'ulu maika stones, one stone mirror, one grooved sinker for fish net or line.
70. Three shark tooth implements and one shell ornament.
71. Two tattooing implements, one kukui (?) nut necklace, two shell ornaments and two turtle ornaments.
72, 73. Two drawings, each of two gourd containers.
74. One dance rattle or 'uli 'uli and a wooden bowl (of unknown origin).
75. One dance rattle or 'uli 'uli and a wooden bowl (Tonga or Fiji).
76. One bowl (Society Islands), and a Maori canoe bailer (New

Zealand).
77. Four head rests (Tonga).
78. Five head rests (Tonga and Tanna, New Hebrides).
79. One paddle club (Fiji) and a club (Society Islands) and a Maori Taiaha (New Zealand).
80. One paddle club (New Zealand), one paddle club (Fiji/Tonga) and a paddle (Hawaii).
81. One Maori paddle (New Zealand), one 'Pandanus' club (Fiji) and a club (New Caledonia).
82. Two Maori paddles (New Zealand) and one "Lotus" club (Fiji).
83. One food hook (Tonga), and a carving of a bird.
84. One food hook (Tonga) and a carving (pipe or whistle?).
85. One mask, and an unidentified object (both Pacific Northwest Coast).

VOLUME 3
(Accession number 1964.019,002)

Items 1-29 are from Hawaii:
1. Two feather images of a head, signed "Sarah Stone". Left: tall, double crest, adam's apple, crescent eyes, and bump on nose; right: small, low forehead and crescent eyes.
2, 3. Each a feather image of a human head and neck.
4. One feather "ANUU, or temple oracle".
5. Two feather helmets or mahiole. Top: red with green and yellow stripes and long yellow fringe across crest; bottom: green base, red crest with white and green stripe.
6. Two feather helmets or mahiole. Top: red with yellow crest fringe, spotted band near forehead; bottom: red with yellow and red rectangular crest, black spots along side of crest.
7. Two feather helmets or mahiole.

Top: black with elaborate red and yellow crown, red cords attached along crest, yellow, red and dark feathers sewn in pattern around face edge; bottom: red base, wide crown with white crest, yellow edging around face edge.
8. One helmet, two feather lei. Top: helmet shows twining pattern, no feathers attached, human hair crest; middle: red feather lei with yellow/dark patterned lines; bottom: feather lei with shark teeth.
9. One red and yellow feather cloak or 'ahu'ula.
10. One feather cloak or 'ahu'ula, predominantly brown feathers with red, yellow pattern along top edge, partial view of netting on inside. (Hawaii)
11. One feather cloak or 'ahu'ula, predominantly green with red V, yellow and red border,

netting visible, and an 'akialoa bird. Force and Force tentatively identified the bird drawn by Sarah, underneath this cloak, as being the subspecies Hemignathus obscurus procerus from Kauai (extinct ca.1965), but three other subspecies, from Hawaii, Lanai and Oaku, are also now extinct. A specimen of Hemignathus obscurus was in the LM (see notes under NMHL (3) 51 and Dixson Library). Unfortunately, the specimen in the Liverpool Museum appears to have been lost.
12. One feather cloak or 'ahu'ula made with cocks' tail feathers, shorter yellow and red feathers along top and side edges. (Bottom half of this page cut.)
13. One feather cloak and one feather cape or 'ahu'ula. Top: cloak with wide horizontal red

and yellow stripes; bottom: cape with predominantly brown and white feathers, yellow trim at top edge.
14. Two feather capes or 'ahu'ula. Top: yellow, red and black repeat triangle pattern at top edge with white feathers beneath trim; bottom: dark feathers surround yellow shape at centre, red and yellow edges.
15. Two feather capes or 'ahu'ula. Top: rectangular shpe with red and yellow trim above white, brown, and black feathers; bottom: red and yellow bands at top, predominantly white beneath bands with red shapes at edges, dark feathers along bottom edge.
16. Two feather capes or 'ahu'ula. Top: red background with yellow pattern across cape; bottom: rectangular shape, exposed netting at top, white

rectangle edged with dark feathers.

17. Two feather capes or *'ahu'ula*. Top: green with red and yellow band at top; bottom: long dark feathers (cock feathers?) with red, black and yellow band at top and sides.

18. Two feather capes or *'ahu'ula*. Top: predominantly red with yellow trim, draping at top corners; bottom: short cape, predominantly yellow with red.

19. Two feather capes or *'ahu'ula*. Top: long brown feathers, red and white trim at top edge; bottom: rectangular shape, red and white bands at top and black and brown feathers below.

20. One red and yellow feather cloak or *'ahu'ula* with exposed netting on side, and an 'i'wi bird. The I'iwi, *Vestiaria coccinea* (G. Forster) (see Dixson Library and Private Collection B) is a Hawaiian honeycreeper, still surviving. The first specimen in The Natural History Museum, London, came from the Royal College of Surgeons. Most of the red feathers used in featherwork came from the i'iwi, but the young of this species have greenish-yellow feathers similar to those of the 'akialoa, which

originally caused some confusion in identifying the species.

21. One red and yellow feather cloak or *'ahu'ula* and one 'o'o bird, *Moho nobilis* (Merrem), a honey-eater, extinct *ca.* 1934. (See Dixson Library notes. The specimen in the Liverpool Museum came from the Bullock Museum.)

22. Two feather mats.

23. Three feather *lei*. Left: red with yellow; middle: red with yellow and black; right: yellow.

24. Three feather *lei*. Left: green, yellow, red, white and black; middle: red and black; right: red and yellow.

25. Three feather *lei*. Left: red, green and black; middle: red, green yellow and black; right: red, green, yellow and black.

26. Three feather *lei*. Left: red and green; middle: red, black and yellow; right: red, black and yellow.

27. Two multi-strand *lei*. Left: seven strands tied together at ends, each strand, with sections of yellow, black, red and white feathers, of same design; right: six strands tied together at ends, each strand a different design, using red, yellow and black feathers.

28. Three dog hair wands with

feather trim, each different in size and feather design.

29. Two feather standards of royalty or *kahili*. Left: black, brown and white with red and yellow base; right: black and brown with red and yellow base.

30. Two cloaks, one with whale/fish design (Pacific Northwest Coast).

31. One Tahitian mourning costume (Society Islands).

32. One sled (Pacific Northwest Coast).

33. One "Venetian lady's chopine (shoe), 16th century" (Europe).

34. One "Tahiti chest" (Society Islands).

35. Two sculpted heads (Europe/Asia).

36. One bowl and one dated trim (both Europe/Asia).

37. Three ornaments (Europe/Asia).

38. Two ornaments (Europe/Asia).

39. Four ornaments (Europe/Asia).

40. One dagger, and one unidentified artefact (both Pacific Northwest Coast).

41. One unidentified artefact (Europe?) and two Eskimo snow spectacles (Pacific Northwest Coast).

42. One abacus (Asia), one Chinese razor, one unidentified object.

Items 43-78 from (Europe/Asia):

43. Two vessels.

44, 47. Each a drawing of one vessel.

48. Two vessels.

49. Three vessels.

50. Three sculpted figures.

51, 52. Each a drawing of one vessel.

53. One container and one tea pot.

54. One cone-shaped object.

55. Two smoking implements.

56. Four pipes(?).

57. Three implements for holding coals(?).

58. Five unidentified artefacts.

59. One sculpted mythical bull.

60, 61. Each a drawing of two objects (for light?).

62. Five timepieces.

63. One bowl, three emblems and one compass.

64. Ten buckles, three rings, one pin.

65. One vessel.

66. Eight keys.

67. Four items of hardware.

68. One painted vase.

69, 70. Each a drawing of one plate.

71. One "Tazza" majolica wine-cooler.

72. One urn with lion on lid (Asia).

73. One illustrated plate (Europe).

74. One vessel.

75. One bowl.

76. One vessel with lid.

77. One plate with bird design.

78. One weapon or walking stick?

A volume of drawings by Sarah Stone, with an inscription: *Sarah Stone Drawings: Collection of 132 original water-colour drawings by Miss Stone of the principal objects of curiosity in the Ashton Lever Museum, consisting of Natural history Subjects, and the Arms Ornaments and dresses of the inhabitants of New Zealand and other countries discovered by Captain Cook, with 132 leaves containing the drawings ... folio, crimson straight grained morocco ... £35.*

These drawings are of the greatest importance, as they illustrated the heads and feet of birds, curious old bags, and other dress ornaments, native arms, implements, horns etc and furnish a permanent record of many of the vastly interesting and varies objects which were collected by that odd Manchester character Sir Ashton Lever ... By the generosity of George Robertson of Angus & Robertson, Limited, these were donated to the Australian museum (in May 1928). (Ref: RB 101 C11 22820)

The ethnographical objects, nos. 1–35, 69–93, 99–130, 132, will be described by Adrienne L. Kaeppler, Curator of Oceanic Ethnology, Smithsonian Institution, Washington, in a forthcoming book. Some of the watercolours have previously been noted in her *Artificial Curiosities: being an exposition of native manufactures collected on the three Pacific voyages of Captain James Cook, R.N.*, Bishop Museum Special Publications, 65, Honolulu 1978. The mammalian specimens, and horns and antlers, were identified by Richard Sabin of The Natural History Museum, London, from the microfiches of the watercolours in the Australian Museum Research Library deposited at the British Museum, Department of Ethnography.

Folios numbered 1–10 are labelled with the bird names in Sarah's handwriting. On folios no. 10, beginning with Carrier pigeon, and no. 11, the bird names are in a different hand.

Nos 1–11 are heads and feet of the birds only:

1. *Pied Ousle*
   A variety of blackbird?
   Black throated Parroquete
   Sea Lark in December
   [LM 203 Sea-lark, variety of Canary-bird, and a variety of the sky-lark – 3 cases, T. Walker 9/-; 2562 Sea Lark, Gibraltar, Salto 1/6]
   Scarlet loury
   [LM 4074 Scarlet loury, E. Indies, Blackman 10/6]
   Peregrine falcon
   = *Falco peregrinus*, Linnaeus 1758. [LM 3135 Rev. Mr Vaughan £1.12.0; Last day but one 41 Peregrine falcon falco peregrinus, Kirkpatrick 13/-]
2. *Cock curroso, young curroso, Cushew bird*
   = *Crax pauxi* Linnaeus 1766. [LM 746 Cushew birds, Crax pauxi; two fine specimens, male and female, rare, Vaughan £4.7.0]
   Fire finch
   [LM 639 Fire Finch, Africa, one of three birds in three cases, 10/6; 2579 Firefinch, Africa, two specimens, Latham £1.0.0]
   Large Kings Fisher Surinam
3. *Bittern*
   = *Botaurus stellaris* (Linnaeus 1758). [LM 188 two fine specimens of the bittern in one case, Ardea stellaris, 19/-; 4255 Bittern, Kirkpatrick 18/-.]

Cornish Chough
= *Pyrrhocorax pyrrhocorax* (Linnaeus 1758).
[LM 4267 Cornish chough, Corvus graculus, Fichtel 8/-; 5125 A very fine specimen of the Cornish chough, Corvus graculus, P.Walker 15/-]
Mandarin Drake
= *Aix galericulata* (Linnaeus 1758). [LM Last day 30 Mandarine Duck, Anas galericulata, Linn., Fillingham £7.0.0]
Stork
= *Ciconia ciconia* (Linnaeus 1758). [LM 647 Storks, Holland, m. and fem. Ardea ciconia Linn. Hall £1.13.0; 2217 Ardea ciconia, N. America (crossed through and replaced with handwritten) Holland stork, Cummings £1.12.0]

4. *Loon*
   = *Gavia*, sp. of Divers. [LM 362 Large speckled loon, N. America, 5/-; 1495 Speckled loon, N. America, m. and f., Ellis, Dr Sillers 14/-; 3121 Lesser speckled loon, Sivers 7/6; 5387 Red throated loon, one specimen, without case (colymbus septentriolis) rare, Thompson £6.10.0 (not for Lord Stanley); 5800 Red throated loon, Colymbus septentrionalis, rare. £1.11.0]
   Vultur
   Vulture sp.
   Lesser cockatoo

[LM 4841 Lesser cockatoo (without case) 5/-; 4944 Lesser cockatoo 3/6 ("Fichtel" written in then scored through)]
Pheasant
= *Phasianus colchicus* (Linnaeus 1758). [LM 1391 Very fine specimens of the ring-necked pheasant, phasianus colchicus, var. m. and fem. Kirkpatrick £4.4.0; 4259 Ring pheasant (in mahogany case) Burrel £1.13.0; 4826 Common pheasant, m. and fem. and young, Burrel £1.5.0.]
5. *Mino*
   = *Acridotheres cristatellus* (Linnaeus 1766), Crested mynah. [LM 1757 Mino grackle, Gracula religiosa 3/-]
   Silky fowl and hen [LM 4477 Silky fowls, a pair, East Indies 11/-]
   Golden pheasant
   = *Chrysolophus pictus* (Linnaeus 1758). [LM 1832 Golden pheasant, m. and fem. China, Kirkpatrick £2.3.0; 1936 Golden pheasant, China, without case, Smith £1.1.0; 3392 Golden pheasant, m. fem. and two young, Phasianus pictus, Bostock £2.2.0; 4948 Gold pheasant, female 10/6; 5135 Phasianus pictus]
6. *Red-legged partridge*
   = *Alectoris rufa* (Linnaeus 1758). [LM2784 Red-legged partridge, Solto 12/-; 4614 Red-legged

partridge, m. and fem., Kirkpatrick £2.5.0; 5369 Red-legged partridge, 9/-; 5804 Red-legged partridge, Guernsey; 5861 Red-legged partridge, barbary; 6011 Red-legged partridge, Portugal]
Black Cock
= *Lyrurus tetrix*, Linnaeus 1758. [LM 59 Tetrao tetrix, black Grous, Clark 16.0; 5614 Black grous, m. and fem. tetrao tetrix, Fichtel £3.13.6.]
Cinnamon Dove
= *Zenaida aurita zenaida* (Bonparte 1825). [LM 2049 Cinnamon-coloured turtle dove, S. America, Laskey 10/0; 3131 Cinnamon dove, Jamaica, Fichtel 16/- (see Pelzehn 1873, p. 34); 5380 Cinnamon dove, Jamaica (the male and female were bought at the LM sale by Fichtel, lot 3131 Cinnamon dove, jamaica, for 16/-, and lot 5380 Cinnamon dove, Jamaica, for 6/6, but they are no longer in the Vienna museum (see Pelzehn 1873, p. 35)); 6046 Cinnamon Dove, Jamaica 8/6]
Sea eagle
= *Haliaetus albicilla* (Linnaeus 1758). [LM 545 Sea eagle, Donovan £4.4.0.]
Golden eagle
= *Aquila chysaetos* (Linnaeus 1758). [LM Last day but two 26 Golden eagle Falco chrysaetos, Linn.]

7. *Touraco*
   = *Touraco persa* (Linnaeus 1758), Guinea turaco. [LM Last day but two 27 Cuculus Persa, Linn, tauraco bird]
   Mandarine Drake
   (see no. 3)
   Flight Falcon
   = *Falco peregrinus*, Linnaeus 1758, Peregrine. [LM 1403 Flight falcon, m. and fem. (hooded) Falco peregrinus, Donovan £3.7.0.]
8. *Macaw*
   Macaw sp. = *Ara ararauna* (Linnaeus 1758), Blue and yellow macaw. [LM 50 Blue and yellow Maccaw, without case, Psittacus ararauna, Hall 11/-; 537 Psittacus ararauna (out of case) and Goosander £1.3.0; 727 Psittacus ararauna; 1111 A very finely preserved specimen of psittacus ararauna, Brazil, Sedgliken £1.11.6; 1491 Psittacus ararauna Sillers £1.2.0; 4621 Psittacus ararauna, in mahogany glazed case, Latham £1.1.0]
   Gambo Goose, male
   = *Plecropterus gambensis*, Linnaeus 1758, Spur-winged goose, African. [LM 1755 Gambo goose, Cape of Good Hope, Fichtel 10/6; 4082 Gambo goose, Donovan 12/-; 4950 Anas Gambensis, spur-winged goose, S. America, extremely rare and fine, £4.4.0; 5386 Gambo Goose, Cape of Good Hope, Clark 15/-; 5397 Gambo duck, Surinam, Fenton 14/-]
   Water hen South America
   Perhaps [LM 6189 Small spotted water hen, S. America m. and fem., Fichtel 6/-]
   Gull sp.
9. *Parroquete, Isle of Borneo*
   [LM 6177 Two most beautiful specimens of the Borneo parroquet, £2.12.6.]
   Swan
   = *Cygnus olor* (Gmelin 1789). [LM 2312 A very fine female swan, Donovan £1.8.0; 2313 A ditto male swan Sivers £1.14.0.]

Bittern
(see no. 3)
Stone Curlew
= *Burhinus oedicnemus* (Linnaeus 1758). [LM 3586 Thick kneed plover, m. fem. and young, Donovan £1.1.0; Appendix 214 Thick-kneed plover, bought with 213 Shearwater petrel, Scotland, by Laskey 4/6]
10. *Iceland Falcon*
    Falcon sp.?
    Carrier Pigeon
    [LM 3127 Carrier pigeon, m. and fem. Sivers 7/-; 4432 Carrier pigeon, male and female, 13/-; 5827 Carrier pigeon; 5954 Carrier pigeon; 6335 Carrier pigeon, 3/-]
    White Cuckow
    = *Cuculus canorus*, Linnaeus 1758. [LM Last day but two 22 White variety of cuckoo, Cuculus canorus, Thompson £1.11.0.]
11. *White Turkey hen*
    [LM 1933 White variety of the turkey, m. and fem., Sivers 11/-]
    Brazilian Finch
    Goosander
    = *Mergus merganser*, Linnaeus 1758. E. Donovan, *The Natural History of British Birds*, III, 1796, pl. LXV, *Mergus meganser*, Female goosander or Dun diver: "In the Leverian Museum, the Dun-Diver and goosander are placed together as male and female ... Yet Latham has endeavoured to prove, by the most satisfactory experiments, that they are distinct species." [LM 728 Goosander, Mergus Merganser, female; and an avocet, two cases, 10/6; 5110 Goosander, fem., Swainson 8/-; 3395 Goosander, and young woodcock, two cases, 11/-; 4073 Goosander, m. and fem., Donovan 11/6]
    Turkey
    [LM 869 Mottled turkey, m. and fem. £1.2.0]

Nos. 12–35 are ethnographical items (see initial notes above).

Nos. 36–68 are of horns and antlers:
36. Giant Irish elk = *Megaloceros giganteus*
37. Greater kudu = *Tragelaphus strepsiceros*
38. Asian water buffalo = *Bubalus bubalis*
39. Left: Gemsbok = *Oryx gazella*; right: Nyala = *Tragellaphus* sp.
40. Domestic ox = *Bos taurus*
41. Moose/elk = *Alces alces* [LM Appendix 667 Pair of horns of the American moose, Donovan £3.3.0]
42. Red deer = *?Cervus elaphus*
43. Moose/elk = *Alces alces* [LM see no. 41]
44. Reindeer skull with antlers = *Rangifer tarandus*; Deer single antler = *Cervus* sp.
45. Red deer? = *Cervus elaphus*
46. Eland, possibly giant eland = *Taurotragus* sp. (*T. derbianus?*)
47. Deer = *Cervus* sp.
48. Ibex = *Capra ibex*
49. Two pairs of rhinoceros horns, probably either White rhinoceros, *Ceratotherium simum*, or Black rhinoceros, *Diceros bicornis*. [LM 1330 Double horns of rhinosceros, Fichtel 9/-; 1453 Remarkably fine and large double horns of rhinosceros, Rowe £1.2.0; App 657 Curious double horn of rhinosceros, Fillingham 5/6]
50. Rhinoceros horns [LM see no. 49]
51. Left: unidentified; right: Gemsbok = *Oryx gazella*
52. Left: Blackbuck = *Antilope cervicapra*; right: unidentified
53. Horns unidentified
54. Horns unidentified
55. Horn pieces bound together
56. Narwhal skull = *Monodon monoceros*
57. Narwhal skull, double tusks = *Monodon monoceros* [LM 1450 Tusk of the Narwal whale, monodon monceros, £1.7.0.]
58. Roe deer = *Capreolus capreolus*
59. Three horns unidentfied
60. Deer antler

61. Goat = *Capra* sp., probably Domestic goat *C. hircus*
62. Musk ox = *Ovibos moschatus*
63. Deer antlers
64. Sheep = *Ovis* sp., possibly Bighorn sheep, *Ovis canadensis*
65. Reindeer/caribou = *Rangifer tarandus*
66. Deer antler
67. *?Rangifer* antler
68. Domestic ox = *?Bos taurus*

Nos. 69-93 are ethnographical subjects:
94. Shark?
95. Sword fish and head of sword-fish, *Xiphius gladius?* [LM 1452 Snout of the sword-fish, 4/6]
96. Manatee? = *Trichechus* sp. [LM ?5461 Round-tailed seal, bought in £1.1.0.]
97. Dolphin (Common? = *Delphinus delphis*). Cook (Beaglehole 1961, p. 564), "Off New Caledonia 9 October 1774 Mr Cooper struck a Porpoise with a Harpoon, it was necessary to have two boats in the water before we could kill him and get him on board. It was six feet they differ from the other sort in the head and jaws, which in these are long and pointed: this one had teeth in each jaw [The Common Dolphin, *Delphinus delphis* (Linnaeus), described in detail by J.R. Forster (*Descr. An.*, p. 280 and painted by his son]. The crew welcomed this as a feast and ate it."

98. Seal, probably southern phocid, Mediterranean monk seal? = *Monachus monachus*.

99–130, 132 are ethnographical subjects including spears and clubs, axes, rapiers and daggers, head-dresses and necklaces, fly-whisks, pipes and fans, with some other unidentified artefacts.

131. Two heads of primates: (a) Old World primate; (b) Madril male = *Mandrillus sphinx*.

4. BRITISH MUSEUM
(DEPARTMENT OF ETHNOGRAPHY)

(Ref: MM 034 227/3)

Forty ethnographical drawings by Sarah Stone.

Dr Jonathan C. H. King wrote two articles, identifying the items on each folio drawing by Sarah, and linking them with items in the LM sale of 1806. His first article, 'Woodlands art as depicted by Sarah Stone in the collection of Sir Ashton Lever', appeared in *American Indian Art Magazine*, 18 (2), 1991, pp. 35–45. The second article, 'New evidence for the contents of the Leverian Museum', in *Journal of the History of Collections*, 8, 1996, pp. 167–86, surveyed the history of Sir Ashton Lever and his museum, and then described (with black and white illustrations) nine folios depicting eleven non-ethnographical objects, followed by a group of ethnographical objects, the first North American, and then thirteen folios of Asian and African musical instruments.

In addition, the British Museum owns a painting that is most probably a copy of Sarah's painting of the Leverian Museum, 1786 (see frontispiece), the original of which is now in a private collection: *Sir Ashton Lever's Museum (Leicester House, Leicester Square)*, copied "From a drawing made on the spot", watercolour, *ca.* 40 × 43 cm, with a watermark *J Whatman 1835*.

1. Oval majolica plate
2. Round majolica glass
3, 4. German enamelled glass
5. English clay pipe
6-23. Native North American artefacts
24. Shark hook, almanac and whet stone
25. Two curios of wood
26. Sarinda, string instrument
27. Rabab, string instrument
28. Valiha, zither
29, 30. Each a drawing of an Asian drum
31. Chinese cloud gong
32. Chinese mouth organ
33. Three Chinese wind instruments
34. African rattle
35, 36. Each a drawing of a Chinese lute
37. Two Chinese wind instruments
38. Asian lute
39. Hiberno-Viking brooch
40. Mineral specimen

5. THE DIXSON LIBRARY, MITCHELL LIBRARY, STATE LIBRARY
OF NEW SOUTH WALES, SYDNEY, AUSTRALIA

This library has one signed watercolour by Sarah Stone, and several similar but unsigned watercolours which may be her work. These are among a number of added illustrations, either bound in or pasted into sets of Captain Cook's published accounts of his voyages, which once belonged to Thomas Pennant.

James Cook, *A Voyage to the Pacific Ocean* (3 vols., 2nd edn., London 1795) (Dixson Library ref: Q77/35–37.)

Vol. III, opposite p. 118, I'iwi; watercolour signed *Sarah Stone* = *Vestiaria coccinea* (Forster 1781), I'iwi. A specimen of this bird was in the British Museum (Natural History collection), ex Royal College of Surgeons, in 1969 (Whitehead 1969, p. 195) [LM 3070 *Certhia vestiaria*, very rare, m. and fem. Sandwich Islands, Latham £1.17.0; Last day 33 Red certhia, Sandwich islands, *Certhia vestiaria*].

PLATE 11

Other watercolours in this copy of the *Voyage*, which may be by Sarah:

Vol. I, opposite p. 148, South Island Kokako: *Callaeas cinerea cinerea* (Gmelin 1788), Cinerous wattlebird [LM 2698 Cinerous wattle bird, S. Seas, Glaucopis cinera, Lord Stanley £1.16.0. A syntype is present in the Liverpool Museum (Largen 1987, pp. 277, 286).]

Vol. I, opposite p. 333: Red-breasted musk parrot = *Prosopeia tabuensis tabuensis* (Gmelin 1789), Red shining parrot. Latham described this bird from his own specimen and another in the LM. Captain James Cook described the finding of this bird in October 1773, when on the island of Tong-tabu, and wrote in his journal, "The land Birds found here are of the same sort as at Otaheite and the neighbouring isles (viz) Pigeons, Turtle Doves, Parrots,[10] Perrokets and several other small Birds". Beaglehole (1961, p. 262) identified note 10 as *Prosopeia tabuensis* (Gm.), the Red-breasted Musk Parrot. [LM 2427 Psittacus tabuensis, a very fine specimen, £1.3.0; 4434 Tabuan parrot, Psittacus tabuanus, Fenton 13/-; Lot 4747 Pompadour-fronted parroquet, South Seas, in fine plumage, Fichtel £2.3.0. (this specimen was noted as being present in the Vienna Museum by Pelzehn (1873, p. 30), who said it was the type of Latham's and Shaw's descriptions and figures of *Platycercus tabuensis* (Gmelin 1789))].

Vol. II, opposite p. 90: Long-billed warbler = *Conopodera caffra longirostris* (Gmelin 1789).

Whitehead (1969, p. 195) listed the specimen collected by Anders Sparrman as still being present in the Universitets Zoologische Museum, Stockholm.

Vol. III, opposite p. 117: another, unsigned, drawing of the I'iwi. (See above, III, opposite p. 118, signed by Sarah Stone.)

Vol. III, opposite p. 119: Hawaiian akialoa = *Hemignathus obscurus obscurus* (Gmelin 1788). (See NHML (3), no. 51.)

Vol. III, opposite p. 120: Hawaiian O-o, Sarah's hook-billed green creeper = *Moho nobilis* (Merrem 1786).

Vol. III, opposite p. 121: Hawaiian Ou = *Psittirostra psittacea* (Gmelin 1789). No one has seen an Ou since 1992, when a hurricane hit its Hawaiian island home (*Birds*, Winter 1996, p. 41, comment on *Endangered Birds*, published by World Book International). A specimen of the Moho (Ou) was present in the Liverpool Museum, ex Bullock Museum, in 1969 (Whitehead, p. 195). [LM 4270 Parrot-billed grosbeak, Loxia Psittacea – very rare]. This was bought by Fichtel for the Vienna Museum, where the type of Latham's description of the

male had remained in the collection (Pelzehn 1873, pp. 21–22).

James Cook, *A Voyage towards the South Pole and round the world* (2 vols., London 1777)

Vol. II, opposite p. 205: Sheath bill = *Chionis alba* (Gmelin 1789). This watercolour is similar to the engraving of the Sheath bill by Peter Mazell in James Cook's *A Voyage to the Pacific Ocean*, I, p. 88. A specimen of a young bird bought from the LM sale by Fichtel was present in the Vienna Museum collection in 1873 (Pelzehn 1873, pp. 37–38). (See also NHML (3), no. 146.)

Ethnographical watercolours pasted into vol. II of James Cook's *A Voyage to the Pacific Ocean*, which may have been painted by Sarah:

Opposite p. 20: Two fish hooks, octopus lure and trolling hook. Four pencil sketches on one sheet.

Opposite p. 45: Adze, chisel, bread-fruit pounder and axe of Tahiti. Four pencil sketches on one sheet.

Opposite p. 78: Tongan club, flint blade and haft, flint blade harpoon and ceremonial mace. Five pencil sketches on one sheet.

6. NATIONAL LIBRARY OF AUSTRALIA, CANBERRA

(National Library ref: R 11196-11208.¹)
A collection of fifteen watercolours in an album, with the title page *Natural History Specimens of New South Wales by Sarah Stone*, 1790: being a collection of original watercolours painted after specimens sent by John White to England in 1789, used for illustrations in his *Journal of a Voyage to New South Wales*.

The watercolours were purchased by an American collector in the 1920s, and obtained by the National Library of Australia when they came on to the market in Australia in 1992.

There are several features of these watercolours that are curious. There is clear evidence that Sarah Stone made her drawings in 1789, and the title page ought to bear the date 1789. The contents page, which reads, "Natural History specimens of New South Wales copied from nature by Sarah Stone 1790" also bears the wrong date. Furthermore, Sarah married on 8 September 1789, and by 1790 was Sarah Smith. The engravings were done for plates that bear the copyright date 29 December 1789, with the name of the publisher, I. (= John) Debrett. The watercolours are unsigned, although the plates to which they correspond in White's *Journal* are signed *S Stone delin*.

Evidence pointing to the paintings being the work of Sarah Stone is based on her characteristic use of sized paper, her stylistic treatment of trees and branches, her manner of painting feathers and claws of birds, and the placement of shadows under the bodies of animals.

In the eighteenth century, artists who prepared drawings to be engraved by craftsmen, drew in such a manner that every line could be copied, and shading interpreted. Sarah was not used to preparing work for book

illustrations and did not draw in this way. The engraver, Milton, employed to copy her drawings, was heavy-handed and, on the evidence provided by these attributed drawings, made several changes. He not only altered the size of the figure (frequently enlarging it), but the size of the shadows, even adding one or two extra shadows.

The paintings are both softer and more lively than the engravings, and in every case each watercolour is superior in its representation of the bird, fish, snake or lizard. Unusually, most of the drawings and engravings of the species face in the same direction; an engraving is normally in reverse. When the original drawing and the engraving face the same way, a tracing was used by the engraver, resulting in the drawing and engraving being exactly the same size. These watercolour drawings are not the same size and were not traced onto the metal plate. One of the two C. Catton junior mammal paintings also faces the same way as the engraving, and the tail of the Tapoa Tafa is twice as thick and bushy in the engraving as in the painting. It is most unusual for the paintings to differ to this degree from the engravings done from them.

One can only conclude that either the engraver took unusual liberties, or was working from a set of drawings other than these now in Canberra; Sarah may have made two sets, this one unsigned. Alternatively, the drawings are skilful copies and improved versions of the engravings. In the three examples of figures in the paintings and engravings facing in opposite directions, the differences between the figures are so great as to create the impression that while the paintings might well be original Sarah Stone portraits, they may not be the basis of all the engravings.

1. Banksian cockatoo, pl. 3 (in the *Journal*).
2. Great brown kings fisher, pl. 2.
3. The Tabuan parrot, female, pl. 12.
4. Motacilla, pl. 42.
5. The crested goatsucker, p. 29.
   PLATE 9

6. Pennantian parrot, pl. 13.
7. The crested cockatoo, pl. 26.
8. Superb warbler, upper figure, pl. 41.
9. The red shoulder"d paroquet, pl. 49.
10. The pungent chetodon and Granualate baliste, pl. 39.

11. The fasciated mullet and Doubtful sparus, pl. 53.
12. Snake and Muricated lizard, pl. 31.
13. Ribbon lizard and Broad-tailed lizard, pl. 32.
A further thirty-one watercolours associated with the plates in John

White's *Journal of a Voyage to New South Wales* are now in a private collection in Australia (see p. 136). For notes on the species, see 'John White's *Journal of a Voyage to New South Wales*', in 'Sarah Stone's Book Illustrations', p. 140.

7. ALEXANDER TURNBULL LIBRARY, WELLINGTON, NEW ZEALAND

There is one signed watercolour by Sarah Stone in the Raper Collection, of *Parokets of Otehaete = Vini peruviana* (P.L.S. Müller 1776), Tahitian lory

[LM 4748 Otaheitan blue parrot. Ps. Taitanus, Vaughan £3.11.0.].
PLATE 7

8. YALE CENTER FOR BRITISH ART, NEW HAVEN, USA

Watercolour of a red parrot = *Psittacus erithacus*, Linnaeus 1758, African grey

parrot, signed and dated 1786, sold Sotheby's, London, 1962. PLATE 8

9. SEDGWICK MUSEUM, DEPARTMENT OF EARTH SCIENCES, UNIVERSITY OF CAMBRIDGE

Twenty-eight watercolours of echinoderms, molluscs and fossil plants, stones and marbles, identified by Mike Dorling and Debbie Wharton. The drawings came to light in 1978 and are part of the series of ninety watercolours in The Natural History Museum, London (see NHML (1)), which were presented to the then British Museum (Natural History) in 1931 by the Superintendent of the Univeristy Museum of Zoology, Cambridge.

1. *S. Stone*
   Two fossil fishes in stone
   (a) *Myripristis homopterygius* Upper Eocene: Monte Bolca, near Verona.
   (b) ?*Leptolepis* sp. Lithographic slate: Solenhofen, Bavaria.
2. Twelve shells:
   (a) ? *Fusivoluta pyrrhostoma* (Watson 1882), Fire-mouthed volute.

(b) *Buccinulum pallidum* Finlay 1928, Powell's lined whelk.
(c) *Vexillum rugosum* (Gmelin 1791), Rugose mitre.
(d) *Vexillum balteolatum* (Reeve 1844).
(e) *Vexillum formosense* (Sowerby 1890), Formosan mitre.
(f) *Cancilla (Tiara) filaris* (Linnaeus 1771), File mitre.
(g) *Vexillum sanguisugum*

(Linnaeus 1758), Bloodsucker mitre.
[LM 4604 Three varieties of mitra sanguisuga, two striated spotted needles, and a singular ladder, all from China, and rare, Latham 12/6; 2192 A spotted obelisk, S. Seas; the wheater-ear cuma, Guinea; two orange clouded needles, China; the banded subula, and a

sanguineous mitre – all rare, Sivers 6/6]
(h) *Vexillum plicarium* (Linnaeus 1787), Plaited mitre.
[LM 2702 Two plaited and two other mitres, with four other shells, Sivers 5/-; 4314 Two of the plaited mitre, and a scarce banded mitre, all from China, G Humphrey 2/6]
(i) *Cancellaria balboae*, Pilsbry

1931, Balboa nutmeg.
(j) ? *Pseudovertagus* sp.
(k) *Vexillum sanguisugum*, Linnaeus 1758. [For LM see (g)]
(l) *Vexillum amanda* (Reeve 1845), Amanda mitre.

3. *Sarah Stone*
Six shells:
(a) *Terebra strigata*, Sowerby 1825, Zebra auger.
(b) *Terebra crenulata* (Linnaeus 1758), Crenulated auger.
(c) *Terebra dimidiata* (Linnaeus 1758), Dimidiate auger.
(d) *Terebra subulata* (Linnaeus 1767), Subulate auger.
(e) *Terebra dimidiata* (Linnaeus 1758), Dimidiate auger.
(f) *Turritella terebra cerea* (Linnaeus 1758), Screw turritella.

4, 5. Each one shell of *Fasciolaria lilium hunteria*, Perry 1811, Banded tulip.

6. Two shells, similar to *Astraea heliotropium*, Martyn 1784, Sunburst star turban.

7. Three fish teeth *Ptychodus* sp. Chalk: Kent/Sussex.

8. Twelve shells:
(a) *Cipangopaludina chinensis malleata*
(b) *Natica* sp.?
(c) *Euspira poliana* (Chiaje 1826), Poli's necklace shell.
(d) *Calinaticina oldroydii* (Dall 1897), Oldroy's fragile moon.
(e) and (f) *Neritina communis* (Quoy and Gaimard 1832), Zigzag nerite.
(g) ?*Polinices mammatus* (Röding

1798), Breast-shaped moon.
(h) *Neritodryas dubia* (Gmelin 1791), Dubious nerite.
(i) *Heliacus variegatus*, Gmelin 1791. [LM 1785 Two of helix variegata, China; the ribband land snail, Granada; two scarce pyrae, Tranquebar; and four others, G Humphrey 4/-; 1786 Two of helix variegata, China, three bullae, a small richly coloured guinea music, and three others, 5/6; 3233 The onyx lamp, W. Indies; a purple variety of helix variegata, China, and another rare land snail, McLeay 11/-; 3408 Two of helix variegata, (citrina, Linn.) two orange mouth olives, two brown caterpillar clubs, and three others – all from China, Sivers 7/6]
(j) *Natica tigrina* (Röding 1798), Tiger moon.
(k) *Nerita versicolor*, Gmelin 1791, Four-toothed nerite. [LM 5503 Nerita versicolor, W. Indies, with with 13 other shells, 3/-]
(l) *Nerita exuvia*, Linnaeus 1758, Snake-skin nerite.

9. Four shells ?*Donax faba*, Gmelin 1791, Pacific bean donax.

10. Four shells:
(a) *Argonauta hians*, Lightfoot 1786, Brown paper nautilus.
(b) *Volva volva* (Linnaeus 1758), Shuttlecock volva. [LM 585 Licium textorium, the weaver's shuttle, (Bulla volva Linn) Japan extremely scarce, Playter 5/-]
(c) and (d) *Neoberingius turtoni*

(Bean 1834), Turton's neptune.
11. Two shells, both *Limaria ?inflata* (Gmelin 1791), Inflate lima.
12. Echinoderm *Dorocidaris papillata*.
13. Echinoderm *?Heterocentrotus* sp.
14. Echinoderm *Heterocentrotus trigonarius*.
15. Echinoderm, two views of *Echinometra* sp.
16. Echinoderm *Heterocentrotus mammillatus* (Linnaeus 1758). [LM 3403 A mammillated echinus, Arabia; and two other diadem echini – both having their spines, Horne 15/-; 3549 A mammilated echinus, Arabia; and two other diadem echini, one having its spines, Sicily, Brent 4/6]
17. Echinoderm (another view of no. 16?).
18, 19. Starfish (two views of the same species), both signed *Sarah Stone: 1780*
20. Three plant fossils:
(a) *Neuropteris* sp., counterpart of (c). Coal Measures, British.
(b) *Mariopteris* sp., Coal Measures, British.
(c) *Neuropteris* sp., counterpart of (a). Coal Measures, British.
21. *Sarah Stone July 8 – 1778*
Four plant fossils:
(a) and (b) part and counterpart of *Williamsonia* sp. pecten. Stonesfield slate.
(c) *Adientites/Sphenopteris* sp. Coal Measures, British.
(d) *Neuropteris/Sphenopteris* sp. Coal Measures, British.
22. *Sarah Stone July 9 – 1778*
Two plant fossils:

(a) and (b) part and counterpart of *Alethopteris lonchotica*. Middle Coal Measures, Yorkshire/Derbyshire.
23. *Sarah Stone July 9 – 1778*
Two plant fossils:
(a) and (b) part and counterpart of *Alethopteris lonchotica*. Middle Coal Measures, Yorkshire/Derbyshire.
24. *Sarah Stone July 10 – 1778*
Two plant fossils:
(a) and (b) part and counterpart of *Neuropteris* sp. Coal Measures, Yorkshire/Derbyshire.
25. *Sarah Stone Sepr 4 – 1778*
Four square pieces of marble:
(a) and (c) Onyx
(b) and (d) indeterminate
26. *Sarah Stone Sept 23 – 1 – 1778*
Four square decorative stones:
(a) and (c) indeterminate
(b) ?Tuscany
(d) Fluorite
27. *Sarah Stone Oct 10 – 1778*
Two square pieces of granite and two of onyx
28. *Sarah Stone Dec 9 – 1778*
Four square pieces of marble:
(a) *Portoro macchia larga*: La Spezia, which is still available in Italian trade catalogues.
(b) *Brecchia* sp.
(c) ?*Brecchia violetto: seravezza*, Tuscany (widely used in Ancient Rome)
(d) indeterminate

Watercolour of a beetle, signed and dated 1781, bequeathed by Sally, Duchess of Westminster to the collection in 1990.

PRIVATE COLLECTION A

Birds

1. *S. Smith*
   Amazon, yellow-headed, watching a fly. = *Amazona ochrocephala* (Gmelin 1788). [LM 3293 Yellow headed parrot, Brazils, Brogden 17/-; 6092 Yellow-headed parrot, Brazils]

2. *Sarah Smith 1801*
   Amazon, yellow-headed with Salmon-crested cockatoo. Yellow-headed amazon = *Amazona ochrocephala* (Gmelin 1788); Salmon-crested cockatoo = *Cacatua moluccensis* (Gmelin 1788).

3. *Sarah Stone, 1782. 35*
   Ardea caerulescens. = *Egretta caerulea* (Linnaeus 1758), Little blue heron.

4. *Sarah Smith*
   Bee-eater, with hoopoe and Pompadour cotinga Bee-eater = *Merops apiaster*, Linnaeus 1758. [LM 636 Goldfinch, m. and fem.; Merops apiaster; Woodcocks, young, two specimens; Pit wren, four specimens – four cases £3.4.0; 2570 Merops apiaster, m. and fem. Mrs Higgins 11/6; 5358 Common bee-eater Merops apiaster, P.Walker 10/6] Hoopoe = *Upupa epops*, Linnaeus 1758. [LM 3290 Common hoopoe Davis? Prayter 18/-; 4923 Common hoopoe Kirkpatrick 14/-; 5837 Hoopoe male] Pompadour cotinga = *Xipholena punicea* (Pallas 1764). [LM 5398 Pompadour chatterer, Ampelis pompadora, m. and fem. Thompson £3.3.0.]

5. *Sarah Smith*

Ibis, scarlet = *Eudocimus ruber* (Linnaeus 1758). [LM 4079 Scarlet ibis, tantalus ruber, Smith £2.2.0; 4837 A capital specimen of the scarlet ibis, Tantalus Ibis, Triphook £2.10.0.]

6. *Sarah Smith*
   Macaw, blue and yellow = *Ara ararauna* (Linnaeus 1758), Blue and yellow macaw. [LM 50 Blue and yellow Maccaw, without case, Pisittacus ararauna, Hall 11/-; 537 Psittacusa rarauna (out of case) and Goosander, £1.3.0; 727 Psittacus ararauna; 1111 A very finely preserved specimen of psittacus ararauna, Brazil, Vaughan £1.11.6; 1491 Psittacus ararauna Sillers 11/-; 4621 Psittacus ararauna, in mahogany glazed case, Latham £1.5.0.]

7. *Sarah Smith*
   Barn owl = *Tyto alba* (Scopoli 1769). [LM 308 Golden-eye duck, and two barn owls – two cases, Donovan 17/-; 1493 Red godwit, and barn owl, Sivers 11/-; 1922 Black and white smew and young barn owl, Sivers 10/-; 3141 A case, containing three young barn owls, Thompson 3/6; 5128 Young barn owls, two specimens, Thompson 5/6] Partridge still life, with a carrier's label against a board background *Sarah Smith* = *Perdix perdix* (Linnaeus 1758).

9. *Sarah Smith*
   Peacock pheasant = *Polyplectron bicalcaratum* (Linnaeus 1758). [LM Last day but one 50 Phasianus bicalcaratus, peacock pheasant

China, a most beautiful specimen, very rare]

10. *Sarah Smith*
    Golden pheasant with beetle = *Chrysolophus pictus* (Linnaeus 1758). [LM 1832 Gold pheasant, m. and fem. China, Kirkpatrick £2.3.0; 1936 Golden pheasant, China, without case, Smith £1.1.0; 3392 Gold pheasant, m. fem. and two young. Phasianus pictus, Bostock £2.2.0; 4948 Gold pheasant, female, 10/6; 5135 Phasianus pictus]

11. *Sarah Smith*
    Bronze-winged pigeon = *Phaps chalcoptera* (Latham 1790). The specimen was collected in Adventure Bay, Van Dieman's Land, January 1777, on Cook's third voyage of 1776-80 (Beaglehole 1967, p. 792). Sarah also painted this pigeon under the eagle's foot in a painting in the same collection (see no.16). [LM 4080 An uncommonly fine specimen of the male bronze winged pigeon, (columba chalcoptera) and a female, New Holland. Bought in £1.11.0.]

12. *Sarah Smith*
    Quetzal = *Pharomachus moccino*, de la Llare 1832, Resplendant quetzal.

13. *Sarah Smith*
    Touraco = *Tauraco persa* (Linnaeus 1758) Guinea turaco. [LM Last day but two 27 Cuculus Persa. Linn, tauraco bird, Thompson £2.2.0.]

14. *Sarah Stone 1785*
    Tropicbird, red-tailed = *Phaethon rubricauda*, Boddaert 1783. [LM 2580 Red-tailed tropic bird, Phaeton

phoenicurus, Thompson £1.8.0. (Largen 1987, pp. 282-83).

15. *Sarah Stone 1785*
    Brown bird, undetermined.

16. *Sarah Smith 1806*
    Golden eagle with bronze-winged pigeon = *Aquila chrysaetos* (Linnaeus 1758), and *Phaps chalcoptera* (Latham 1790), (see no. 11).

17. Yellow-shouldered amazon *Amazona barbadensis* (Gmelin 1789) with blue-crested and blue-headed parrot (unidentified).

18. Demoiselle crane, *Anthropoides virgo* (Linnaeus 1758). [LM Last day but one 45 Demoiselle crane, Ardea virgo]

19. Painting of birds' feathers.

Insects

Several sheets with insects and some inscriptions:

Stag beetle Sarah Stone

Scarabeus Sarah Stone January 7–1778

Mantis Sarah Stone Dec 8–1777

Grasshoppers Sarah Stone January 10–1778

Cicada Sarah Stone

Gryllus Sarah stone Feb 19–1778 with others, unsigned

Cerambyx Sarah Stone January 12–1778

Cemax (unsigned)

Nepa (unsigned)

Pap. Dan. Cand., Alcmeone, Hab. in Asia Sarah Stone March 4–1778 = *Delias candida*; *Papilio alcemeone,* Cramer 1777. [LM 4642 Twenty-two Papiliones, chiefly Danai candidi, Hepworth 3/-]

Pap. Dan. Cand., Amasene, Hab. in Asia Sarah Stone March 4–1778 = *Papilio amasene,* Cramer 1775.

Phal. Attai. Hab. in Afric Sarah Stone March 6–1778

= *Phalaena (Attai) promothea*, Drury 1773.
Papil. Heliacon, Charithonia fam., Hab. in Jamaica Sarah Stone
= *?Ionolyce helicon*, Felder 1860, *Heliconius charitonia*, Linnaeus 1767. [LM 3925 Papilio

Heliacon, rare, McLeay 11/6; 4405 Papilio Heliacon, rare, McLeay £1.11.6.]
Pap. Heliacon, Mopsa, Hab. in Indies Sarah Stone
= *Phalaena mopsa*, Drury 1773.
Pap. Dan. Candid., Glaucippe, Hab.

in China Sarah Stone
= *Hebomia glaucippe* (Linnaeus 1758). [LM 4396 Papilio glaucippe + two more butterflies, Haworth 7/-; 4399 Papilio glaucippe Agamemnon and four more, Sivers 1/-]

Butterfly (unnamed and unsigned)
Butterfly showing the four stages of metamorphosis (unnamed and unsigned).

PRIVATE COLLECTION B

This has "54 drawings of birds by Miss Stone done for Sir Ashton and sold at N. Alkrington after Ld (*sic*) Lever's death; 1 drawing of butterflies; 2 drawings of molluscs; 5 drawings of quadrupeds; 4 drawings of minerals and 2 drawings of fossils." Sheets of watercolours have been pasted on to a folio, sometimes two on the recto, and others on the verso.

The birds were identified by Clemency T. Fisher and George Phillips; mammals by Clemency T. Fisher and George Phillips; the geological drawings by Wendy Simpkiss and Alan Bowden; the reptiles by Malcolm J. Largen; hydroids by Ian Wallace; and the insects by Steve Cross and Chris Felton.

1. *Sarah Stone*
Three fossils
2. *Sarah Stone 1779*
(a) Two fossils
Lithographic limestone (Upper Jurassic).
(b) Pebbles
Nine agates, Chalcedony, 2 Onyx, Bumastus sp. (Sp. of trilobite, Ordovician/Silurian), and limpet?
(c) Two specimens of landscape marble (Rheatic).
(d) One fossil; 1 marked pebble.
Dendritic limestone (or very fine grained sedimentary rock); Lithographic limestone.
(Verso): *Sarah Stone 1780*
Kingfisher = *Halcyon smyrnensis* (Linnaeus 1758), White-breasted kingfisher. [LM 3529 Smyrnensis Kingfisher S. Seas Alcedo Smyrnensis var. Oliphant 9/6]
3. *167*
Three young barn owls
= *Tyto alba* (Scopoli 1769). [LM 3141 A case containing three young barn owls, Thompson 3/6]

3. *Sarah Stone No. 8*
Teal, male and female, two paintings
= *Anas crecca*, Linnaeus 1758. [LM 4487 Common teal, a pair, 11/-]
4. *Sarah Stone Febr 27 1779*
Two birds, one with a butterfly and a lizard
= *Chlorophanes spiza* (Linnaeus 1766), Green honeycreeper. [LM 2786 Black-headed creeper, Certhia spiza, Blackman 17/6; 3139 Certhia spiza, Sivers 8/-; 3294 Certhia spiza, Breedon 9/-]
= *Phoenicopterus ruber junior avis.* [LM 377 Red flamingo, Phoenicopterus ruber, Jamaica, 4/-; 2053 A most beautiful specimen of the flamingo, Phoenicopterus ruber, with red and white variegations, Butt £4.5.0.; 4091 The flamingo, a young bird bred in Osterley Park, Heslop 10/6; Last day but one, 60, Flamingo, a singularly fine and high coloured specimen, Phoenicopterus ruber. Parkinson advertised the addition of a "Flamingo, from

South America, one of the most rare and beautiful of its species ever seen, and which belonged to the late Mr Bond of Clapham", 20 May 1788 (*Morning Post and Daily Advertiser*, p. 1. [LM 377 Red flamingo, Phoenicopterus ruber, Jamaica, 4/-; 2053 A most beautiful specimen of the flamingo, Phoenicopterus ruber, with red and white variegations, Butt £4.5.0; 4091 The flamingo, a young bird bred in Osterly Park, Heslop 10/6; Last day but one, 60, Flamingo, a singularly fine and high coloured specimen, Phoenicopterus ruber]
Lizard (too small to identify).
Moth = *Euchromia* sp.
Sarah Stone 1780
Parakeet *Alexandri* Var *V*
= *Psittacula alexandri* Linnaeus 1758, Alexandrine parakeet. [LM 64 Alexandrine parrot, male and female, Psittacus Alexandri, Bassino 10/-; 186 Psittacus Alexandri, the Alexandrine parrot, Birchell 15/-; 3137 Psittacus Alexandri,

Sivers 7/-; 3386 Ring parroquet, Psittacus Alexandri, Sivers 7/6; 3507 Rose-ringed parroquet, m. and fem. Psittacus Alexandri, var. Mrs Oliphant £2.2.0; 4069 Alexandrine parakeet, 2/6; 4083 A pair of Alexandrine parroquet, Psittacus Alexandri, Sivers 6/-; 4833 Psittacus Alexandri, Carrudes 5/6; 5603 Psittacus Alexandri, Col.Thompson 10/-]
5. *Sarah Stone March 17 1779*
Psittacus: an aestivus
Blue-fronted amazon, with a cricket
= *Amazona aestiva* (Linnaeus 1766), Turquoise-fronted parrot. [LM 2211 Blue-fronted parrot, Brazils, Vaughan 10/6]
African grey parrot, with a Nymphalid bird-wing butterfly
Sarah Stone March 26 1779
= *Psittacus erithacus*, Linnaeus 1758. [LM 187 Psittacus erithacus, Gray parrot, 12/-; 1299 Gray parrot, Africa, Psittacus erithacus, 5/-; 4941 Gray parrot, Sugden 9/-; 5869 Grey parrot]
6. *Sarah Stone*

Pigeon = *Treron waalia* (F.A.A. Meyer 1793), Yellow-bellied fruit pigeon.

Common Cuckow Sarah Stone 20 = *Cuculus canorus*, Linnaeus 1758. [LM 1516 Cuckow y[oun]g with least brown grebe. Stanley 8/6 (Largen 1987, p. 282); 3608 Cuckow, m. and fem., 17/-; 4628 A large case containing the common cuckow in its various stages of growth, with the respective birds by which it is fed. W. Swainson £3.3.0]

Grous Tetrao scotica La. Sarah Stone and Gregson's Sale 1830 Oct 2 = *Lagopus lagopus scoticus* (Latham 1787), Red grouse. [LM 4253 Grous, Donovan £1; 5376 Grous, m. and fem. Donovan p. Lockee £2.2.0.]

7. *Sarah Stone June 26 1778*
A pair of Capercaillies = *Tetrao urogallus*, Linnaeus 1758. [LM 1419 Cock of the wood and hen, Tetrao urogallus, P.Walker £4.0.0.]

8. *Sarah Stone June 26 1778*
Buzzard and heron
Buzzard = *Buteo buteo* (Linnaeus 1758). [LM 883 blue and white fronted parrot and bald buzzard hawk – without case, Vaughan £2.2.0; 4411 Common buzzard, Falco buteo, Sivers 12/-; 1393 Buzzard hawk, male, and common pigeon, Segeltin 14/-]

Heron = *Ardea cinerea*, Linnaeus 1758. [LM 300 Heron, female, Ardea major, Newman 11/-; 1835 Heron, male, N Carrudes 17/6]

Red-fronted finch New Species? Sarah Stone 1784 p. 268
= *?Lagonosticta senegala*, Linnaeus 1766, Red-billed firefinch. [LM 639 a lot with three birds including Fire Finch, Africa; 2579 Fire finch, Africa, two specimens, Latham £1.16.0.]

9. *Todus viridis*
= *Todus todus* (Linnaeus 1758), Jamaican tody. [LM 5272 Green tody, Todus viridis, Thompson

8/6 (Largen 1987, pp. 284–85)]
Malacca Grosbeak La. Syn. 3 p. 140 Loxia malacca Sarah Stone No 16 and "Gregson's Sale 1830" = *Lonchura malacca* (Linnaeus 1766), Black-headed munia.

10. *Trochilus Sarah Stone* = *Selasphorus rufus* (Gmelin 1788), Rufous hummingbird.

11. *Sylvia Sarah Stone 1784* = *Fringilla montifringilla*, Linnaeus 1758, Brambling. [LM 190 Bramble finch, and a sandpiper; 3055 Bramble finch, and canary bird, m. and fem. Kirkpatrick 6/6; 5834 Brambling and another; 6006 Brambling, and wheatear.
(Verso): *Sarah Stone*
A Bee-eater and a Jacamar with three Hymenoptera, wasps = *Merops apiaster*, Linnaeus 1758, Common bee-eater. [LM 2570 Merops apiaster, m. and fem., Mrs Higgins 11/6], and *Galbula dea*, Linnaeus 1758, Paradise jacamar. A specimen was also in Vienna in 1873 (Pelzehn 1873, p. 108), perhaps LM 6033 Jacamar, m. and fem. (fine) (with the note), "A specimen called Alcedo paradisesa, from Cayene or Surinam. According to Latham this species was represented in the Leverian Collection." [LM 4485 Paradise jacamar, Alcedo Paradisea, a pair, Vaughan £1.11.6]

12. Parrot finch, *Fringilla psittacea* and one unnamed = *Erythrura psittacea*, Gmelin 1789, Red-throated parrot-finch. [5488 Loxia psittacea, m. and fem. Sandwich Island-rare, Thompson £1.12.0.] A specimen from New Caledonia was collected September 1774, two syntypes of which are currently in the Liverpool Museum, from Lord Stanley's collection (Largen 1987, p. 286). [LM 4270 Parrot-billed grosbeak Loxia Psittacea-very rare, Fichtel £1.12.0.] The unnamed

black and yellow bird is probably *Euplectes* sp.

13. Pair of Great crested grebes with one striped young = *Podiceps cristatus* (Linnaeus 1758), Great crested grebe. [LM 875 Crested grebe, Colymbus cristatus; gentle falcon-two cases, Donovan £1.12.0; 1833 Crested grebe, m. and fem., Colymbus cristatus, Sivers 5/6; 5371 Crested grebe, Colymbus cristatus, (without case) Donovan £1.3.0; 5723 Knot bird, and young of the great crested grebe; Appendix 210 Great crested grebe young, sold with 2 yellow-breasted larks, Kirkpatrick 10/6]

14. Bustard? Possibly = *Eupodotis humilis* (Blyth 1856) Little brown bustard.

15. *Bucco calcaratus Sarah Stone 1781* Drawing of *Monasa atra* (Boddaert 1783), Black nunbird.

16. Two unnamed birds. Pencil: *Black sparrow Duchis of Portland's* = *Sporophila luctuosa*, Lafresnaye 1843, Black-and-white seed-eater, and ? immature *Piranga rubra* (Linnaeus 1758), Summer tanager.

17. *Lanius Sarah Stone 1781* = *Lanius tigrinus*, Dapriez 1828, Tiger shrike.

18. *Ampelis Pompadora Pompadour chatterer* = *Xipholena punicea* (Pallas 1764), Pompadour cotinga. [LM 199 Ampelis Pompadora, Pompadour chatterer, Zennetty 8/-; 5398 Ampelis pompadora m & f Thompson bought £3.3.0.]

19. *Paradisea Sexsetacea – avis incomplete Sarah Stone*
Painting of *Parotia lawesii exhibita*, Iredale 1948, Six-wired bird of paradise, with the six wire-like plumes growing from the sides of the head missing.

20. *King bird of paradise Paradisea regia* = *Cicinnurus regius* (Linnaeus 1758). [LM 4412 King bird of

Paradise, Paradisea regia, very fine and rare, without case, Vaughan £5.7.6.] Latham (*Gen. Syn.* I, p. 475) said that the "Dutch call it King Bird, and get it from Banda to which place it is brought by the natives of the islands where it is found" (in New Guinea and Papua).

21. *Psittacus accipitrinus Sarah Stone* = *Deroptyus a. accipitrinus* (Linnaeus 1758), Red fan parrot. [LM 5749 Hawk-headed parrot, rare]

22. *Sylvia S Stone* accompanied by a nest. Unidentified.

23. *Sylvia superba Sarah Stone 1782* = *Malurus cyaneus*, Ellis 1782, Superb blue wren (not in full breeding plumage). [LM 1032 Superb warbler, Botany Bay, Sylvia superba, Vaughan 9/-; 2224 Silvia superba Botany Bay Stanley 16-0 (Largen 1987, p. 276; Sarah's drawing now identifies this species); 2767 Superb warbler, male, New Holland, Silvia superba (crossed out in the auctioneer's catalogue as having been listed twice); 3288 silvia superba, New Holland, Kirkpatrick 6/6]

24. *Emberiza vidua* = *Vidua macroura*, Linnaeus 1758, Pin-tailed whydah. [LM 6061 Pin-tailed whydah]

25. *Psittacus – lory Sarah Stone* = *Lorius lory* (Linnaeus 1758), Black-capped lory. [LM 4514 Purple capped lory, 'East indies, Psittacus domicella, Carrudes £1.0.0.]

26. *Falco Sarah Stone January 27 1778* = *Falco peregrinus*, Tunstall 1771, Peregrine falcon. [LM 3135 Peregrine falcon, Rev.Mr Vaughan £1.12.0; Last day but one 41 Falco peregrinus, Peregrine falcon.]

27. *Falco Nissus* = *Accipiter nisus* (Linnaeus 1758), Sparrowhawk. [LM 5116

Sparrow hawk, 13/6; 5617
Sparrow hawk, hen, Sivers 11/-;
Last day but two 32 Sparrow
hawk, m. and fem. and young,
Falco nisus, Linn.; Last day 24
Sparrow hawk, Falco nisus,
Linn. and green parrot,
S.America]

28. *Sylvia Sarah Stone 30*
= *Dacnis cayana*, Linnaeus 1766,
Blue dacnis (female).

29. *Sarah Stone*
A juvenile Auk, an insect, and a
Scarlet-crested cockatoo
= *Cacatua moluccensis*, Gmelin
1788. This was a very similar
drawing to no. 30.

30. *Psittacus rosaceus Sarah Stone 1788*
= *Cacatua moluccensis*, Gmelin
1788, Salmon-crested cockatoo.

31. Two parrots:
Sarah Stone Feb 19 – 1779
Psitt. Pacificus
= *Cyanoramphus n. novaezelandiae*
(Sparrman 1787). Pacific
parrakeet of Latham's *Gen. Syn.*
I, p. 252 is LM 3510 Red
fronted parroquet, S. Seas,
Fichtel 15/-, the type of
Gmelin's *Psittacus pacificus*. [LM
4246 Pacific parrot, Psittacus
pacificus, Fichtel 6/6 (Pelzehn
(1873, pp. 30–31); 6041 Psittacus
pacificus, South Seas; 6586
Pacific parrot, var., Sir Henry
Martin 8/6]
Psitt Cy ... Aratinga leuteo sive
Guarouba Spix = *Aratinga guarouba*
(*the Brazilian yellow parrot Latham*)
= *Aratinga solstitialis* (Linnaeus
1758), Sun conure. [LM 4256
Angola yellow parrot Psittacus
solstitialis, very fine and rare,
Dr Shaw £1.6.0.]

32. *Sarah Stone 1780*
= *Ptilonopus purpuratus* (Gmelin
1789), Grey-green fruit dove,
probably the nominate species
from Tahiti. [?LM 6094
Beautiful grey and green dove,
S. Seas]

33. *Columba nicobarica Sarah Stone*
= *Caloenas nicobarica* (Linnaeus
1758), Nicobar pigeon. [LM
5400 A most beautiful specimen

of the Nicobar pigeon Columba
nicobarica. Laskey £6-12-6; 4828
A most beautiful specimen of
the Columba nicobarica, very
rare, Fichtel £5.2.6 (still in the
Vienna Museum in 1873
(Pelzehn 1873, p. 35)); Last day
but two 25 Nicobar pigeon,
Columba nicobarica, Vaughan
£4.15.0; Last day 29 (entered
twice so deleted)]

34. *Smooth-billed toucan Ramphastos*
glaber(?) Sarah Stone 1782
= *Pteroglossus viridis* (Linnaeus
1766), Green aracari. [LM 4097
Rhamphastos laevirostris,
smooth-billed toucan,
Thompson 5/6]

35. Two parrots:
Psitt: garrulus var ju[?]
= *Lorius garrulus* (Linnaeus
1758), Chattering lory.
Psitt: chrysopterus Sarah Stone Feb 22
– 1779
= *Brotogeris chrysopterus* (Linnaeus
1766), Golden-winged parakeet.
[LM 2761 Parroquet
Brazils,Thompson 16-0 (Largen
1987, pp. 282-83)]

36. *Psitt: purpuratus? Sarah Stone*
1781
= *Touit purpurata* (Gmelin 1788),
Sapphire-rumped parrotlet.
Pelzehn (1873, p. 32) reported
that the *Psittacula purpurata*
(Gmelin), Purple-tailed
parakeet (Latham, *Gen. Syn.* I,
p. 312), bought by Fichtel [5377
Psittacus porphyrurus, 9/6],
was no longer in the Vienna
Museum. [LM 6198 Small
purple rumped lory, E. Indies,
Laskey £1.11.6.]

37. *Perdix cineracea nov. Sarah Stone*
1783
= *Perdix perdix* (Linnaeus 1758),
Partridge. [LM 733 Green
Shanks, Widgeon female,
common starling m & f,
common Partridge, – four cases,
£1.1.0; 4629 The common
partridge, m. fem. and seventeen
young most beautifully
preserved, Harrison £6.6.0; 4925
Partridge, m. and f., Bostock

£1.4.0; 5118 Common partridge
var. Thompson 10-6; 5900
Young of the common
partridge; 5904 Variety of the
common partridge]

38. *Ampelis/Carnifex [Linn] Red*
chatterer Sarah Stone 1781
= *Phoenicircus nigricollis*, Swainson
1832, Guianan red cotinga. [LM
4501 Red chatterer, Ampelis
carnifex, both sexes, Vaughan
£1.4.0.]

39. Two parrots with one
unidentifiable butterfly:
Psitt: Sonneratii? Psitt: Alexandri var
V. Ginginianus
= *Psittacula eupatria* (Linnaeus
1758), Alexandrine parakeet,
and *Psittacula krameri* (Scopoli
1769), Rose-ringed parakeet, or
another Alexandrine parakeet.
[LM seven lots had an
Alexandrine parakeet (see
no. 4)]

40. *Alcedo sacra*
Drawing of the Tongan
subspecies of *Halcyon chloris sacra*
(Gmelin 1788), Mangrove
kingfisher. [LM 5612 Alcedo
sacra m & f Thompson £1 (this
is a specimen of *Halcyon tuta*
(Gmelin 1788) in the Liverpool
Museum (Largen 1987, p. 286));
sp. uncertain for LM [2778
Sacred kingfisher, Alcedo sacra,
from New Holland, Sivers 8/6;
6590 Alcedo sacra, Fenton 5/-]

41. *Psitt: Papuensis Papuan lory Sarah*
Stone
= *Charmosyna papou* (Scopoli
1786), Papuan lory.

42. *Sarah Stone 1781*
Todus nasutus (Latham),
Great-billed tody
= *Cymbirhynchus m. macrorhynchos*
(Gmelin 1788), Black and red
broadbill from Borneo. [LM
3400 Great billed tody, *Todus*
nasutus, extremely rare, Fichtel
£2.17.0. (Pelzehn (1873, p. 19)
mentioned Latham's type
specimen of the Great billed
tody as being in the Vienna
Museum collection)]

43. *Angola vulture Sarah Stone Feb 27th*

1777
= *Gypohierax angolensis* (Gmelin
1788), Palmnut vulture. Pelzehn
(1873, p. 106), reporting on
specimens bought by Fichtel in
the LM sale, stated that
according to Latham this bird
was described by Pennant from
the fine collection of birds at
Bryn y Pys, the seat of Richard
Parry Price, Esq.. There were
two of them, which came from
Angola. They were, he said,
"very restless and querulous,
and more active than is usual
with this sluggish race". They
were later "finely preserved in
the Leverian Museum". Pelzehn
goes on to say, "Our individual
agrees pretty well with Latham's
and Shaw's description and
figure; but the great remiges are
white, as represented in Shaw's
plate, and not black tipped with
white, as erroneously described
by Latham and Shaw". Sarah
got the remiges (primary and
secondary flight feathers)
correct. [LM 2059 Falco
angolensis, a very fine specimen
and rare, Vaughan £3.13.6.]

44. *Certhia coccinea juv avis Red creeper*
Sarah Stone 1780
= *Vestiaria coccinea* (Forster 1780),
Hawaiian honeycreeper, I'iwi.
There was a specimen in the
BM (Natural History) in 1969,
donated at an earlier date by the
Royal College of Surgeons
(Whitehead, p. 195). [LM 3070
Certhia vestiaria, very rare, m.
and fem. Sandwich islands,
Latham £1.17.0; Last day 33 Red
certhia, Sandwich islands,
Certhia vestiaria]
Crested oriole Gen Syn 2. p. 421
Oriolus maximus La Sarah Stone
1778
= *Psarocolius decumanus* (Pallas
1769), Crested oropendola. [LM
3922 Oriolus cristatus, crested
oriole, m. and f. Sivers 15/-;
4089 Oriolus cristatus, crested
oriole, Cayenne, Vaughan 6/6]

45. *Turdus roseus Rose color'd Ouzel or*

Thrush Sarah Stone 1780
= *Sturnus roseus* (Linnaeus 1758),
Rose-coloured starling. [LM
3916 Rose coloured ouzell,
turdus roseus, extremely rare,
£3.3.0.]

46. *Picus: an viridis?*
= *Picus viridis*, Linnaeus 1758,
Green woodpecker.

47. Two pairs of parrots on one
sheet:
Sarah Stone Feb 11 1779
Psitt: galgulus [Linn]
= *Loriculus galgulus* (Linnaeus
1758), Blue-crowned hanging
parrot. [LM 6070 Sapphire-
crowned parroquet, Psittacus
galgulus, very fine and rare, m.
and f.]
Psitt: canus [Gm]
= *Agapornis cana* (Gmelin 1788),
Grey-headed lovebird. [LM
2679 Gray-headed parrot, E.
Indies, m. and fem. Vaughan
£1.5.0.]

48. *Psittacus Macar L Sarah Stone 1780*
= *Ara macao* (Linnaeus 1758),
Scarlet macaw. [LM 4067
Scarlet and blue macaw,
Vaughan 17/-; 4510 Red and
blue macaw. Psittacus macao,
Bostock £1.11.0.]

49. *Psittacus asiaticus See Edwards 1,
pl. 6.*
= *Loriculus beryllinus* (J.R.Forster
1781), Ceylon hanging parrot.
[LM 4254 The red-faced
parrotlet, the [Indian] roller
and another rare bird, W
Comyns 4/6]

50. *Coracias Bengal roller Sarah Stone
1782*
= *Coracias benghalensis indica*
(Linnaeus 1766), Indian roller.
[LM 4254 A most beautiful
specimen of the Indian roller,
Coracias Indica, Brogden
£4.13.0; Appendix 203 The red-
faced parrotlet, the [Indian]
roller and another rare bird, W
Comyns 4/6]

51. *Upupa superba Grand promerops
Sarah Stone 1782*
= *Epimachus fastuosus* (Hermann
1783), Black sicklebill.

52. *Scolopax Helius Paon des Roses
Caurale Snipe. In the collection of
Ashton Lever Esquire*
= *Eurypyga helias* (Pallas 1781),
Sunbittern. It inhabits Guiana,
where the inhabitants give it
the name of the "Paon des
Roses" (Leroy de Barde 1814, p.
11, no. 20). [LM 6029 Scolopax
Cauralia, South America, rare,
£3.3.0.]
On reverse: Nine eggs labelled:
*Hobby, Bittern Honey Buzzard,
Sparrow Hawk, Guillemot, Heron,
Stannel* (= Kestrel), *Razor Bill,
Buzzard*. Several lots of eggs
were sold in 1806 (lots 5176,
5178, 5182, 5183, 5426–32). The
group painted by Sarah Stone
was not sold as a composite lot
in that sale.

53. Composite picture of four birds
of prey: Red kite, Peregrine
falcon, Hobby and Buzzard
Red kite = *Milvus milvus*
(Linnaeus 1758). [LM 4504
Common kite, Donovan £1.0.0;
4623 The common kite, Sivers
£1.6.0.]
Peregrine = *Falco peregrinus* (see
no. 26).
Hobby = *Falco subbuteo*,
Linnaeus 1758. [LM 4245
Hobby, Falco Subbuteo, Sivers
12/6; 4630 Hobby, m. fem. and
young, Falco subbuteo
Donovan £2.8.0; 5817 Hobby
hawk and stannel hawk]
Buzzard = *Buteo buteo* (see no.
8).

54. Ten hummingbirds in pairs but
numbered 1-10 on the drawing,
listed in faint pencil, some
rubbed out:
Phaethornis minimus, Least h-b
(numbered 2, 3), (Latham II, p.
788)
= *Mellisuga minima* (Linnaeus
1758), Vervain hummingbird.
*Phaethornis maculata Patch'd necked
hummingbird* (numbered 4, 5, 6),
(Latham supplement I, 1787,
p.135). Latham said of the
Patch-necked hummingbird
that it was the size of the Red-

throated hummingbird and he
had described it "from the
drawings of Sir Ashton Lever".
Since Sarah made the drawings
for Lever, the description in
Latham in all probability was
taken from this drawing.
Ruby Topaz (numbered 7, 8) =
Chrysolampis mosquitus (Linnaeus
1758), Ruby-topaz
hummingbird.
Fork-tailed (numbered 1, 9, 10) =
Thalurania furcata (Gmelin 1788),
Fork-tailed woodnymph.

55. Composite picture of ten
hummingbirds, with faint
pencil notes
(1), (2). *Trochilus colubris Linn
Red-throated HB Latham Syn II, p.
769*
= *Archilochus colubris* (Linnaeus
1758), Ruby-throated
hummingbird.
(3). *Trochilus aurita Linn Violet-eared
HB Latham Syn II, p. 767?*
= *Heliothryx auritus* (Gmelin
1788), Black eared fairy.
(4), (6). *Trochilus ourissia Linn Green
& Blue HB Latham Syn II, p. 766*
= *Chlorostilbon maugaeus*
(Linnaeus 1758), Puerto Rican
emerald.
(5). *Trochilus cristatus Linn, Latham Syn
II p. 783*
= *Orthorhynchus c. cristatus*
(Linnaeus 1758), Antillean
crested hummingbird, with
nest. [LM 6161 A fine specimen
of trochilus cristatus, or crested
humming bird on the nest; 5133
A fine specimen of the crested
humming bird, on the nest.
Fenton £3.14.0.]
(7). *Trochilus polytmus Linn Black-
capped B Latham II, p. 748*
= *Trochilus polytmus* (Linnaeus
1758), Streamertail. [LM 6355
Trochilus polytmus]
(8). *Trochilus pella Linn Topaz HB
Latham II, p. 746*
= *Topaza pella* (Linnaeus 1758),
Crimson topaz.
(9). = *Nectarinia violacea* (Linnaeus
1766), Orange-breasted sunbird.
(10). = *Nectarinia afra* (Linnaeus

1766), Greater double-collared
sunbird.

56. Composite painting of a
peacock, black-capped lory,
crane, small finch, sunbird, and
an eagle.
Peacock = *Pavo cristatus*,
Linnaeus 1758. [LM 4070 A
beautiful specimen of a
peacock, Donovan 18/6 (and
note that the auctioneer crossed
out the words in this lot, "A
large case containing"; 4835 A
fine specimen of the peacock
(without case), £2.2.0; 5139 A
capital specimen of the peacock
and peahen, £1.1.0.] In the sale
catalogue of the Donovan
Museum, 1818, Lot 293 Crested
peacock Pavo cristatus. Both
sexes in large glazed case: finest
of the Leverian Gallery.
Black-capped lory Psitt:
domicella = *Lorius domicellus*
(Linnaeus 1758), Purple-naped
lory. [LM 4514 Purple-capped
lory, East Indies, Psittacus
domicella, Carrudes, £1.0.0.]
Crane = *Anthropoides virgo*
(Linnaeus 1758), Demoiselle
crane. [LM Last day but one 45
Demoiselle crane, Ardea virgo]
A small finch, unidentified
Sunbird = *Aethopyga nipalensis*
(Hodgson 1837), Green-tailed
sunbird.
Eagle = *Aquila chrysaetos*
(Linnaeus 1758), Golden eagle.
[LM Last day but two 26
Golden eagle Falco chrysaetos]

57. Two Swallowtail butterflies =
Papilio ulysses (Linnaeus 1758).
[LM 4475 Papilio ulysses, in
fine condition, very rare Milne
£1.17.0; Papilio ulysses, fine and
rare, one specimen, Last day
82]
Two Birdwing butterflies =
Ornithoptera priamus (Linnaeus
1758). [LM Last day 87 Papilio
priamus, East Indies, very rare
and in fine condition]
Two Owlet moths *Thysania* sp.

58. Ten anemones and two
octopuses.

59. Coral (unidentified) and Tamandua = *Tamandua ?mexicana* (Bechstein 1800), Collared anteater.

60. Pangolin sp. = *Manis* sp. [LM Last day but two 47 Long-tailed pangolin, *Manis tetradactyla,* very rare; and Last day but one 68 a Five-toed pangolin *Manis pentadactyla*] Shell and shell cluster = brachiopods?

61. Ant-eater, giant = *Myrmecophaga tridactyla,* Linnaeus 1758. [LM Sale 1806 Lot 2300 An extremely large and fine

specimen of the great ant-eater, south America, Myrmecophaga jubata, bought Fichtel £12]

62. Goat (with white patch on its back) = *Ovis orientalis* (Linnaeus 1758).

63. Small deer = ?*Sylvicapra grimmia,* Common duiker (Ogilby, 1837). [LM 1347 Moschus grimia, very rare, Fichtel 5/-; 5473 A beautiful specimen of Moschus Grimmia, very rare, bought in £2.2.0]

Sarah Stone watercolours in a folio of Thomas Davies watercolours

p. 125 *Mundie Sarah Stone 1784* Mineral specimen, fluorite showing a high proportion of twinned crystals. Carboniferous plant fossil *Pterodosperm ?neruoptis* sp. from Coal Measures period.
Long spiked oyster from E. Indies = *Spondylus,* Thorn oyster.
Fools cap from ditto in the collection of Ashton Lever Esq. (The above two are unsigned but have inscriptions in Sarah's

handwriting.)

p. 126 Fossils, seven fishes and, on the reverse, two leafbugs, unsigned, that may be by Sarah Stone

p. 127 *Sarah Stone 1783* Hydroid – Plumularian type? *Sarah Stone 1783* Hydrocoralline coral or Hydroid growing on a shell with Arc Shells or Pteriid oyster attached (not British).

p. 129. *Sarah Stone 1783* [Two sheets] Sertularian Hydroid, Gorgonian precious coral.

PRIVATE COLLECTION C, AUSTRALIA

Thirty-one watercolours associated with the plates in John White's *Journal of a Voyage to New South Wales* (London 1790). Twenty-five of the images face the same way as the corresponding plate; six face the opposite way. All are painted on the sized paper, of approximately the same size as the watercolours in the National Library of Australia's complementary set of watercolours for the same title (see p. 131). Ruled pencil borders outline an area of 23 × 17 cm. Seven of the watercolours have associated plates with no attribution printed in the captions. Four watercolours have three associated plates with *C. Catton delin* printed on the plate. Two of the watercolours are signed *Sarah Smith* and one other *S Smith*.

If this were the set of watercolours on which the engravings were based, nos. 4, 22, 25, and 28 ought to be original watercolours by Charles Catton for the corresponding engraved plates 61, 54 and 59. However, all the watercolours appear to be by the same hand, and that of the Hepoona Roo (pl. 61) with its tail curled upwards, bears the signature *S. Smith*. Pl. 61

in the book is captioned *C. Catton junr delin* and the watercolour of the same animal in the Australian National Library, and on the corresponding plate, has the tail curled downwards. The existence of two drawings for the same mammal confirms the suspicion that this was such an important collection of skins that more than one set of drawings was made from it. Catton's drawing of this mammal was either done first, or preferred, for the engraver to copy.

For notes on the corresponding specimens in the Leverian Museum, see *Sarah Stone's Book Illustrations,* p. 139.

The watercolours are listed here in the order in which they appear in the private collection, with a reference to the corresponding plate no. in John White's *Journal of a Voyage to New South Wales.* The watercolour and plate images face the same way unless indicated otherwise. The three watercolours bearing Sarah's signature are indicated in italics.

1. *Sarah Smith* Anomalous hornbill (pl. 5)
2. Cyprinaceous labrus and Hippocampus (pl. 50)
3. *Sarah Smith* Knob-fronted bee-eater (pl. 16)

4. *S Smith* Hepoona Roo (pl. 61; *C. Catton Junr delin,* the plate and watercolour face the same way, and in the opposite direction to Sarah's)

5. New Holland creeper (pl. 65)
6. Variegated lizard (pl. 38; the watercolour image faces the opposite way to that of the engraving)
7. New Holland cassowary (pl. 1)

8. Doubtful lophius (pl. 51)
9. Blue frog (pl. 33)
10. Tapoa tafa (pl. 58)
11. Insects of New South Wales (pl. 47)
12. Scinc-formed lizard (pl. 30; has

no signature on the plate)

13. Atherine, Tobacco-pipe fish, Remora fish (pl. 64)
14. Yellow-eared flycatcher (pl. 10)
15. Golden-winged pigeon (pl. 8; has no signature on the plate)
16. White fulica (pl. 27)
17. Wattled bee-eater (pl. 6)
18. Small paraquet (pl. 48)
19. New Holland creeper male (pl. 15; has no signature on the plate)
20. Snake (pl. 43)
21. Snakes no. 1 and 2 (pl. 46)
22. Kangaroo (pl. 54; with C. Catton's signature on the plate (see also no. 25)) Watercolours nos. 22 and 25 (kangaroo) were the bases for pl. 54 but show differences: no. 22 shows a pouch, and sexual feature omitted on pl. 54.
23. White hawk (pl. 35)
24. Fuliginous petrel (pl. 37)
25. A kangaroo (pl. 54; *C. Catton* (see also no. 22))
26. Wattled bee-eater, female (pl. 7; the image on the watercolour and plate face in opposite directions)
27. Poto roo or Kangaroo rat (pl. 60; the image on the watercolour and plate face in opposite directions)
28. Spotted tapoa tafa (pl. 59; the image on the watercolour and plate face in opposite directions)
29. Port Jackson thrush (pl. 9)
30. White-vented crow (pl. 36; the image on the watercolour and plate face in opposite directions)
31. Muricated lizard (pl. 40)

PRIVATE COLLECTION D

Paul Mellon Collection, Upperville, Virginia, USA

A scarlet ibis, *Eudocimus ruber* (Linnaeus 1758), watercolour heightened with white 37 × 26.5 cm, signed *Sarah Stone*. Sold Sotheby's, London 1962 to P. & D. Colnaghi, who sold it to Paul Mellon.

Watercolours by Sarah Stone in Auction Sales

WATERCOLOURS

Sarah Stone's watercolours have passed through the sale rooms, in the UK, the USA and Australia. The watercolours listed below were registered in E. Mayer, *International Auction Records*, 1969–, and in *Art Sales Index*, 1972–.

This list does not include the private sales by dealers.
The size of each painting is given in cm.

1995 Bird perched on a branch, watercolour 32 × 24. Sotheby's Melbourne 21 August 1995, lot 149, £1,691.

1995 Spoonbill – sold with copies of Latham's books in the Fattorini sale, Christie's, London, 25 October 1995, lot 21, illustrated. Original watercolour, s & d 21 Sept. 1777.

1994 Eastern rosella of New South Wales, watercolour 36 × 27. Sotheby's, Melbourne, 19 April 1994, £9,709.

1992 A pink flamingo, watercolour 35.8 × 25.1. Christie's, London, £1,210.

1991 Variety lark, Blue grosbeak, pair of watercolours 36 x 25, one signed, one dated 1795. Youngs Fine Art Gallery, Maine, USA, Oil Paintings and Watercolours, 23 November 1991, lot 279, illustrated, £689.

1991 A Little blue heron, watercolour 40.3 × 29.2, s & d 1782. Christie's, London, 12 November 1991, lot 49, illustrated, £1,200.

1991 A pink flamingo, pencil and watercolour 36 × 25. Christie's, London, 12 November 1991, lot 47, illustrated, £1,100.

1991 A Crowned crane, watercolour 38 × 27, s & d 1783. Christie's, London,12 November 1991, lot 50, illustrated, £1,100.

1991 Night heron, watercolour 38 × 28, s & d 1782. Christie's,

London, 12 November 1991, lot 48 illustrated, £1,100.

1989 Red-billed tropic bird, watercolour 41.9 × 31.8, s & d 1785. Christie's, London, 22 March 1989, lot 27, illustrated, £1,100.

1988 An album of 175 watercolours of birds, by Sarah Stone, fifteen signed, majority 25 × 35, Sotheby's, London, 2 November 1988, lot 77, illustrated, unsold.

1987 Studies of exotic birds and an insect, watercolour 37 × 35, s & d 1779. Bonham's, London, 1 July 1987, lot 3, illustrated, £600.

1987 A portfolio of watercolours of beetles and other insects, fourteen sheets, 27 × 37.5 (13); 21 × 14 (1); six signed, five dated 1777 or 1778, twelve inscribed. Bearne's, Torquay, 20 May 1987, lot 80, illustrated.

1987 A portfolio of studies of butterflies, seven sheets 26.5 × 37.5, four signed, three dated 1778, five inscribed. Bearne's, Torquay, 20 May 1987, lot 81, illustrated.

1985 Rose-coloured tropical bird, watercolour 41 × 31. Sotheby's, London, 14 March 1985, lot 33, illustrated; also a pair (of a Purple-backed toerako, and Rainbow lorikeet with a Goldfinch) watercolour and ink, by John Collet, £520.

1982 Tropical birds, a pair,

watercolour over pencil 41.5 × 32 and 39.5 × 29, s & d 1785. Sotheby's, London, July 1982, £400.

1981 Portrait of Charles I, watercolour 103 × 84. Sotheby's, London, 9 December 1981, £1,300.

1979 Butterflies and moths, watercolour 35 × 48. Sotheby's, London, 19 July 1979, lot 131, £400.

1979 Butterflies and moths, watercolour 35 × 48. Sotheby's, London, 19 July 1979, lot 130, £450.

1977 Parrots and a butterfly, and Three parrots in a tree, pair of watercolours 24 × 36.8, s & d 1779. Sotheby's, London, 7 July 1977, £500.

1977 Two parrots and butterfly, watercolour 24 × 37, s & d, 24 February 1779. Sotheby's, London.

1977 Butterflies, watercolour 38 × 46. Bonham's, Glasgow, 14 September 1977, lot 845, £240.

1977 Sea bird, watercolour 36 × 25. Bonham's, Glasgow, 14 September 1977, lot 849, £320.

1977 Hermit crab, watercolour 13 × 10. Bonham's, Glasgow, 14 September 1977, lot 851, £400.

1977 Spoonbill, watercolour 36 × 23, Bonham's, Glasgow, 14 September 1977, lot 847, £450.

1977 Secretary bird, watercolour 31 × 23. Bonham's, Glasgow, 14 September 1977, lot 846, £450.

1977 Seven butterflies, watercolour 20 × 25. Bonham's, Glasgow, 14 September 1977, lot 848, £520.

1977 A pair of tropical birds, watercolour 35.5 × 23. Bonham's, Glasgow, 14 September 1977, lot 850.

1968 Bufflehead drake, Dodo, Dotterel, King eiderduck, Lark, Woodcock, watercolours. Sotheby's, New York, cat. 2688, April 1968, of which:

Woodcock, 28.3 × 30, lot 159, $275.

King eider drake, 24 × 34.2, lot 159, $350.

1962 A giraffe led by a Negro page, watercolour 48.3 × 3. Sotheby's, London, 14 March 1962, lot 34, £260.

1962 A red parrot, watercolour 44.5 × 34.3, s & d 1786. Sotheby's, London, 14 March 1962, lot 34, £110.

1962 A Scarlet ibis, watercolour 37 × 26.5. Sotheby's, London, 14 March 1962, lot 36, £120.

1962 A Cock of the rock with a Blue humming-bird, watercolour 24.5 × 36.5, s & d 3 March 1779. Sotheby's, London 14 March 1962, lot 37, £130.

1962 A Peahen, watercolour 43.5 × 30.5. Sotheby's, London, 14 March 1962, lot 38, £60.

1962 Tanagra rubra; Loxia capensis, a pair of watercolours 43.5 × 31, s & d 1785. Sotheby's, London, lot 39, £120.

The birds are listed in alphabetical order, with the present scientific name and [LM sale 1806 references].

Bufflehead drake = *Bucephala albeola* (Linnaeus 1758). [LM 5801 Buffalo-headed duck].

Cock of the rock (probably = *Rupicola rupicola* (Linnaeus 1766)).

Crane, crowned = *Balearica pavonina* (Linnaeus 1758). [LM 1406 Crowned African crane, Ardea Pavonina, one specimen, without case, Jackson £3.11.0; 5280 Ardea pavonina, in very fine preservation £4.4.0.]

Dodo = *Raphus cucullatus* (extinct *ca*.1680). [LM 1575 A framed and glazed drawing of the Dodo, 5/-]

Dotterel = *Eurodromus morinellus* (Linnaeus 1758). [LM 316 Dottrel, sparrow and starling variety, Smith 13/-; 371 Dottrell, one of four birds, each in its own case, Smith 13/-; 1102 Dottrel, one of three birds, each in its own case, £1.13.0; 1501 Dottrell, and goldfinch, m. and fem. Hall 8/6; 1751 Dottrel, m. and fem. and ring turtle dove,m. and fem. Laskey 10/6; 2429 Dottrel, and marten, m. and fem. – two cases, Kirkpatrick 10/6; 4825 Dottrel, m. and fem. Donovan £1.4.0.]

Eider, king = *Somateria spectabilis* (Linnaeus 1758). [LM 51 Anas spectabilis, king duck, America, Latham £3.3.0.]

Flamingo = *Phoenicopterus ruber* Linnaeus 1758. [LM377 Red flamingo, Phoenicopterus ruber, Jamaica, 4/-; 2053 A most beautiful specimen of the flamingo, Phoenicopterus ruber, with red and white variegations, Butt £4.5.0; Last day but one 60 Flamingo, a singularly fine and high coloured specimen, Phoenicopterus ruber, Laskey £12]

Grosbeak, blue = *Passerina caerulea* (Linnaeus 1758). [LM 5375 Loxia caerulia, Blackman 7/6; 5494 Loxia caerulea m. and f. Thompson £1.5.0 (listed by Largen 1987, p. 284); 6036 Blue grosbeak, America: m. and fem.; 3396 Blue grosbeak, S. America, Loxia coerulea, var. B. cyanea.5/-]

Heron, little blue = *Egretta caerulea* (Linnaeus 1758). [LM 6195 Ardea caerulea, small black heron, Fichtel] No longer in the Vienna Museum (Pelzehn 1873, p. 38).

Heron, night = *Nycticorax nycticorax* (Linnaeus 1758). Latham mentioned one in the LM, shot not many miles from London in May 1782. Sarah drew this species in 1782, probably shortly after it was deposited in the LM. Also known as a Night raven in the eighteenth century. [LM 739 Falco ossifragus, and a Night Raven, Ardea Nycticorax, Donovan £2.3.0; 202 Night heron, Ardea nycticorax, Laskey 31/6; 372 Night heron – Ardea Nycticorax, Donovan 39/-]

Ibis, scarlet = *Eudocimus ruber* (Linnaeus 1758). [LM 417 Scarlet ibis – Tantalus ruber, Jennings 25/; 4079 Scarlet ibis, Tantalus ruber Smith £2.2.0; 4493 Scarlet ibis, Tantalus ruber, a fine specimen, without case, Sivers £1.2.0; 4837 A capital specimen of the scarlet ibis, Tantalus ibis, Triphook £2.10.0.]

Lark (variety unknown).

Loxia capensis = *Euplectes capensis* (Linnaeus 1766). [LM4084 Cape grosbeak, Loxia capensis, both sexes, Ld S,Thompson 14/-] No longer in the Liverpool Museum (Largen 1987, pp. 282-83).

Peahen = *Pavo cristatus* Linnaeus 1758. [LM 5139 A capital specimen of the peacock and peahen, Donovan £1.1.0.] or perhaps lot 2310 A fine and curious specimen of the pea-hen, which in its eleventh year put forth the plumage of the male bird] It cost £3. 3s. od., and Bullock stated in the catalogue of his sale in 1818 (lot 372) that "It was bred by Lady Tyne, and presented to Sir Ashton Lever".

Rosella, eastern, New South Wales, *Platycercus eximius* (Shaw 1792). [LM 44 Rose-hill Parrot, Botany Bay, Psittacus eximius, Monsado £1.2.0.; 4823 Rose-hill parrot Psittacus eximius, Thompson 8/6. This bird was collected at Rose-hill, Botany Bay]

Secretary bird = *Sagittarius serpentarius* Latham 1790. [LM Last day but two 31 Secretary vulture Vultur Secretarius, one specimen without case. Laskey £3.10.0; Last day 31 Secretary vulture, £1.11.6.]

Spoonbill = *Platalea leucorodia* Linnaeus 1758. [LM 4273 White spoonbill, Platalea leucorodia, Vaughan £2.2.0; 4744 White spoonbill, Platalea leucorodia, Sivers £1.1.0.]

Tanagra rubra (sp. uncertain).

Tropic-bird, red-billed = *Phaethon aethereus* (Linnaeus 1758). [LM 1396 Tropic bird Phaeton aetherius, Fichtel £1.19.0. In the Vienna Museum (Pelzehn 1873, p. 52)].

Tropical bird, rose-coloured (unknown).

Tropical birds (unknown).

Woodcock = *Scolopax rusticola* Linnaeus 1758. [LM 636 Goldfinch m. & f., Merops apiaster, Woodcocks, young, two specimens, Pit-wren, four specimens – four cases, 11/-; 1497 Young woodcocks, with next and egg, taken at Marston, the seat of the Earl of Corke, near Froome, Dr Latham 15/6; 2307 Gray plover, and woodcock – two cases, Kirkpatrick £1.1.0; 4257 Common woodcock, m. and fem. Kirkpatrick 17/-; 5584 Woodcock variety, Col. Thornton 10/6; 5589 Young barn owls, and woodcock, two cases, Col. Thornton £.1.2.0; 5823 Woodcock]

Hermit crab (sp. unknown). [LM 5320 Muricated lizard, banded lizard, atherine, hermit crab, and two more, Prater 5/-]

Giraffe = *Giraffa camelopardalis* E.A.W. Zimmermann 1780.

Portrait of Charles I. The only known portrait by Sarah, and painted in oils, a medium she very rarely used.

Sarah Stone's Book Illustrations

Sarah provided illustrations for three natural history books, over the period 1789–98, and hand-coloured the plates in two titles. Her illustrations were simple watercolours of the species, with little background, for they were designed to be accurate pictorial records. Great care and attention to detail of diagnostic marks, and any peculiar characteristics of the species, whether bird, mammal or reptile, was required. Sarah was obviously well qualified to undertake this work. Her connection with Sir Ashton Lever and examples of her paintings done in his museum combined to recommend her for employment by John White, Thomas Pennant and George Shaw.

Sarah's most significant contribution, not only in terms of the number of drawings but of the importance of the species she depicted, was to John White's *Journal of a Voyage to New South Wales* (1790). In this book, some of her bird, mammal and reptile drawings, on which the engraved plates were based, became the type of the species.

JOHN WHITE'S *JOURNAL OF A VOYAGE TO NEW SOUTH WALES*

Journal of a Voyage to New South Wales with Sixty-five plates of non descript Animals, Birds, Lizards, Serpents, curious Cones of Trees and other natural productions, by John White Esq., Surgeon General to the Settlement. London Printed for J. Debrett Piccadilly MDCCXC. Advertisement: "The Public may rely, with the most perfect confidence on the care and accuracy with which the Drawings have been copied from nature, by Miss Stone, Mr Catton, Mr Nodder, and other artists ... engraved by Mr Milton."

John White (1756–1832) was appointed surgeon-general to the First Fleet under Captain Arthur Phillip in 1786, and sailed for Australia in May 1787 to found a new colony.[1] The "First Fleet" consisted of two King's ships, six convict transports and three store ships with a cargo of convicts and supplies.

Before White left, his naturalist friend Thomas Wilson (died 1829) had suggested that he keep a journal,[2] and volunteered to prepare it for publication. White sent Wilson his *Journal of a Voyage to New South Wales*, recording the first ten months in the settlement Sydney Cove, near Botany Bay, nine miles north of Port Jackson ("the finest harbour in the world, in which a thousand sail ... may ride in the most perfect security"): tending the sick, overseeing the construction of a hospital, accompanying Phillip on two expeditions into the interior, and collecting specimens of flora and fauna.

One of the few pleasures in this unexpectedly bleak and barren land was the wealth of brightly coloured and totally novel birds. Many of these they thankfully caught for food, but John White had a keen interest in natural history and saw further possibilities. He collected specimens, and sent back plants, shells, bird and mammal skins, fishes and some reptiles to Wilson in England.

Although White's account of events in the new colony are of great interest, the notes accompanying the specimens were meagre. Wilson sorted the notes to some extent, and got artists to paint watercolour records of the specimens, before displaying them at Debrett's publishing premises in Piccadilly. He was a member of the Society for Promoting Natural History[3], and on 5 October 1789, exhibited "several drawings which Miss Stone has made from birds sent to England by Mr White from Botany Bay".

Recognizing that he needed expert assistance with the identification of these specimens, Wilson enlisted the help of James (later Sir James) E. Smith of the Linnaean Society (who also acted as literary administrator for White's *Journal*) for the plants, the anatomist-surgeon John Hunter for the seven mammals,[4] and George Shaw for the birds, reptiles and fishes. The scientific names of birds, reptiles and fishes that appear for the first time in White's *Journal* are alternatively attributed to Shaw or to "White, ex Shaw ms".

A Journal of a Voyage to New South Wales contained some of the earliest illustrations of Australian birds, reptiles and mammals, drawn and painted from the skins that White sent back to England. There were sixty-four plates in John White's book, seventeen of which were unsigned. Sarah signed thirty-six, and has been attributed, stylistically, with the drawing of about ten more. Others were executed by Frederick Polydore Nodder, who drew the plants; Edward Kennion (or Kenyon, 1744–1809) who only contributed one plate, the root of the yellow gum tree; Charles Catton (junior, 1756–1819), who signed three mammal plates; and Mortimer, two mammal plates. The first 128 pages of the book were taken up with the journal of the voyage and of setting up the first settlements on land, up to 11 November 1788. From page 129, the plates appeared, the first twenty-six of which had no text or scientific name attached to them. From plate xxvii onwards, a scientific name was given in most instances. In an appendix, some of the species figured are described and named for the first time.

Interest in the new colony and its natural productions was so great in Britain that Wilson obtained 120 subscribers, including book dealers who ordered multiple copies, so that over 700 copies were sold. Within a few years there was also a demand for the book to be translated into German (1792), Swedish (1793) and French (1795 and again 1798).

The plates in White's book were dated 29 December 1789 (the date by which they were engraved and ready for insertion in the text). Sarah Stone would have painted the watercolours of the thirty-six plates which bear her signature, earlier in the year.[5]

In the *Morning Post and Advertiser*, for both 26 August 1790, p. 1, and 11 November 1790, p. 1, the collection was advertised by Parkinson as being in the LM at the Rotunda: "Recently presented to the Museum, by Thomas Wilson, Esq., of Gower-street, upwards of Forty Nondescript and other Animals from Botany Bay, collected and sent over by John White, Esq., Surgeon General to the Settlement, and are figured in his Journal of a Voyage to New South Wales, lately published by Mr Debrett". Seven of the mammals, however, had been placed in John Hunter's hands for him to describe, and were incorporated in his collection (Waterhouse 1841, p. 46).

16 *Portrait of John Latham* (1740–1837), lithographed for the frontispiece to the fourth volume of *The Naturalist*, 1838–39, edited by Neville Wood

17 William Home Lizars, *Portait of Thomas Pennant*, 1833, engraving after Thomas Gainsborough's full-length oil portrait (National Museum of Wales, Cardiff) done in 1776, when Pennant was fifty years old

The *Journal* was reviewed in the *Gentleman's Magazine* in August 1790, and in the *Monthly Review* of March 1791.

The illustrations in two copies of John White's *Journal of a Voyage to New South Wales* were hand-coloured by Sarah for Thomas Wilson to give as presents. One copy has an inscription on the verso of the title-page, "This copy was presented to me by The Editor Thomas Wilson Esq. The plates were selected with great care and coloured by the hand of Miss Stone", signed D. Pitcairn. This eventually came into the G.M. Mathews collection, and is now in the National Library of Australia, Canberra. Thomas Wilson presented a copy of "Mr White's Voyage to Botany Bay with the plates coloured by Mrs Smith" at the 114th meeting of the Society for Promoting Natural History, on 25 July 1791.[6] The location of this copy is unknown.

Another copy of the *Journal* was presented by Wilson to the Linnean Society, 17 January 1792, but this copy was stolen about twenty-five years ago. Thomas Wilson of Gower Street had been elected to the Linnean Society at a meeting on 21 February 1792, and his death was reported to the society in May 1829.[7]

The following list of plates, all signed "S Stone delin", gives the number of the plate; name of species as given on the plate; and the scientific name

from the text (from pl. XXVII onwards). The modern scientific names have been assigned by Robert Prys-Jones, of The Natural History Museum, using Leslie Christidis's and Walter E. Boles's *The Taxonomy and Species of Birds of Australia and its Territories* (Royal Australian Ornithologists Union, Victoria 1994).

Thirteen original drawings attributed to Sarah (and two to Catton), bound into a volume entitled *Natural History Specimens of New South Wales copied from Nature by Sarah Stone, 1790*, are now in the National Library of Australia (see p. 128). They were watercolours corresponding to pls. ii, iii, xii (attrib.), xiii (attrib.), xxvi, xxix, xxxi, xxxii, xxxix, xli, xlii, xlix, liii. The watercolours are approximately 35 × 26 cm, with livelier and more elaborate and realistic foliage on the tree branches, and much better bird portraits and textural details for the fishes' and reptiles' skins.

Thirty-one original drawings attributed to Sarah Stone, three of which were signed by her, either *Sarah Smith* or *S. Smith*, are now in a private collection in Australia (see p. 136). These are watercolours corresponding to pls. i, v–x, xv, xvi, xxvii, xxx, xxxiii, xxxv–xxxviii, xl, xliii, xlvi–xlviii, and two watercolours for pls. liv, lviii–xi, lxiv and lxv. The watercolours are 34 × 25 cm, with greater detail than the corresponding prints.

BIRDS

2. *Great Brown King's Fisher S. Stone delin.*
= *Dacelo novaeguineae* (Hermann 1783), Laughing kookaburra. (One of the earliest names for the Kookaburra.) [LM 5370 Great brown kingfisher Alcedo fusca, Brodgen 16/-]

3. *Banksian cockatoo S. Stone delin.*
= Female *Calyptorhynchus lathami* (Temminck 1807), Glossy Black Cockatoo. [LM 1097 Banksian cockatoo, psittacus banksii, New Holland (bought by Fichtel for the Vienna Imperial Museum) £2.2.0] was a young or female genuine Banksian cockatoo, *Calyptorhynchus Banksi* (Pelzehn 1873, p. 33).

4. *Blue bellied parrot S. Stone delin.*
= *Trichoglossus haematodus* (Linnaeus 1771), Rainbow lorikeet or Blue Mountain parrot. R. J. Willis[8] said that a specimen (alive?) was taken to England and given to Marmaduke Tunstall in whose museum Peter Brown painted it for his *New Illustrations in Zoology*, the engraved plate dated 3 November 1774. Willis found a gouache on vellum, in London, of this species, signed "Moses Griffith pinxt 1772". This drawing, which predates that by Sarah, is in a private collection. [LM 4506 Blue-bellied parrot, Psittacus haematodus, Mason 13/6]

6. *Wattled bee-eater* and 7. *ditto female S. Stone delin.*
= *Anthochaera carunculata* (Shaw 1790, Red wattlebird bird, a new species "not hitherto" described. [LM 1035 Wattled bee-eater, Merops carunculatus, Botany Bay, Vaughan 9/6, and 1036, ditto the female, Constable 5/6. A specimen was present in the Vienna Imperial Museum in 1873 (Pelzehn 1873,

pp. 109–10), but the female or young were no longer in the collection.

10. *Yellow eared flycatcher S. Stone del*
= *Lichenostomus chrysops* (Latham 1801), Yellow-faced honeyeater. In his *Journal*, White wrote on 30 May 1788, "We this day caught a yellow-eared flycatcher". [LM 2769 Yellow-eared flycatcher, from New Holland, William Swainson 2/6]

13, 14. *Pennantian parrot female* (13, male, unsigned; 14 *S. Stone delin.*)
= *Platycercus elegans* (Gmelin 1788), Crimson rosella, also known in White's day as Scarlet lory. Pl. 13 was unsigned but attributed to Sarah (see Watercolours attributed to Sarah Stone, no. 13, p. 144). [LM 2776 Pennantian parrot, female from New Holland, Sivers 5/-; 4095 Pennantian parrot, both sexes, Botany Bay, Sivers 13/-]

16. *Knob fronted bee-eater S. Stone delin.*
= *Philemon corniculatus* (Latham 1790), Noisy friarbird. In White's *Journal* for 29 July 1788, he recorded, "We this day shot a Knob-fronted Bee-eater". [LM 2779 Knob-fronted bee-eater, from New Holland, Merops corniculatus, Thompson 3/6]

26. *Crested cockatoo Psittacus cristatus Linn. S. Stone delin.*
= *Cacatua galerita* (Latham 1790), Sulphur-crested cockatoo. There were plenty of these birds in England, usually imported alive. They appeared in the LM sale under various names: [LM 729 Lemon-crested cockatoo, Psittacus cristatus, with a Royston crow, two cases 6/6; 734 Orange-crested cockatoo Psittacus cristatus, Hall 11/-; 1927 Large orange-crested cockatoo,

Psittacus cristatus, 8/-; 2777 Crested cockatoo Psittacus cristatus from New Holland, Sivers 7/6; 4841 Lesser cockatoo (without case) 5/-; 4944 Lesser cockatoo, 3/6; 6833 Yellow-crested cockatoo]

27. *White fulica Fulica alba S. Stone delin.*
= *Porphyrio albus* (Shaw 1790), White gallinule. The bird was restricted to Lord Howe Island, slaughtered for food by sailors, and possibly extinct before the island was settled in 1834. Only two skins were known. One, in the LM, was drawn by Sarah. [LM 2782 White fulica, Fulica alba, New Holland, Fichtel 14/- (for the Imperial Museum, Vienna)] (Pelzehn 1873, pp. 44-45). Pelzehn sent a drawing of the Vienna specimen, "ad nat pinx" by Theodor Franz Zimmerman in 1873, to the editor of *Ibis*, who had it redrawn on a slightly larger scale when lithographed by John Gerrard Keulemans to form pl. X (*Ibis* 1873, opposite p. 295). Another illustration was made of it, in 1790, by George Raper (Smith and Wheeler 1988, pl. CLVIIIIX). A second skin, owned by Lord Derby, was purchased by him from William Bullock's museum sale in 1818. Because of its great rarity, this extinct species became the subject of other drawings (surveyed by K.A. Hindwood (1940)[9]).

28. *Southern Motacilla Motacilla Australis S. Stone delin.*
= *Eopsaltria australis* (Shaw 1790), Eastern yellow robin. [LM 2768 Motacilla Australia. The southern motacilla, from new Holland, Thompson 7/-]

29. *Crested goatsucker Caprimulgus cristatus S Stone delin.*
= *Aegotheles cristatus* (Shaw 1790),

Australian owlet-nightjar. Sarah's drawing of this species was slightly anticipated by that published in 1789 in Phillip's *Voyage to Botany Bay* (p. 270). [LM 2774 Crested goatsucker, Caprimulgus cristatus, N. Holland, Fichtel 7/- (in the Vienna Imperial Museum in 1873 (Pelzehn 1873, p. 107))]

35. *White hawk Falco albus S Stone delin.*
= *Accipiter novaehollandiae* (Gmelin 1788), Grey goshawk. [LM 2789 White hawk, Falco albus, from new Holland, Thompson £1.2.0.] Pelzehn (1873, p. 107) suggested "A specimen in white plumage is perhaps the type of White's description and plate"; Fichtel may have purchased it from Thompson after the sale.

36. *White Vented crow Corvus graculinus S Stone delin.*
= *Strepera graculina* (Shaw 1790), Pied currawong. [LM 2788 White-vented crow. Corvus graculinus, very rare, New Holland, 7/6] The bird marked *Corvus graculinus*, purchased for the Vienna Imperial Museum, was found to be in poor condition and therefore not preserved (Pelzehn 1873, p. 27).

41. *Superb warblers Motacilla superba S Stone delin.*
The two birds on this plate were different species. The top one was *Malurus cyaneus* (Latham 1783), Superb fairy wren, and the lower figure *Malurus lamberti* (Vigors and Horsfield 1827), Variegated fairy wren. [LM 2224 Silvia superba, Botany Bay ("blue-headed" written in by hand), Lord Stanley 16/- (Largen (1987, p. 276) discusses the identity of this bird, which he could not determine because Lord Stanley's specimen had been lost. Largen refers to this species as *Malurus cyaneus* (Ellis

1782)); 2767 Superb warbler, male, New Holland, *Silvia superba* (crossed out by the auctioneer as having been listed twice)] There was a specimen in the Vienna Imperial Museum in 1873 (Pelzehn 1873, p. 111); Pelzehn quoted Latham as saying it was in the LM, but Latham's own figure did not agree with Sarah's.

42. *Motacilla, a warbler Motacilla pusilla S Stone delin.*
= *Acanthiza pusilla* (Shaw 1790), Brown thornbill. [LM 2772 Brown warbler, New Holland; *Motacilla pusilla*, Smith 2/-]

48. *Small parroquet Psittacus pusillus S Stone delin.*
= *Glossopsitta pusilla* (Shaw 1790), Little lorikeet. A specimen in the Vienna Imperial Museum, implied to have been obtained in the LM sale, was listed by Pelzehn (1873, p. 117), with the comment that the Vienna bird "does not well agree with the plate in White's Journal".

49. *Red shouldered parroquet Psittacus discolor S Stone delin.*
= *Lathamus discolor* (Shaw 1790), Swift parrot, drawn from a poorly feathered specimen. Sarah's drawing was predated by the one in Phillip's *Voyage to Botany Bay* (1789, p. 269). A Viennese specimen was noted by Pelzehn (1873, p. 117) who said it differed "somewhat in coloration from the plate in White's Voyage". [LM 3277 Red-shouldered parroquet, Sivers 10/6]

65. *New Holland creeper, female S Stone delin.*
= *Phylidonyris nigra* (Bechstein 1811), White-cheeked honeyeater. [LM ?2780 New Holland creeper, Certhia nov. Hollandiae, mas. Thompson 5/6, and 2781 Ditto. fem. Thompson 7/-. Largen (1987, p. 280), discusses lot [6587 Yellow-winged creeper, New Holland] as potentially this

bird, but in the auctioneer's catalogue, reprinted in 1979, the name of Thompson against this lot is heavily scored through.

REPTILES

Sarah's signed (or attributed) paintings of the Copper-tailed skink, *Ctenoltus taeniolatus* (Shaw 1790), Leaf-tailed gecko, *Phyllurus platurus* (Shaw 1790), and Blue-tongued lizard, *Tiliqua scincoides* (Shaw 1790), represent the types of these species. The original specimens from which the drawings were made were formerly in the collections of The Natural History Museum, London, but only one, the Blue-tongued lizard, is now certainly identifiable.[10] Either the original drawings, or copies of the original drawings, are now in the National Library of Australia.

31. *Muricated lizard Lacerta muricata and snake S Stone delin.*
= *Amphibolurus muricatus* (Shaw 1790), Tree dragon, and ?barred form of young *Pseudonaja textilis* (Duméril, Bibron and Duméril 1854), Eastern brown snake. [LM 248 Lacerta muricata, two other lizards, and a fish, all in three bottles, Carfrae (an Edinburgh dealer) 2/-; 3667 A very curious and rare muricated lizard, with a spotted snake, and a fish, Fichtel 4/-; 5320 Muricated lizard, banded lizard, atherine, hermit crab, and two more, Prater 5/-]

32. Fig 1. *Ribboned lizard Lacerta taeniolata*
= *Ctenotus taeniolatus* (Shaw 1790), Copper-tailed skink.
Fig. 2. *Broad-tailed lizard Lacerta platura Sarah Stone delin.*
= *Phyllurus platurus* (Shaw 1790), Leaf-tailed gecko.

33. *Blue frogs Rana caerulea S Stone delin.*
= *Hyla caerulea* (Shaw 1790), Green tree-frog. This is not a particularly good English name because the frog may be blue or

green. [LM 3251 Rana caerulea, blue frog, from New Holland, Fichtel 9/6]

38. *Variegated lizard Lacerta varia S Stone*
= *Varanus varius* (Shaw 1790), Goanna. [LM 3250 Variegated lizard Lacerta varia, New Holland, Vaughan 16/-; 4156 The variegated lizard, and another, Fichtel 6/6; 5678 Variegated lizard, East indies, very rare, Fichtel 12/6; 5316 Variegated lizard, and a curious snake, Prater 7/-]

40. *Muricated lizard, variety Lacerta muricata S Stone delin.* (see no. 31)

43. *Snake, no. 1. S Stone delin.*
= *Pseudonaja textilis* (Duméril, Bibron and Duméril 1854), Eastern brown snake.

44. *Snake, no. 2. S Stone delin.*
= *Dendrelaphis punctulatus* (Gray 1827), Common tree or Common bronze back snake.

45. *Snake, no. 3. S Stone delin.* (no. 5 on pl.)
= *Morelia spilota* (Lacépède 1804), Carpet python.

46. *Snake no. 1 and 2. They belong to the Linnean genus Coluber S Stone delin.*
No. 1. *Morelia spilota* (see no. 45), young diamond snake.
No. 2. *Vermicella annulata* (Gray 1841), Bandy-bandy. The natives of New South Wales eat this snake. [LM 6531 Three curious snakes, New Holland, three cases, Sir Henry Martin 9/-] suggests that these were dried specimens, the identity of which Donovan could not make out; many of the snakes were sold unnamed and unidentified.

INSECTS

47. *Insects of New South Wales S Stone delin.*
Large Scolopendra (centipede)
= *Scolopendra morsitans* (Linnaeus 1758). [LM 3098 Scolopendra morsitans, a sepia and a curious labrus, 2/-; 3244 Scolopendra morsitans, and a beautiful blue

snake, c.(= coluber) caerulea, Jackson 6/-; 3940 Scolopendra morsitans, truxalis viridis, locustae, grylli, eight specimens, Sivers 10/6; 4284 Nepa grandis, scolopendra morsitans, blatta heteroclita, altogether seven, Sivers 3/-; 4525/6 part of more composite lots; 4761 Scolopendra morsitans, various tabani, Asilii, &c, Keynes 2/6; 5327 Scolopendra morsitans, silvery labrus, &c. in seven bottles, Prater 5/-]
Spider (*Isopeda* sp.)
Crab (*Mictyris* sp.)
Caterpillar (unidentified)

SPIDERS

47. (see above)
55. *White jointed spider S Stone delin.*
Two figures and three details (unidentified)

FISHES

39. *Pungent chaetodon Chaetodon armatus and Granulated Balistes S Stone delin.*
= *Enoplosus armatus* (Shaw 1790), Long-tailed chaetodon, and
= *Scobinichthys granulatus* (Shaw 1790), Captain Cook's leatherjacket (see *Australian Museum Magazine*, III, 1929, p. 421). [LM several chaetodon, but none of this species separately listed]

50. *Cyprinaceus S Stone delin.* and *Hippocampus or Sea Horse Syngnathus hippocampus Linn*
= *Pseudolabrus cyprinaceus* (Shaw 1790), Wrasse or parrot-fish, and *Hippocampus whitei* (Linnaeus 1766), Sea-horse, whose scientific name commemorates John White; the seahorse was classified as a fish at this date. [LM 772 Gobius minutus, Sygnathus Hippocampus, a small Exocaetus, another-fish, and two lizards, Laskey 13/-; 774 Sygnathus Hippocampus, a julus, a spider, fishes, etc — in six bottles. 8/-; 3091 Atherina japonica, an hippocampus, and

syngnathus, or pipe fish, in three bottles, Breedon 6/-; 5311 Sygnathus hippocampus, pipe fish, spotted snake etc in 8 bottles, Prater 4/-]

53. *Fasciated Mullet Mullet fasciatus and Doubtful, or compressed sparus S Stone delin. Sparus? compressus* = *Lovamia fasciata* (Shaw 1790), and *Pempheris compressa* (Shaw 1790), Bulls-eye.

64. *Atherine, Tobacco Pipe, and Remora Fish S Stone delin. Southern Atherine Atherina Australis* = *Austranchovia australis* (Shaw 1790), Anchovy; *The Tobacco Pipe Fish*

= *Fistularia immaculata* (?Cuvier 1816), Flute-mouth [LM 5311 Syngnathus hippocampus, pipe fish, spotted snake, &c in 8 bottles, Prater 6/-; 5342 Pipe fish, and two snakes, Dick 2/6] *Remora or Sucking-fish (Echensis Remora of Linnaeus)* = *Remor remora* (Linnaeus 1758), Sucking-fish [LM 114 The sucking fish-Echineis Remora 2 1/2 feet long, Zenetty 8/6; 3609 The sucking fish echeneis remora, and the blue snake, in two bottles, 3/6; 4021 A sucking or remora fish, and another, Fenton 2/-; 4883 A

large remora, or sucking fish, Fichtel 5/6; 4978 A large sucking fish or remora, Sugden 7/6]

MAMMALS

58. *The Topoa Tafa S Stone delin.* = *Phascogale tapoatafa* (Meyer 1793), Brush-tailed phascogale.

60. *A Poto or Kangaroo Rat S Stone delin.* = *Potorous tridactylus* (Kerr 1792). The original scientific description was based on Sarah's signed drawing, engraved for this plate, and that drawn and etched by Peter

Mazell from a drawing sent from Australia for Arthur Phillip's *Voyage to Botany Bay*, pl. XLVII (4 September 1789), "Kangaroo rat, young, jaws". The skull of White's specimen, a female, was present in the museum of the Royal College of Surgeons, where it was recorded by Waterhouse (1841, p. 175). [LM 262 Kangaroo rat, out of case, Macrous minor, was purchased with "Kangaroo, young," by Hall for 10/-]

ILLUSTRATIONS WITH NO SIGNATURE, COMMONLY ATTRIBUTED TO SARAH STONE

(See corresponding watercolours in *Australia*, pp. 128 and 136)

1. *New Holland cassowary* = *Dromaius novaehollandiae* (Latham 1790), Emu. A New Holland cassowary was shot some two miles from the Sydney Cove settlement, in Australia, at the end of February 1788, and drawn on the spot by Lieutenant Watts. The skin was sent to England in spirits, and was presented by Lord Sydney to Sir Joseph Banks, who deposited it in the collection of John Hunter in Leicester Square, according to Arthur Phillip (*Voyage to Botany Bay*, 1789, p. 272). Now named Emu, the national bird of Australia. The drawing, and the plate in White's *Journal*, were unsigned, and though frequently attributed to Sarah Stone, are most probably not by her. [LM 2700 Cassuary, N. Holland (without case) Casuarius nov. Hollandiae, Hall 16/-; 2058 Cassuary, a fine specimen (without case) Hall 18/-]

5. *Anomalous hornbill.* = *Scythrops novae-hollandiae*

(Latham 1790), Channel-billed cuckoo. [LM 2783 Scythrops novae Hollandiae, very rare, psittaceous hornbill, Fichtel £1.12.0. (Pelzehn 1873, p. 34, "It seems not improbable that our specimen is the type of the figure in White's *Journal*")]

8. *Golden-winged pigeon* = *Phaps chalcoptera* (Latham 1790), Common bronzewing. [LM 4080 An uncommonly fine specimen the male bronze winged pigeon (Columba chalcoptera), m. and a female, New Holland, bought in £1.11.0.]

9. *Port Jackson thrush* = *Colluricincla harmonica* (Latham 1801)

11, 12. *Tabuan parrot, male and female* = *Alisterus scapularis* (Lichtenstein 1818), Australian king-parrot. A watercolour of the female Tabuan parrot is now in the National Library of Australia, Canberra, bound in a volume of *Natural History Specimens of New South Wales copied from nature by Sarah Stone 1790.* [LM 2427 Psittacus tabuanus, a very fine specimen, £1.3.0; 4434 Tabuan parrot, Psittacus

tabuanus, Fenton 13/-]

13. *Pennantian parrot, male* = *Platycercus elegans* (Gmelin 1788), Crimson rosella. Named for Thomas Pennant by Latham, but Gmelin 's name had preference. A watercolour of the male Pennantian Parrot is now in the National Library of Australia, Canberra, bound in a volume of *Natural history Specimens of New South Wales copied from nature by Sarah Stone 1790* (see 'Illustrations by Sarah Stone', no. 14; and 'George Shaw' below). [LM 2776 Pennantian parrot, female, from New Holland, Sivers 5/-; 4095 Pennantian parrot, both sexes, Botany Bay, Sivers 13/-]

15. *New Holland creeper male* = *Phylidonyris novae-hollandiae* (Latham 1790), New Holland honeyeater (see also no. 65).

17. *Sacred King's fisher* = *Todiramphus sanctus* (Vigors and Horsfield 1827), Sacred kingfisher. [LM 2778 ?Sacred kingfisher, Alcedo sacra, from New Holland, Sivers 8/6]

30. *Scinc-formed lizard Lacerata scincoides* = *Tiliqua scincoides* (Shaw 1790). [LM 3255 Scincoid Lizard,

Lacerata scincoides, New Holland, Fichtel 12/6]

37. *Fulliginous petrel Procellaria fuliginosa* = *Procellaria aequinoctialis* (Linnaeus 1758), White-chinned petrel. [LM 2775 Fuliginous petrel Procellaria fuliginosa from New Holland, Fichtel £1.10.0.]

51. *Doubtful Lophius Lophius dubius* = *Batrachomaeus dubius* (Shaw 1790) Angler fish.

52. *Southern Cottus Cottus Australis and Flying fish* = *Centropogon australis* (Shaw 1790), and *Exocoetus volitans* (Shaw 1790) [LM 771 Exocaetus volitans, or flying fish, Pleuronectes, and a silurus, Walker 4/-; 3473 Exocaetus aevolans, flying fish, and a marine fasciculated worm, Fenton 3/6; 4014 Exocoetus evolans, flying fish, Mediterranean, 4/6; 5257 Exocetus volitans, mullet, chaetodon, & six specimens collected by Captain Cook in the S. Seas, Fichtel 6/6]

The second book to contain illustrations after Sarah Stone's watercolours was George Shaw's *Museum Leverianum (Musei Leveriani explicatio anglica et latina) containing select specimens from museum of the late Ashton Lever with descriptions in Latin and English*, published by James Parkinson, proprietor of the collection (London 1792), vol. I (5 parts), vol. II (6th part), with 72 plates – all that were published.

The artists who were employed by James Parkinson were C.R. Ryley, S.T. Edwards (for one plate only), Philip Reinagle, and Mrs Smith (née Stone). In this book, Charles Reuben Ryley supplanted Sarah as the chief illustrator for Parkinson. Ryley painted over thirty birds for plates in the six parts, and Sarah contributed two plates. Parkinson hoped to interest the scientific world in the collection by employing George Shaw of the British Museum to write a descriptive text and so reveal not only the extent of his collection, but also the uniqueness of some of the specimens.[11] However, the detailed catalogue ceased publication after only six parts had been published. The scientific world had showed indifference.

Sarah had been married three years before the catalogue began publication. Her two bird plates were the orange-coloured Cock of the rock from the Guianas and northern Brazil, and the Crimson rosella. This last painting, of what was then the Pennantian parrot, differed from that of the same species, which Sarah had painted for John White's *Journal of a Voyage to New South Wales*, in 1789.

1. Vol. II, p. 13 *Pipra rupicola The rock manakin. Mrs Smith late Miss Stone delin.* = *Rupicola rupicola* (Linnaeus 1766), Guyanan cock-of-the-rock. [LM 52 Pipra rupicola, cock of the rock, male, South America, Vaughan £3.15.0; 4784 A very fine specimen of the rock manakin, Pipra rupicola, Burchell £3.3.0.]

2. Vol. II, p.27 *Psittacus splendicus Splendid parrot Miss Stone delt.* = *Platycercus elegans* (Gmelin 1788), Crimson rosella. Latham called this the Pennantian parrot (and see under 'John White', nos. 13 and 14). [LM 184 Splendid Parrot, Psittacus splendicus, mas. New Holland, Burchell 15/-]

THOMAS PENNANT'S *A VIEW OF HINDOOSTAN*

The third book, with one illustration by Sarah Stone, was Pennant's *A view of Hindoostan* (4 vols., 1798–1800).

Sarah's employment by Thomas Pennant is unequivocally recorded by Pennant himself in his book.[12] In the first volume, on page 156, he wrote, "In gratitude I must mention the several friends to whom I am indebted for information respecting the natural history of this riche province [Bengal]. Sir Elijah Impey and his lady, gave me the most liberal access to their vast and elegant collection of drawings made with much fidelity on the spot; to them I was indebted for permission to have several copies made by my paintress, Miss Stone, taken from the most curious subjects in their cabinet."

In the second volume, a coloured engraving of *Moory Mamoorei or bright bird* (pl. xii, opposite p. 340), *The Napaul pheasant*, is inscribed *S Stone del. J. Barlow sculp.* Pennant said that "Lady Impey favoured me with drawings of several [birds] of the gallinaceous tribe", and this Satyr tragopan was probably drawn by Sarah from an Indian drawing executed for Lady Impey.[13]

1. Vol. II, pl. xii (opposite p. 344) *Moory Manmoori or bright bird S Stone delin.* = *Tragopan satyra* (Linnaeus 1758). PLATE 6

The first two volumes of *A View of Hindoostan* were very sparsely illustrated with engravings by Barlow; the third and fourth volumes contained no engravings. The only other illustrations that could possibly have been drawn by Sarah were a Passarage plover (vol. II, pl. viii, opposite p. 271), and a Cheetal, taken near Dacca (vol. II, pl. xi, opposite p. 318).

Pennant paid a number of artists to work for him, both to paint pictures to hang on the walls of his house, and to record new or rare natural history objects that particularly interested him. He sometimes grangerized books in his library, using watercolours that he had commissioned from his artists. He owned the published accounts of Captain James Cook's voyages, *A Voyage towards the South Pole and round the World* (2 vols., 1777), and *A Voyage to the Pacific Ocean* (3 vols, 2nd edn, 1795). He extra-illustrated these by inserting watercolour paintings of birds and artefacts that had been seen or acquired on the voyages, in the appropriate page openings. The Dixson Library (see p. 127) now owns Pennant's copies of the accounts of these voyages, and with them pasted-in watercolour drawings commissioned from Sarah and other artists.

John Latham (1740–1837) documented all the new bird species discovered at the end of the eighteenth century.[14] His aim was to make a complete record of all known bird species, and he illustrated many of these himself, with the assistance of his daughter, Ann. Sarah's role was not in the provision of drawings for Latham, but she was asked to hand-colour the etched plates in a few special, deluxe copies of his *A General Synopsis of Birds* (6 vols., and 2 vols. of supplements) "in a superior manner". William Lowndes, in his *Bibliographer's Manual of English Literature* (6 vols., 1864, vol. III, p. 1314) notes four copies coloured by Sarah: one purchased by Sir M.M. Sykes for £110. 5s., which had upwards of 1,000 coloured figures of birds; a copy bought by John Dent for £43. 1s.; another by John North for £44. 2s.; and a fourth by Colonel Stanley for £56. 14s. It is believed that six of these deluxe copies were originally coloured by Sarah.

The plates were very lightly printed counter-proofs which resulted in a faint reversed image on the page. Sarah painted the plates with watercolours and gouache, which resembled more closely an original watercolour painting than a coloured print. Colourists in the nineteenth century were paid between 3d. and 6d. to colour a quarto plate. Latham was an old friend of Sir Ashton Lever, well aware of Sarah's capabilities, having seen her work at the Lever Museum.[15] He could give her the job of painting the deluxe editions with every confidence, but whether Sarah got a good price for her work, or was capable of driving a hard bargain, we may never know.

In June 1989, at the Sotheby's, New York, sale of the Bradley Martin collection of fine books, the copy originally purchased by John Dent was sold for $23,100. The copy originally bought by John North for 42 guineas, was sold in October 1995 by Christie's, London, with an original watercolour of a spoonbill by Sarah, from the Fattorini collection, for £27,600.

NOTES

1 John White was born *ca.* 1756 at Drumaran, county Fermanagh, Ireland and entered the navy on 26 June 1778 as third surgeon's mate. He worked his way up the ranks until appointed surgeon-general of the First Fleet in 1786 at a salary of £182. 10s. per annum.
His journal of his voyage and the settlement ended in 1788. He took a convict woman to be his housekeeper and she was the mother of a son named Andrew Douglas[s] White. John White set sail for home on the Daedalus, 17 December 1794, then served with the navy until 15 January 1820 and died at Worthing on 20 February 1832, aged 75, leaving the substantial legacy of £12,000. In 1797 he sent a draught of a proposed second book, with a collection of drawings, to his friend Lambert, but this was never published and the ms is now lost. (Biographical introduction, pp. 17–34 by Rex Rienits to John White's Journal of 1790, edited and re-issued by Alex H. Chisholm, Sydney, 1962; Nelson, 1998.

2 Thomas Wilson of Gower Street, Bedford Square, London, was a minor naturalist. In November 1788 White sent Wilson skins of birds, mammals, fishes and reptiles collected soon after landing in Botany Bay. White also sent Wilson "a quart of oil" from the "peppermint tree *Eucalyptus piperata*" and later a collection of shells.

3 Society for Promoting Natural History, 1782–1822, Minute book, 5 October 1789, Linnean Society Library, London. The committee of the Society met at Leicester House from 6 June 1786 until 2 November 1789, after which the Society moved to new rooms at 19 Warwick Street, Golden Square.

4 John Hunter (1728–1793) was a museum and menagerie owner in London, and employed artists to record his specimens. He was born at Long Calderwood, Lanarkshire and went to London when twenty years old to work for his elder brother, William, in his anatomical school. John later became a surgeon at St George's, and Surveyor Extra-ordinary to George III. In 1783 he acquired 28 Leicester Square and built a museum of comparative anatomy. When he died, this museum was purchased by the government and presented to the College of Surgeons. In 1806 the museum was re-housed in a new building in Lincoln's Inn Fields. Some of the first specimens of kangaroos were presented to Hunter by John White in 1789, one of which was drawn for the Journal (1790). In 1806 the conservator of the museum, William Clift, was directed by the trustees to attend the Leverian Museum sale and spent nearly £100 purchasing some specimens for the Royal College of Surgeons. Clift's marked-up copy of the sale catalogue is a source of information about the purchasers of the lots. Some stuffed birds and mammals from the Hunterian museum's biological collection were subsequently transferred to the British Museum.

5. Ann Latham (born 1772) was an amateur artist in watercolours and drew some birds for her father, John, to be reproduced as illustrations. Several of Ann's watercolours were engraved in 1789 for Arthur Phillip's account of *The Voyage to Botany Bay*, preceding Sarah's illustrations in John White's *Journal of a Voyage to New South Wales* by a few months. Ann sighed eight plates *A Latham delt*, viz. Norfolk Island petrel, Bronze-winged pigeon, White-fronted heron, Wattled bee-eater, Banksian cockatoo variety, Red-shouldered parrot, New Holland goat-sucker, and White gallinule. The engravings were dated by the publisher, J Stockdale, in September, October and November 1789. Sarah's plates (some of these same species) were all dated 29 December 1789. Ann Latham was thus probably the first lady artist to publish illustrations of Australian species, although she and Sarah were painting them at the same time.

6. Society for Promoting Natural History, 1782–1822. Minute book, 25 July 1791. Linnean Society Library, London.

7 The Minute Books of the Linnean Society, London. One final reference to the donated copy of White's *Journal* occurs on a slip of paper dated 18 February 1792, signed by D. Alves Robello, "Having borrowed of the Natural History Society White's Journal to New South Wales, I herby promise to return the same". Dr E.C. Nelson drew my attention to these coloured copies.

8 R.J. Willis, 'The earliest known Australian bird painting: a Rainbow Lorikeet, *Trichoglossus haematodus moluccanus* (Gmelin) by

Moses Griffith, painted in 1772', *Archives of Natural History* 15 (3), 1988, pp. 323–29.

9 K.A. Hindwood, 'The Birds of Lord Howe Island', *Emu* 40, 1940, pp. 1–86.

10 J.H. Calaby, 'The natural history drawings', ch. 4 in B. Smith and A. Wheeler, *The Art of the First Fleet*, Melbourne 1988, pl. CLII, depicting a sheet of drawings from Banks Ms 34, p. 51. G.M. Shea's article on this first Australian reptile to be named, and the largest species of skink, 'The anatomist John Hunter (1728-1793), the Eastern Bluetongue Skink, *Tiliqua scincoides* (Squamata: Scincidae) and the discovery of herbivory in skinks', *Archives of Natural History* 20 (3), 1993, pp. 303–06.

11 George Shaw (1751–1813), see *Dictionary of National Biography*. In February 1791, he became assistant-keeper of the natural history section of the British Museum and in 1807 was promoted to keeper of the section that included botany, zoology, geology and mineralogy as well as ethnography. Despite the wide-ranging responsibility, the salary was meagre and Shaw supplemented his income by publishing natural history books, among them the remarkably well illustrated *General Zoology, or Systematic Natural History*, 14 vols., 1800–26, 1,217 pls. The

commission from James Parkinson to describe the contents of the *Museum Leverianum* would have been welcome and interesting, taking him into a quite differently displayed collection – although the lack of a systematic arrangement of the specimens no doubt impeded his work and sometimes exasperated him.

The engravings in Shaw's *Zoology and Botany of New Holland*, 1794, were done from drawings sent from Australia and did not involve artists in England; nor, as far as the present records exist, did Sarah subsequently paint the species represented in this volume. John White had sent these "coloured drawings, made on the spot" to Thomas Wilson in 1793, along with "a most copious and finely presented collection of dried specimens" (Preface written December 1793).

12 Thomas Pennant (1726–1798) was a prolific natural history author and encouraged artists, other than Sarah Stone (see p. 86, 90), to work on his projects. He used specimens from every source in England and Wales, and visited museums, including Lever's, on his frequent travels. For his biography and account of his artists and books, see Jackson (1985), pp. 103–21.

13 Sir Elijah (1732–1809) and Mary, Lady Impey were back in

England from Bengal in 1783. He had been given the new appointment of Chief Justice of the Supreme Court of Bengal in 1773, and was knighted just before sailing in the *Anson*, in April 1774 for the six-month passage. Impey's wife, Mary, the daughter of Sir John Reade of Shipton Court, Oxfordshire, whom he married 18 January 1768, joined him in Calcutta in 1777. They had five sons, two born in England, one in Bengal, and two more after their return to England. While in Bengal she established a menagerie of birds and mammals and employed Indian artists to make paintings of them from life. The couple amassed sixty-three folios (of which forty-seven depict birds) painted by native artists between 1777 and 1782. John Latham referred to twenty-five birds in the Impey collection, when he had access to them *ca.* 1785. Pennant saw the gallinaceous bird paintings in the collection, when "Miss Stone" copied some for him (therefore prior to her marriage in 1789). The collection was sold in 1810 and dispersed. Collections are now in the Victoria and Albert Museum, London; the Radcliffe Science Library, Oxford; the Binney Collection, San Diego; the Wellcome Institute, London; the Liverpool Museum, as well as

some private collections. The Earl of Derby sold a number at Christie's in May 1998.

14 John Latham (1740–1837) wrote the standard work from which the names of the birds drawn by Sarah at the Leverian Museum were later written on to her drawing sheets, where 'Gen. Syn.' or 'Syn.' referred to Latham's *General Synopsis of Birds* (3 vols., 1781–85, with two supplements by 1801, including 142 illustrations that had been drawn and etched by Latham with some assistance from his daughter, Ann). Latham and Lever corresponded and shared their specimens, and sent one another drawings. A Sarah Stone drawing is among the 888 original watercolours in the Latham folios at the Natural History Museum, London, in which collection some of Ann's watercolours are also conserved. For biography of Latham see Jackson (1985), pp. 136–47.)

15 Latham confirms that he visited the Leverian Museum when in London, in a letter to Pennant, 25 January 1782, "It is now 2 months since I was at Leicester House when there I forgot to attend to the Bill as defined in your Letter, but shall do it next time I visit there" (Warwick County Record Office, Pennant papers, TP277/1-16).

Index to the Species in Sarah Stone's Watercolours, Drawings and Prints

Species are listed under the names on Sarah Stone's watercolours; where there was no name, the modern equivalent has been supplied.

AM Australian Museum, Sydney, Australia (p. 125)
AS Auction sales (p. 138)
AT Alexander Turnbull Library, Wellington, New Zealand (p. 129)
BME Ethnography Dept. of the British Museum (p. 127)
DL Dixson Library, Mitchell Library, Sydney, Australia (p. 127)
GS George Shaw, *Museum Leverianum*, London 1792 (p. 145)
HH Bernice P. Bishop Museum, Honolulu, Hawaii (p. 122)
ICWA International Centre for Wildlife Art, Gloucestershire, UK (p. 131)
L Linnaeus, Carolus, *Systema naturae*, 10th edn., 1758 and 1766
La Latham, John *A General synopsis of birds*, London, 3 vols., 1781–85 (p. 146)
NHML Natural History Museum, London
 NHML (1) A portfolio of 93 watercolours (p. 109)

NHML (2) Collection of 13 watercolours of birds (numbered by the museum 48–60) (p. 113)
NHML (3) Album of 175 sheets on 168 mounts of watercolours approximately 25 × 35 cm (p. 114)
 NHML John Latham Collection of 888 watercolours of birds (1) (p. 122)
NLA National Library of Australia, Canberra (13) (p. 128)
P Pennant (1) (p. 145)
PMC Paul Mellon Collection, Upperville, Virginia, USA (1) (p. 137)
pc Private collections: pcA, pcB and pcC (p. 131ff.)
SMC Sedgwick Museum of Earth Sciences, Cambridge (p. 129)
TD Thomas Davies Collection (in pcB) (p. 136)
W John White *Journal of a Voyage to New South Wales*, London 1790 (p. 140)
YCBA Yale Center for British Art, Paul Mellon Collection (p. 129)

BIRDS

Some birds were auctioned on each of fifty-two out of the sixty-five days of the sale, usually in a compact block of some twenty, thirty or forty lots. There was only one day completely devoted to auctioning birds, when 119 lots were sold on the fiftieth day. Many lots had the male and female of the species, sometimes also the young, and it was common to combine two cases containing different species in a single lot. Most of the bird specimens were sold in their mahogany cases; where "out of a case", this was usually indicated in the catalogue. Occasionally, the identity of the specimen was unknown. There were at least 2,300 bird specimens that came under the hammer. Allowing for some 230 duplications of species and the same species having male and female and some young, this leaves some 1,550 -1,600 species. The museum was particularly rich in parrot specimens, sold in 104 lots. It is not possible to be more acurate about the number of species because the catalogue used so many alternative English names, vague descriptions, and occasionally did not itemize or specify every bird within a composite lot. In addition, at that date Latham and fellow ornithologists described a closely related species as "Var. A" or "Var. B", following the name of the species which the bird most closely resembled. These variants were later given specific names, or not, as they were studied more closely for the purpose of identification.

Edward Donovan bought by far the largest number of birds, some 500; Fichtel bought 204 bird specimens for Vienna; Lord Stanley about 100. In each case, there were new species represented among the skins and type specimens that went to these collections.

Trochilus elatus NHML (3) 58

Trochilus pcB 10

Trochilus pella pcB 55

Trochilus polytmus pcB 55

Trochilus, green and blue pcB 55

Trogon viridis NHML (3) 30

Tropic bird, common NHML (3) 154

Tropic bird, red-billed AS, NHML (3) 154

Tropic bird, red-tailed pcA 14

Tropical bird, rose-coloured AS

Turdus brasiliensis NHML (3) 61

Turdus caudatus NHML (3) 70

Turdus ceylonus NHML (3) 69

Turdus cinclus NHML (3) 66

Turdus dominicus NHML (3) 62

Turdus linearis NHML (3) 67

Turdus merula NHML (3) 63, 64

Turdus nitens NHML (3) 68

Turdus pilaris NHML (3) 60

Turdus roseus pcB 45

Turdus torquatus NHML (3) 65

Turkey AM 11

Turkey hen, white AM 11

Turkey, guan/quan NHML (3) 115

Turkey, marail NHML (3) 116

Turtle, Cape NHML (3) 114

Upupa epops NHML (2) 48, pcA

Upupa promerops NHML (3) 49

Upupa superba pcB 51

Vestiaria coccinea DL

Vidua macroura pcB 24

Vidua paradisaea NHML (2) 58

Vultur AM 4

Vultur percnopterus NHML (3) 2

Vulture, Angola pcB 43

Warbler, blue-headed NHML (3) 99

Warbler, Cayenne NHML (3) 100

Warbler, long-billed DL

Warbler, plumbeous NHML (3) 161

Warbler, sedge NHML (3) 98

Warbler, superb pcB 23, W 41, NLA 8

Warbler, white-polled NHML (3) 108

Water hen South America AM 8

Wattle-bird, cinerous NHML (3) 18

Waxbill NHML (3) 77

Waxen chatterer NHML (3) 71

Waxwing NHML (2) 59

Wheatear, black NHML (3) 67

Woodcock AS

Woodpecker, Cayenne NHML (3) 36

Woodpecker, minute NHML (3) 37

Wren, common NHML (3) 101

Wren, yellow, var A NHML (3) 102

Wryneck NHML (3) 35

Wydah NHML (2) 58

Yanx torquilla NHML (3) 35

Nine birds' eggs pcB 56

MAMMALS

Sarah painted some forty mammals, most of them represented in the LM. In the sale of 1806, there were 334 mammal lots, of which about thirty quadruped and whale/dolphin/seal species were duplicated. Besides these, there were twenty monkey grotesques (monkeys dressed as humans).

Sarah was one of the first artists to draw Australian mammals; her other specimens came from South and North America, Africa and Asia. The original scientific description of the Potoroo, *Potorus tridactylus* (Kerr 1792), was based on Sarah's signed drawing; the skull of this specimen was formerly in the London Museum of the Royal College of Surgeons (B.

Smith and A. Wheeler, *The Art of the First Fleet*, Melbourne 1988). The aboriginal name potoroo was adopted as a generic term, Potorus, for some of the rat-kangaroos, the smallest members of the kangaroo and wallaby family.

Bats were poorly served in the sale catalogue, with few or no distinguishing names, either English or scientific. Sarah painted two watercolours of bats, which are now in The Natural History Museum, London.

Anteater, giant pcB 61

Anteater, pygmy NHML (1) 22

Anteater, silky NHML (1) 22

Ape NHML (1) 17

Bat, fruit NHML (1) 10

Bat, tube-nosed NHML (1) 14

Beaver NHML (1) 4

Bradypus tridactylus NHML (1) 20

Bush buck? NHML (1) 16

Canine, Mus Lev p.48 NHML (1) 18

Capra ibex NHML (1) 5

Civet, palm NHML (1) 13

Coati, white-nosed NHML (1) 3

Didelphis virginiana NHML (1) 9, 23

Dog, Indian red/golden jackal NHML (1) 18

Dik-dik? pcB 63

Dolphin AM 97

Elephant NHML (1) 7

Felis serval NHML (1) 12

Giraffe led by Negro page AS

Gnu, Hottentot or white-tailed NHML (1) 15

Goat of Angora NHML (1) 21

Goat with white patch on its back pcB 62

Hepoona roo W 61, pcC 4

Ibex, Alps NHML (1) 5

Kangaroo W 54, pcC 22, 25

Kangaroo rat W 60, pcC 27

Kinkajou NHML (1) 8

Loris, slender NHML (1) 17

Manatee? AM 96

Manis sp. pcB 60

Mandrill male AM 131

Mongoose NHML (1) 11

Moschus grimmia pcB 63

Musk (deer) of Thibet NHML (1) 6

Narwal skull and tusks AM 57,

NHML (1) 19

Opossum, Virginian NHML (1) 9 and 23

Pangolin pcB 60

Poto roo W 60, pcC 27

Primate, Old World AM 131

Raccoon NHML (1) 3

Seal AM 98

Serval NHML (1) 12

Sloth, three-toed NHML (1) 20

Tafa, tapoa W 58, pcC 10

Tafa, spotted tapoa W 59, pcC 28

Tamandua (mexicana?) pcB 59

Zibet NHML (1) 8

MAMMALIAN HORNS AND ANTLERS

The Lever collection had a large number of horns and antlers, thirty-seven of which were painted by Sarah and are now in the Australian Museum (see p. 128). Only ten horns or antlers, some with incised decorations, were sold, in small groups, during the first forty-seven days of the 1806 sale; the bulk of the collection was sold at the end. On the very last day, Appendix nos. 655–84 were all (nineteen) horns and antlers, most unidentified. The majority were purchased by Fillingham.

Blackbuck AM 52	66	Ibex AM 48	Reindeer AM 44, 65, 67
Buffalo, Asian water AM 38	Eland 46	Kudu, greater AM 37	Rhinoceros AM 49, 50
Caribou AM 65	Elk, giant Irish AM 36	Narwal AM 56, 57, NHML (1) 19	Sheep, bighorn AM 64
Deer, red AM 42, 45	Elk/Moose AM 43	Nyala AM 39	
Deer, roe AM 58	Gemsbok AM 39, 51	Ox, domestic AM 40, 68	
Deer, unidentified AM 47, 60, 63,	Goat AM 61	Ox, musk AM 62	

REPTILES AND AMPHIBIANS

Sarah painted half a dozen snakes, a skink, a gekko, some lizards, and a chameleon. She painted one amphibian, a Blue frog.

When Edward Donovan compiled the sale catalogue of the Leverian Museum in 1806, his own strengths and weaknesses as a naturalist became apparent. He was strong on birds and shells, but not as knowledgeable on the species of reptiles; consequently, many of the lots were not clearly identified. Several lots were formed of a lizard, a fish and a snake, with no identification, others merely listed "snakes", or an identified snake "and others". Over 370 reptiles and amphibians were sold in 1806, but at least a third were duplicates and nearly one half were unidentified in the catalogue.

Lizards	Lacerta varia W 38, pcC 6	Lizard, scincoid, or skinc-formed	Snake, flying? NHML (1) 27
Gekko NHML (1) 26	Lizard pcB 4	W 30, pcC 12	Snakes, nos 1 & 2 W 46, pcC 21
Lacerta muricata W 31, NLA 12;	Lizard, broad-tailed W 32, NLA 13	Lizard, variegated W 38, pcC 6	*Chameleon*
W 40, pcC 31	Lizard, green NHML (1) 26	*Snakes*	Chameleon NHML (1) 28
Lacerta platura W 32, NLA 13	Lizard, muricated W 31, NLA 12;	Coluber spp. W 46, pcC 21	*Frog*
Lacerta scincoides W 30, pcC 12	W 40, pcC 31	Snake W 31, NLA 12; 43, pcC 20,	Blue W 33, pcC 9
Lacerta taeniolata W 32, NLA 13	Lizzard, ribboned W 32, NLA 13	44, 45	Rana caerulea W 33, pcC 9

FISHES

Sarah painted fourteen species of fishes. In the LM sale, there were some 200 named fishes (with approximately thirty duplicates), 130 unnamed; in all, just over 300 lots. However, in that group crabs were included, and several species were joined to form one lot. Mixed lots of fishes, sometimes also with reptiles, were not uncommon.

Atherina Australis W 64, pcC 13	Cottus, southern W 52	Labrus cyprinaceus W 50, pcC 2	NHML (1) 7
Balistes granulatus W 39, NLA 10	Doubtful lophius W 51, pcC 8	Lophius dubius W 51, pcC 8	Seahorse W 50, pcC 2;
Chaetodon armatus W 39, NLA 10	Echeneis remora W 64	Mullet, fasciated W 53, nLA 11	NHML (1) 2
Chaetodon, pungent W 39,	Exocoetus volitans W 52	Pipe fish, tobacco W 64	Shark AM 94
NLA 10	Flying fish W 52	Remora or sucking fish W 64	Sparups, doubtful W 53, NLA 11
Cottus Australis W 52	Hippocampus W 50, pcC 2	Rockling, three-bearded	Sword fish AM 95

CRUSTACEANS

The crabs and lobsters are integrated in the blocks of lots of fishes, often one lot containing a fish, a crustacean and a specimen from another phylum. There were only two dozen or so crustacea.

Crab or cancer W 47	Hermit AS

Sarah painted eighteen sheets of watercolours, containing thirty-six specimens of shells, in The Natural History Museum, London; three watercolours are in the Bernice Puahi Bishio Museum, and forty-two shell watercolours in the Sedgwick Museum.

At the LM sale, almost 850 lots comprised shells, but very rarely was a single shell sold in one lot. Nearly all the lots included several named or unnamed specimens. There were duplicates not only of common shells, but also some rarer species, several of which were not described scientifically for many years.

Argonauta hians SMC 10
Astraea heliotropium SMC 6
Bivalve, Unionacea NHML (1) 61
Brachiopods? pcB 60
Buccinulum pallidum SMC 2
Busycon contrarium NHML (1) 66
Calinaticia oldroydii SMC 8
Cancellaria balboaea SMC 2
Cancilla filaris SMC 2
Carrier NHML (1) 72
Cipangopaludina chinensis
    malleata SMC 8
Clam, bear's paw NHML (1) 54,
    68, 75
Clam, fluted giant NHML (1) 60,
    65
Clanculus pharaonis NHML (1) 69
Conch, common spider NHML
    (1) 70,
Conch, scorpion NHML (1) 55
Conch, spider NMHL (1) 74

Devil's claw (spider conch)
    NHML (1) 74
Donax faba SMC 9
Drupa sp. 69
Euspira poliana SMC 8
Fasciolaria lilium hunteria SMC 4,
    5
Fools cap pcB (TD 125)
Fusivoluta pyrrhostoma SMC 2
Heliacus variegatus SMC 8
Hexaplex duplex NHML (1) 56, 59
Hippopus hippopus NHML (1)
    54, 68, 75
Hyotissa hyotis NHML (1) 57
Lambis chiragra NHML (1) 74
Lambis lambis NHML (1) 70
Lambis scorpio NHML (1) 55
Limaria inflata SMC 11
Mitra papalis NHML (1) 70
Mitre, papal NHML (1) 70
Murex, duplex NHML (1) 56, 59

Natica sp. SMC 8
Natica tigrina SMC 8
Natica turtoni SMC 8
Nerita exuvia SMC 8
Nerita versicolor SMC 8
Neritina communis SMC 8
Neritodryas dubia SMC 8
Oyster Crassostrea sp NHML (1)
    73
Oyster, honeycomb NMHL (1) 57
Oyster, long spiked = thorn pcB
    (TD 125)
Oyster, regal thorny NHML (1) 71
Oyster, thorny NHML (1) 60, 65
Pecten sp. NHML (1) 68
Polinices mammatus SMC 8
Pseudovertagus SMC 2
Rock shell NHML (1) 69
Scallop NHML (1) 68
Spondylus NHML (1) 60, 65, pcB
    (TD 125)

Spondylus ?regius NHML (1) 71
Terebra crenulata SMC 3
Terebra dimidiata SMC 3
Terebra strigata SMC 3
Terebra subulata SMC 3
Thais sp. NHML (1) 69
Tibia, delicate NHML (1) 67
Top, strawberry NHML (1) 69
Tridacna squamosa NHML (1) 60,
    65
Turritella terebra cerea SMC 3
Vexillum amanda SMC 2
Vexillum balteolatum SMC 2
Vexillum formosense SMC 2
Vexillum plicarium SMC 2
Vexillum sanguisugum SMC 2
Vexillum rugosum SMC 2
Volva volva SMC 10
Whelk, lightning NHML (1) 66
Xenophora ?conchyliophora
    NHML (1) 72

INSECTS

The insects in the LM were very numerous, and mostly unidentified in the 250 lots devoted to them. There were sometimes up to thirty in a single lot, and it is impossible to count the number of specimens accurately because of the frequency with which the phrase "and others" recurs for this particular phylum. Spiders were intermingled with insects. A rough count revealed 2000 unnamed specimens, and 400 named species. Only 228 named species of insects occurred in the lots. It is impossible to assess the number of duplicates. Sarah painted groups of insects, arranging species from various genera to form a pleasing design. She also included several insects in her bird pictures.

Beetle NinA
Beetle, dynastine NHML (1) 24, 25
Beetle, horned scarab NHML (1)
    24, 25
Beetle, stag pcA
Birdwing butterfly pcB 55, 57
Butterflies pcA, pcB (3)
Butterfly larva W
Cerambyx pcA

Cicada pcA
Cimex pcA
Danai Candidi pcA
Dragonfly pcB
Dynastes hercules NHML (1) 24,
    25
Euchromia sp. pcB 4
Grasshoppers pcA, pcB 5
Gryllus pcA

Hymenoptera pcB 11
Insects of New South Wales W
    47, pcC 11
Mantis pcA
Moth, owlet pcB 57
Nepa pcA
Nymphalid butterfly pcB 55
Ornithoptera priamus pcB 57
Papilio alcmeone pc A

Papilio amasene pcA
Papilio glaucippe pcA
Papilio ulysses pcB 57
Phalaena mopsa pcA
Phalaena promothea pcA
Scarabaeus pcA
Swallowtail butterfly pcB 57
Thysania sp. pcB 57
Wasps pcB 11

CHILOPODA MYRIAPODS

These were scattered indiscriminatingly among the lots of insects in the LM sale catalogue.

Centipede W 47, pcC 11

Scolopendra morsitans W 47,
    pcC 11

ARACHNIDAE

There were approximately fifty named or unnamed spiders among the 250 lots of insects in the LM sale catalogue.

Isopeda sp. W 47, pcC 11   Spider W 47, pcC 11   Spider, white-jointed W 55

STARFISHES

Two drawings of the same specimen SMC 18, 19

MADREPORES – CORALS

Very few genus names were used for corals in the LM sale catalogue. They were mainly classified in *Gorgonia*, the sea fans or horny corals; *Madrepora* corals of the reef-building type; *Millepora*, the corals with many pores or polyp-cells; only one lot contained *Alcyonium*, the sea-pens, sea-fans, red coral and organpipe coral. Sarah painted four corals, but the scientific names were not inscribed on the watercolours and it is almost impossible to relate her drawings to named species in the sale catalogue.

Acropora sp. NHML (1) 76
Diploria sp. NHML (1) 93
Gorgonian precious coral pcB (TD 129)

Gorgonian, (Coelenterate) *Isis* sp. NHML (1) 78
Gorgonian NHML (1) 77, 80
Hydroid pcB (TD 127, 128, 129)

Hydroid (Plumularian?) pcB (TD 127)
Hydroid, Sertularian pcB (TD 129)
Turbinaria sp. NHML (1) 92

Unnamed pcB 59

ZOANTHARIA

Anemones pcB 58

PORIFERA – SPONGES

Only nineteen sponges were named in the thirty-one lots in the LM sale catalogue that included sponges. Sarah painted a group of sponges on one sheet.

Aplysina sp. NHML (1) 79
Callyspongia sp. NHML (1) 79

Chalinopsilla sp. NHML (1) 79
Dactylochaliia sp. NHML (1) 79

Ianthella ?basta NHML (1) 79
Niphates ?digitalis NHML (1) 79

CEPHALOPODS

Octopus pcB 58

ECHINODEA

Dorocidaris papillata SMC 12
Echinometra sp. SMC 15

Heterocentrotus sp. SMC 13

Heterocentrotus mammillatus SMC 16

Heterocentrotus trigonarius SMC 14

Fossils were becoming less of a minor interest when Lever collected so many in the third quarter of the eighteenth century. There were just over 500 fossil lots in the 1806 sale, many of such vague description that it is now impossible to relate them to Sarah's drawings. Some were catalogued with the name of the area from which they had been obtained.

Minerals Just over one thousand lots at the LM sale were composed of minerals, and each lot was a composite of three, four or more specimens. Occasionally, an expecially valuable piece of ore, or a gemstone, constituted a single lot. The minerals had been the subject of the second part of *A Companion to the Museum* (1790).

Sarah painted some "pebbles" of agates, onyx etc, a fluorite and some polished specimens of marble. Marbles were listed in the *Companion to the Leverian Museum*, with references to Da Costa's *Natural History of Fossils*. It is not possible to identify the marble specimens in the sale catalogue because of the number of occasions when "Fifteen various polished marble" specimens were contained in a single lot. There was even one lot (6555) that consisted of "Ninety-seven ancient and modern beautiful specimens of marble, &c, cut and polished". Another lot contained samples of 187 "modern and ancient marbles". Altogether, there were some thirteen lots containing marble. At the sale, lot 3117 was sold to Sivers for 10/6: "Two elegant drawings of agates, by Miss Stone, framed and glazed".

Adientites sp. SMC 21
Agates pcB 2
Ammonite NHML (1) 40, 51, 53
Ammonite, ribbed NHML (1) 29
Bivalve, caritid NHML (1) 37
Bivavle, Ceratomya sp. NHML (1) 35
Bivalve, Gryphaea arcuata NHML (1) 33
Bivalve, Inoperna scalprum NHML (1) 36
Bivalve, Plagiostoma gigantea NHML (1) 29
Bivalve, Spondylus sp. NHML (1) 35
Bones, bird, pterodactyl tibia, NHML (1) 84
Bones, fish NHML (1) 89
Bones, mammal NHML (1) 85
Bones, reptile, ichthyosaur NHML (1) 86
Brachiopods NHML (1) 37, 91
Buccinites Thama NHML (1) 31
Bumastus sp. pcB 2
Cadoceras sp. NHML (1) 51

Calamite sp. NHML (1) 44
Chalcedony pcB 2
Crinoid NHML (1) 88, 90
Dalmanites NHML (1) 47
Devil's claw NHML (1) 30
Echinoid: Phymostoma sp. NHML (1) 36
Fish: Leptolepis SMC 1
Fish: Myripristis homopterygius SMC 1
Fluorite pcB (TD 125), SMC 26
Gastropod, globose NHML (1) 37
Gastropod, high-spired Turrilitid NHML (1) 37
Granite SMC 27
Ichthyomorphite NHML (1) 47
Isocrinus sp. NHML (1) 90
Lepidodendron sp. NHML (1) 41, 42, 43, 45, 48
Lepidodendron aculeatum NHML (1) 45, 46
Lepidodendron mannabachense NHML (1) 45
Lithographic limestone pcB 2
Lithophyte NHML (1) 43

Marble pcB 2
Marble: Brecchia SMC 28
Marble: Portoro macchia larga SMC 28
Nautiloid NHML (1) 52
Nautiloid, orthoconic NHML (1) 38
Nautilus from Dorset NHML (1) 52
Neuropteris sp. plant NHML (1) 58, SMC 21
Onyx pcB 2, SMC 25, 27
Overtonia fimbriata NHML (1) 91
Pebbles pcB 2
Pecten, large fossil NHML (1) 29, 34
Pecten-type bivalve NHML (1) 29
Plagiostoma sp.? NHML (1) 34
Plant, Adientes/Sphenopteris SMC 21
Plant, Alethopteris lonchotica SMC 22, 23
Plant, Maropteris SMC 20
Plant, Neuropteris SMC 20, 24
Plant, Neuropteris/Sphenopteris

SMC 21
Pterodactyl phalange NMHL (1) 8
Pterodosperm ?neuropteris pcB (TD 125)
Pugnax acuminata NHML (1) 91
Spaniodon? sp. NHML (1) 79
Stigmaria ficoides NHML (1) 32, 39
Teeth, Equus sp. NHML (1) 50
Teeth, fish SMC 7
Teeth, fish, Ptychodus sp. NHML (1) 83
Teeth, fish, ray, Ptycnodontida NHML (1) 83
Teeth, fish, shark, Carcharodon sp. NHML (1) 84
Teeth, fish/reptile NHML (1) 87
Teeth, mammal, part of molar of Mammut americanum NHML (1) 50
Teeth, reptile NHML (1) 83
Tree rootstock, Stigmaria ficoides NHML (1) 32
Trilobite fragment NHML (1) 37, pcB 2

ETHNOGRAPHICAL

Just over 800 lots were of ethnographical objects, including items of clothing, jewellery, implements of war, drinking and food vessels, ceremonial regalia and other effects from the South Seas, Africa, South America and many islands. Some of the objects had been taken to England in ships from Cook's three world expeditions, but crews from many other ships contributed to the huge collection at the museum. Sarah completed 285 sheets of watercolours of ethnographical subjects, now in the following museums:

Forty artefacts, including a fine collection of drawings of musical instruments. BME. Listed by Jonathan King in two periodical articles.

Two sketchbooks with 164 ethnographical drawings. HH. Listed by Force and Force 1968.

A sketchbook with 132 watercolours, some zoological, 81 ethnographical. AM.

For lists of ethnographical objects, see published accounts listed in the Bibliography, and the three museums in London, Honolulu and Sydney listed under 'Watercolour Drawings in Public Institutions', pp. 109ff.

MISCELLANEOUS

Charles I portrait AS

Painting of Sir Ashton Lever's museum AS

Carrots and radishes growing in intertwined spirals NHML (1) 81

Bibliography

Allen, Lewis, 'An Old World Diary', *Universal Review*, London 1890, VI, pp. 572–84.

Allingham, E.G., *A Romance of the rostrum:* being the business life of Henry Stevens and the history of 38 King Street, together with some account of famous sales held there during the last 100 years, London 1924.

Anderson, C., 'A link with the Leverian Museum', *Australian Museum Magazine* 1928, 3 (8), pp. 225–26.

Beaglehole, J.C., *The Endeavour Journal of Joseph Banks, 1768–1771*, 2 vols., London 1962

Beaglehole, J.C., *The Journals of Captain Cook on his voyages of discovery*, 4 vols., London 1955–67:
1. *The Voyage of the Endeavour, 1768–1771*, London 1955
2. *The Voyage of the Resolution and Adventure, 1772–1775*, London 1961
3. *The Voyage of the Resolution and Discovery, 1776–1780*, 2 vols, London 1967

Bearne's and Waycotts, *Important works of art and artefacts including items which relate to the voyages of Captain Cook and the collection of Sir Ashton Lever:* a list of items purchased in the name of Rowe, Roe and Rhodes at the sale of the Leverian Museum in 1806 as annotated in the catalogue of that sale at the Cuming Museum, Walworth

Braquehaye, A., *Un peintre d'histoire naturelle. Leroy de Barde et son temps (1777–1829)*, 44 pp., 4 pls, Abbeville (Fourdrinier) 1896.

Burney, Frances, *The Early Diaries of Frances Burney, 1768–1778*; A. R. Ellis (ed.), new edn. 2 vols., London 1907.

Burney, James, *With Captain Cook in the Antarctic and Pacific: the private journals of James Burney, second lieutenant of the Adventure on Cook's Second Voyage, 1772–1773*; Beverley Hooper (ed. and with an introduction), Canberra (National Library of Australia) 1975

A Companion to the Museum (late Sir Ashton Lever's) removed to Albion Street, the Surrey end of Black Friars Bridge, 2 parts, 4 pls., 1790

Delany, Mary, *Mary Delany: the autobiography and correspondence of Mary Granville, Mrs Delany*; Lady Llanover (ed.), London Series I, 3 vols., 1861, Series II, 3 vols., 1862

Dictionary of National Biography.

Donovan, Edward (compiler), *Catalogue of the Leverian Museum*, 7 parts and Appendix, 1806. Complete copies are conserved at The Natural History Museum, London, Zoology Library, with a hand-written alphabetical list of the names of the purchasers (many lots have the sale price written in, and an Appendix to the sale 14–17 July 1806, with ms notes of the purchasers and prices paid for many of the lots); Newton Library, Cambridge Zoology Museum, with the prices written in; Liverpool Free Library, annotated with some names and prices; British Library, London; Middleton Central Library, Manchester (formerly the property of Captain John Laskey); Library of Thomas Parkin of Hastings (annotated)

Ella, Anthony, *Visits to the Leverian Museum; containing an account of … its principal curiosities … for young persons*, London 1805

Farington, Joseph, *The Farington Diary, 1793–1821*; James Grieg (ed.), London 1922–28

Fenn, Eleanor, Lady, *A short history of insects … designed as an introduction to the study of that branch of natural history, and as a pocket companion to those who visit the Leverian Museum*, 14 pls., Norwich [1797], several edns.

Fenn, Eleanor, Lady, *A short history of quadrupeds extracted from works of credit, designed as an introduction to the study of that branch of natural history and as a pocket companion to those who visit the Leverian Museum*, London 1780, and several other edns.

Force, R.W. and Force, M., *Art and artifacts of the 18th century: objects in the Leverian Museum, as painted by Sarah Stone*, Honolulu 1968

Graves, Algernon, *Royal Academy of Arts: a complete dictionary of contributors and their work, 1769–1904*, 8 vols., London 1905–06

Graves, Algernon, *The Society of Artists of Great Britain, 1760–1791; The Free Society of Artists, 1761–1783* (a complete dictionary of contributors and their work), London 1907

Hindwood, K.A., 'The Birds of Lord Howe Island', *Emu*, 40, 1940, pp. 1–86

Hodgson, Mr, Sale catalogue (included some contents from Leverian Museum), 18 May 1832

Jackson, Christine E., *Bird paintings: the eighteenth century*, Woodbridge 1995

Jackson, Christine E., *Bird etchings: the illustrators and their books, 1655–1855*, Ithaca 1985

Kaeppler, Adrienne, *Artificial curiosities: being an exposition of native manufactures collected on the three Pacific voyages of Captain James Cook, R.N. at the Bernice Pauahi Bishop Museum January 18, 1978–August 31, 1978, on the occasion of the bicentennial of the European discovery of the Hawaiian Islands by Captain Cook – January 18, 1778*, Bishop Museum Special Publications no. 65, Honolulu 1978

Kaeppler, Adrienne, 'Tracing the History of Hawaiian Cook Voyage Artifacts in the Museum of Mankind', *British Museum Yearbook*, 3, 1979, pp. 167–97

King, Jonathan C.H., 'New Evidence for the Contents of the Leverian Museum', *The Journal of the History of Collections*, 8 (2), 1996, pp. 167–86

King, Jonathan C.H., 'Woodlands Art as depicted by Sarah Stone in the Collection of Sir Ashton Lever', *American Indian Art Magazine*, 18 (2), 1993, pp. 32–45

La Roche, Sophie von, *Sophie in London 1786: being the diary of Sophie von la Roche, translated by Clare Williams*, London 1933, pp. 111–15

Largen, M.J., 'Bird specimens purchased by Lord Stanley at the sale of the Leverian Museum in 1806, including those still existant in the collections of the Liverpool Museum.;' *Archives of Natural History* (14), 1987, pp. 268–88

Largen, M.J. and Fisher, C.T., 'Catalogue of extant mammal specimens from the collection of the 13th Earl of Derby, now in the Liverpool Museum', *Archives of Natural History*, 13, 1986, pp. 225–72.

Lever, Sir Ashton, 'Mr Seaman begs to inform ... has museum with many thousands of natural curiosities ... formerly property of Sir Ashton Lever. Ipswich. 1824

Leverian Museum: Companion to the museum mdccxc. *The Sale Catalogue of the entire collection 1806*: a facsimile reprint of the above two rare volumes with the sale catalogue manuscript annotations, prices, and buyers' names, London (Harmer Johnson and John Hewett) 1979.

Martyn, William Frederick, *A new dictionary of natural history: or, compleat universal display of animated nature* (based on the collection of the Leverian Museum), 2 vols., 100 coloured pls., London 1785. [Lowndes states this was written by William Fordyce Mavor.]

Mullens, W.H., 'Some museums of Old London 1 – The Leverian Museum', *The Museums Journal* (4), 15 October 1915, pp. 123–29, and (5), 15 November 1915, pp.

162–72.

Murray, David, *Museums: their history and their use*, 3 vols., London 1904.

Nelson, E. Charles, 'John White's Journal of a Voyage to New South Wales (London 1790): bibliographic notes', *Archives of Natural History* 25, (1) 1998. pp. 109–130

Nelson, E. Charles 'John White A.M., M.D., F.L.S. (c. 1756–1832), Surgeon General of New South Wales: a new biography of the messenger of the echidna and waratah.' 25, (2), 1998, pp. 149–211.

Newton, Alfred , 'Notes on some old museums' Museum Association *Report of proceedings*, 1891

Pelzehn, A. von, 'On the birds in the Imperial collection at Vienna obtained from the Leverian Museum', *Ibis* 1873, pp. 14–54, 105–24.

Pollard, William, *The Stanleys of Knowsley: a history of that noble family*, London 1868.

Scherren, Henry, *The Zoological Society of London*, London 1905.

The School-room party, out of school hours ... a most pleasing companion to the Lever Museum, Low for T. Hurst, London 1800.

Shaw, George, *Museum Leverianum (Musei Leveriani explicatio anglica et latina) containing select specimens from the Museum of the late Sir Ashton Lever, Kt with descriptions in Latin and English*, by George Shaw, M.D., F.R.S., published by James Parkinson, proprietor of the above collection, 6 parts, 72 pls., London 1792–96.

Smith, Bernard and Wheeler, A., *The Art of the First Fleet*, Melbourne 1988.

Smith, William J., 'A museum for a guinea', *Country Life*, 10 March 1960, pp. 494–95.

Sutton, Denys, 'The Reinagles reconsidered'. *Country Life*, CXVIII, 1955.

Sweet, Jessie M., 'Robert Jameson

in London, 1793. Excerpts from Robert Jameson's *Journal of a Voyage from Leith to London, 1793*', *Annals of Science*, 19 (2), June 1963, pp. 81–114 (London 1965).

Venn, J. A., *Alumni Cantabrigiensis*, 6 vols., Cambridge 1947.

Wagstaff, R. and Rutherford, G., 'Letters from Knowsley Hall, Lancashire', *North Western Naturalist*, 2, 1954, pp. 173–83.

Walford, Edward, and Thornbury, G. W., *Old and New London*, 6 vols., London 1873–78.

Waterhouse, George Robert, *Marsupalia or pouched Animals*, Naturalist's Library series, Edinburgh 1841.

White, Rashleigh Holt, *Life and Letters of Gilbert White*, 2 vols., London 1901, vol. I, pp. 183 (note), 219, 223, 240, 251, 256, 260, 262.vol. I Letters to Rev John White 9 March 1775, 5 March 1776, 26 April 1778.]

Whitehead, P.J.P., 'A guide to the dispersal of zoological material from Captain Cook's voyages', *Pacific studies*, Fall 1978, pp. 52–93.

Whitehead, P.J.P., 'Zoological specimens from Captain Cook's Voyages', *Journal of the Society for the Bibliography of Natural History*, 5 (3), 1969, pp. 161–201.

Wood, Casey, *Introduction to the Literature of Vertebrate Zoology*, Montreal 1931.

Index

N after a page number indicates footnote.